Cultural and Creative Industries of Childhood and Youth

PETER LANG
Bruxelles · Bern · Berlin · New York · Oxford · Wien

ICCA

Industries culturelles, création, numérique

sous la direction de Bertrand Legendre et François Moreau

Sous l'égide du LABoratoire d'EXcellence ICCA (Industries Culturelles et Création Artistique), cette collection réunit les résultats de recherches consacrées aux différentes industries culturelles, traditionnelles comme le cinéma, la télévision, la musique ou l'édition, ou plus récentes comme la vidéo ou le jeu vidéo. Elle privilégie une perspective interdisciplinaire pour étudier les dispositifs de médiation et de promotion, les pratiques de consommation et les mutations induites par des mouvements de fond comme la mondialisation ou la numérisation, qui bouleversent aussi bien les processus de création des contenus que les modes de financement et de distribution de la production.

Valérie-Inés de la Ville, Gilles Brougère
and Pascale Garnier (Eds.)

Cultural and Creative Industries of Childhood and Youth

An interdisciplinary exploration of new frontiers

ICCA – Industries culturelles, création, numérique
Vol. 11

Cette publication a fait l'objet d'une évaluation par les pairs.

1 avenue Maurice, B-1050 Bruxelles, Belgium
brussels@peterlang.com ; www.peterlang.com

ISSN 2506-8741
ISBN 978-2-8076-1601-1
ePDF 978-2-8076-1602-8
ePub 978-2-8076-1603-5
Mobi 978-2-8076-1604-2
DOI 10.3726/b17816
D/2020/5678/77

Information bibliographique publiée par « Die Deutsche Bibliothek »

« Die Deutsche Bibliothek » répertorie cette publication dans la « Deutsche Nationalbibliografie » ; les données bibliographiques détaillées sont disponibles sur le site <http://dnb.ddb.de>.

Acknowledgements

The book *Cultural and Creative Industries of Childhood and Youth – An Interdisciplinary Exploration of New Frontiers*, a selection of research papers presented at the conference "Child and Teen Consumption – Cultural and Creative Industries of Childhood and Youth" held in Angoulême (France) from April 3 to 6, 2018, received financial support from:

- the Maison des Sciences de l'Homme et de la Société of the University of Poitiers
- the CNRS Poitou-Charentes
- the Labex Cultural Industries and Artistic Creation
- European Union, through Feder funds in conjunction with financing from other local institutions:

Special thanks to Michael Kelly for his translation from French and proofreading.

Table of contents

General introduction

Valérie-Inés de La Ville

This book draws on the interdisciplinary conferences "Child and Teen Consumption" that have taken place every two years since their launch by the School of Management of the University of Poitiers in 2004 in Angoulême (France). The "Child and Teen Consumption" conferences aim at facilitating in-depth dialogue between researchers from various disciplines: management, psychology, sociology, information and communication, anthropology, history, education, law, etc. Because of their interdisciplinary focus, the "Child and Teen Consumption" conferences tackle a wide variety of topics relating to the links between childhood and adolescence and consumer environments in different social and institutional contexts. The CTC conferences promote and enhance original research that explores and highlights what children understand about the market experiences in which they participate, and how they use the resources available to them to assert their child status vis-à-vis adults or their peer groups. The conference also welcomes studies that analyze production of goods and marketing techniques used towards young people as well as the socioeconomic mechanisms that shape and control childhood cultures.

An active interdisciplinary community has taken the opportunity to organize the following "Child and Teen Consumption" conferences: Copenhagen Business School in 2006, Norwegian Child Research Centre (NOSEB) in 2008, Linköping University (Sweden) in 2010, Università Libera di Milano (Italy) in 2012, Edinburgh University Business School (Great-Britain) in 2014, Aalborg University (Denmark) in 2016, and Poitiers University (France) in 2018.

The 8th CTC conference returned to the University of Poitiers and Angoulême, and gathered interdisciplinary research and dialogue on broad issues related to children and young people as consumers. Its special focus was on "Cultural and Creative Industries of Childhood and Youth" to highlight research in this field and invite producers of cultural content as well as policy makers to bring their views to the debate. Indeed, Angoulême is a territory that hosts a wealth of creative organizations and initiatives. *Grand Angoulême*, an urban area including 38 communes, set up the Magelis Image Cluster in 1998. Magelis now includes 12 dedicated institutes of higher education that welcome 1300 undergraduate, graduate and post-graduate students, as well as 90 companies from key sectors in the image industry: youth publishing, comic book publishing, audio-visual production studios, post-production studios, producers of video games, serious games, mobile games, and advertising and design agencies, etc. Second to Paris, Magelis in Angoulême is the largest cluster in France producing the greatest number of cartoons each year. Furthermore, *Grand Angoulême* is currently in the process of establishing a technology park – Eurekatech, where the cultural and creative industries are one of three main areas chosen to enhance economic development.

The chapters collected in this volume stem from papers first discussed at the 8th international conference "Child and Teen Consumption" with the purpose to produce a collective effort towards an interdisciplinary dialogue to examine various social issues related to prosumption and transmedial practices of children and adolescents in the cultural and creative industries.

The specificities of cultural and creative industries in relation to other types of economic activities are the subject of important debates which, according to Christian Poirier's longitudinal analysis, have progressively crystallized around five meta-narratives. Firstly, the industrialization of culture, which contrasts legitimate culture and popular culture. Secondly, the neo-liberal approach, which emphasizes that the market allows a plurality of artistic expressions. Thirdly, a relative autonomy of the cultural sphere that tends, through collective and critical appropriations, to reconfigure certain capitalist issues. Fourthly, a growing and unavoidable interpenetration between the spheres of culture and capitalism through new advertising techniques. Finally, a creative economy that considers culture to be an endogenous factor of economic growth (Poirier, 2014). These meta-narratives analyze the complex articulations between cultural and economic issues that accompany the transformations in the balance of power between different types of actors involved in the cultural and creative industries: authors, artists, publishers, distribution platforms, advertising audiences, brands and advertisers, citizens, public authorities, regulators, etc. Numerous research studies from various disciplinary horizons have sought to highlight the specificities of the cultural and creative industries (Martell, 2012) in terms of value creation, entrepreneurial approach and innovation logics, viability of economic models, originality of organization and management modes (Hesmondhalgh, 2012; Bouquillion et al., 2013; Evrard and Busson, 2015; Arsenault and Perren, 2016; Khaire, 2017). Concisely, Bouquillion et al. (2014) remind us that the advent of creative and cultural industries rests on a triple transformation: that of the artist as an entrepreneur; that of the cultural worker as an artist; that of the user as a cultural self-producer.

In this context, the analysis of the place given to children – and more broadly to youth – in the field of cultural and creative industries remains an important scientific issue. Scientific works have brought together different perspectives on the links between childhood and the worlds of culture and media, in order to reveal the presuppositions that guide disciplinary approaches to youth media practices and their recent evolution (Jenkins et al., 2015; Brougère and François, 2018). Yet this field of social, professional and research practices is in constant turmoil, both in developing critical approaches to the equivocal links that cultural industries have with youth, and in raising ethical issues in marketing and management realms and more broadly, in social sciences research (Warde, 2017).

A wide range of topics relating to the links that interweave childhood or adolescence and the worlds of cultural practices and media consumption in different social and institutional contexts call for further interdisciplinary investigation to go beyond the representation of the child as a mere impulsive consumer or a captive prosumer in an attention economy (Johansson, 2004; Buckingham, 2011). Children are active, playing with marketing mechanisms and rehearsing marketing scripts, to the point that the socio-technical networks or platforms they handle have transformed some of them into influencers who now work as marketing practitioners…

Thus, a large array of research on children's media practices highlights either the ambivalence of the figure of children as vulnerable consumers in need of protection or, on the contrary, as involved and creative content producers who are knowledgeable of the commercial offers addressed to them, and are capable of discernment in order to make a relevant choice in the marketplace. In this way, certain cognitive vulnerabilities peculiar to children have been underlined, as well as the skills that children demonstrate by mastering, sometimes better than adults, certain socio-technical devices that the market makes available to them. William Corsaro reminds us of "the importance of appreciating children's active construction of their own peer worlds and cultures. (…) children's construction of and participation in their peer cultures also contributes to the reproduction and change in adult society" (Corsaro, 2011, p. 365). His conceptual contribution about the interpretive reproduction that characterizes children's inventive cultural practices has paved the way for exploring children's media consumption to understand how children's reception of cultural content may differ from that of adults.

While the issues specific to the cultural and creative industries are recognized and explored by different disciplines – economics, sociology, psychology, management sciences, history, information and communication, literature, design, etc. – they are not necessarily the only ones to be addressed. The way in which each of these perspectives defines and problematizes the very notion of "childhood" deserves greater attention and sustained interdisciplinary scientific debate. The collected chapters in this book point to the diverse social and ideological roots of the child consumer and prosumer in cultural and creative industries.

> Rather than thinking in terms of a moment of birth or the progressive unfolding of a universal category, it may be useful to think in terms of the multiple and changing boundaries of the [child][1] consumer. The consumer was bounded in terms of ideas, social composition, representation and, significantly, by consuming practices. (Trentmann, 2006, p. 10)

Indeed, in the field of cultural and creative industries, multiple visions of the child convey the presuppositions of various disciplines:

- an apprentice consumer who gradually becomes more rational in order to achieve a relative optimization of his/her media choices;
- a child who, by nature, is in search of entertainment and gathers playful experiences at the crossroads between media activities and other forms of childlike sociability;
- an essentially vulnerable child whose attention is captured by the media at an early age and to whom the media impose their content through increasingly invasive marketing actions;

1 The word "child" is our addition.

- a "child prosumer," acting as co-creator of innovative cultural content (User-Generated Content) that can be monetized according to the possibilities offered by various commercial socio-technical devices (social networking sites, digital platforms, etc.);
- a child who has become a veritable marketing expert that brands use to promote their innovations targeting children and adolescents on the platforms used by young people: YouTube, Instagram, TikTok, Snapchat, etc.

This is why, in order to highlight these issues in a well-argued way through a rigorous interdisciplinary dialogue, this book is titled *New Frontiers in Cultural and Creative Industries of Childhood and Youth* and is structured in three main parts.

The first part of this volume draws attention to the fact that the child "consumers do not emerge on their own but in dynamic relations with other social actors and agencies. These relationships involve uneven access to expertise, authority and power" (Trentmann, 2006, p. 14). Multiple groups and agencies speak on behalf of children in order to defend their interests against the persuasive discourses and consumer engagement strategies deployed by industrial and commercial interests. By developing the concept of "cultural pedagogy", Shirley Steinberg evidences the fact that "Patterns of consumption shaped by corporate advertising empower commercial institutions as the teachers of the contemporary era" (Steinberg, 2011, p. 18). This invites social researchers to take into account the influence and co-responsibility of media groups in the social construction of contemporary childhood, in relation to other institutions such as family, school, health policies, etc. (Stiegler, 2008; De La Ville, 2007 and 2014; Livingstone, 2017). The influence of social networks and content distribution platforms such as Netflix, YouTube, Amazon Prime or Disney+ over children's cultural and media activities, destabilizes the grounds on which to regulate these powerful economic actors who organize a global circulation of cultural content aimed at young people (Brougère, 2008). Social researchers should pay special attention to unanticipated ethical problems arising from the innovation dynamics interweaving technological advances and cultural practices in the creative and cultural industries aimed at children (Devinney et al., 2010). Could a structured debate about how to guide children's mediated cultural practices help parents, educators, corporations, and public authorities to feel support in the social responsibilities they ought to assume in relation to children's prosumption practices?

The contributions gathered in the second part of this book critically explore what children and adolescents understand about the commercial cultural experiences in which they participate. In order to promote cultural content dedicated to children, the discourse and marketing actions of media groups translate into gender and age logics while taking into account the influence of peer groups on social-digital networks (Corsaro, 2011; Ruckenstein, 2011). By targeting a hybrid "parent-child" consumer, cultural industries take into account adult concerns about family budgets, the tensions and crossbreeding between the logic of entertainment and the logic of academic success or the degree of autonomy left to children in the reception and social use of cultural products. The cultural consumption practices of children and young people are then directly linked to debates about children's agency (Mayall, 2002; James, 2009; Garnier, 2015). As they are increasingly depicted as "active," this also highlights the resistance and transgression practices that they bring to processes of consumption. Young consumers use the resources offered to them by creative and cultural industries to assert their status as children *vis-à-vis* adults, or to individuate themselves by drawing on their peer groups (De Singly, 2006; Jenkins et al., 2015). Conversely, this depiction of the child's agency reveals how children's consumption also brings into play the figure of the "good" parent, a normative figure imposed on them by various institutions, to which parents aspire according to their own educational goals (Martens, 2018).

The third part of the book explores the processes used to create cultural content for young people, as well as the way in which children appropriate, reinterpret, transform and divert it according to various sociocultural contexts. Interactions between these different sectors (audiovisual, publishing, toys, video games, internet, etc.) are already long-standing, as evidenced by the simultaneous presence on different media of the same franchise via cross media, transmedia or "360°" strategies as well as the implementation of licensing policies (Kline et al., 2003; De La Ville and Durup, 2008; Johnson, 2013). Children are then confronted with different media that allow them to appropriate the content. Authors and rights holders must find the path, which is different for each of them, between a control that has become impossible, and a drift in their creation or ownership that would excessively modify its meaning. The series of studies collected in this part of the book analyze the techniques and strategies deployed by cultural industries as well as by the authors in different contexts to underpin and nurture the formation of children's cultures. In a context of globalized circulation of cultural content on multiple media, children's products exemplify emblematic transformations of cultural products, whether it is transmedia scripts (Jenkins, 2006), "media mix" (Ito, 2007; Steinberg, 2012), "circulations" within children's culture (Brougère, 2008) or new innovative and creative combinations between various media that permanently redraw lasting attachments and social ties (Cochoy et al., 2017).

Finally, the interdisciplinary perspective of this volume contributes to a rethinking of the language of separate disciplinary spheres. Indeed, understanding the evolution of cultural prosumption and transmedial practices by children and youth is a complex research endeavor that calls for a subtle and demanding interdisciplinary dialogue. The main scientific challenge social scientists confront is to design innovative research perspectives at the crossroads of various disciplines: sociology of childhood (Garnier, 1995; James and Prout, 1997; Sirota, 2006; Corsaro, 2011), childhood studies (Qvortrup et al., 2009), relational economy (Cochoy, 2012) and marketing and management research (Robertson and Feldman, 1976; McNeal, 1992). By offering a balanced interdisciplinary scientific dialogue about youth culture and media consumption practices, we aim to study the evolutions of several socioeconomic devices that underlie, promote and shape children's expression in cultural and creative industries. This attempt to get out of one's disciplinary comfort zone might enrich our collective understanding of how marketing socio-technical devices transform the meaning of children's cultural practices within their family or peer community.

These changes make it essential to take a different look at children's and teens' prosumption and transmedial practices, in order to go beyond univocal descriptions of children's activities in the media and cultural spheres. Moreover, they underline the importance of developing truly interdisciplinary and critical approaches by mastering the epistemological underpinnings of the competing theoretical frameworks put at work to decipher children's and teens' complex social practices. And finally, deciphering in depth the ambiguity of the prosumption and transmedial practices of children and young people might also help social researchers in grasping the market which is itself "in the process of being made". Moreover, it could help researchers understand how the market is constantly in the process of undoing and redoing institutional, social and cultural ties, and urge them to explore the consequences of such transformations (Zelizer, 1985). A demanding interdisciplinary work on child and teen cultural consumption might help go beyond a pure social critique of economic theories (Polanyi, 1944). What is at stake in child and teen consumption is the need to develop an in-depth interdisciplinary reflection that would make it possible to explore how commercial exchanges produce both "economy" and "society", interwoven realms within which children and teens develop their cultural practices. This raises the question of how the youth market-mediated prosumption and transmedial practices are capable of "producing, evils, or if possible, goods, i.e. entities that can function both as objects and moral contributions" (Cochoy, 2012, p. 15).

This book is also the result of a team effort. We would like to express our warmest thanks to the administrative team of the European Center for Children's Products (CEPE – University of Poitiers) without whose efforts our scientific ideas would remain only vain dreams: Maxine Johnson for her contribution in making the community "childandteenconsumption.org" lively and welcoming; Arnaud Berteau, our gifted computer magician who finds solutions to any technical problem; Carole Boubila, Sandrine Bécaud and Antoine Georget for their unfailing commitment in the preparation of the 8th Child and Teen Consumption conference; Séverine Rouyer, our specialized documentalist who accompanies us on our research projects; and finally, Anita Bhatia, who made the index of this book. This local team also benefited from the administrative support from Rémy Coopman and Françoise Puthon, staff of the CNRS Poitou-Charentes research institute.

References

Arsenault, A., & Perren, A. (Eds.). (2016). *Media industries: perspectives on an evolving field.* CreateSpace Independent Publishing Platform.

Bouquillon, P., Miège, B., & Moeglin, P. (2013). *L'industrialisation des biens symboliques : les industries créatives en regard des industries culturelles.* Presses universitaires de Grenoble.

Bouquillion, P., Miège, B., & Moeglin, P. (2014). Déconstruire la notion de créativité: problèmes et enjeux d'une triple conversion. *Injonction de créativité et création sous contrainte.* 82nd ACFAS Conference, Montréal, May 17–23. https://crea2s.hypotheses.org/

files/2017/10/2014_ACTES_Cr%C3%A9ativit%C3%A9_ACFAS_Montr%C3%A9al.pdf.

Brougère, G. (Ed.). (2008). *La ronde des jeux et des jouets : Harry, Pikachu, Superman et les autres*. Autrement.

Brougère, G., & François, S. (Eds.). (2018). *L'enfance en conception(s) : comment les industries culturelles s'adressent-elles aux enfants*. Peter Lang.

Buckingham, D. (2011). *The material child: Growing up in consumer culture*. Polity Press.

Cochoy, F., & Callon, M. (2012). *Du lien marchand, comment le marché fait société : essai(s) de sociologie économique relationniste*. Presses universitaires du Mirail.

Cochoy, F., Deville, J., & McFall, E. R. (Eds.). (2017). *Markets and the arts of attachment*. Routledge.

Corsaro, W. A. (2011). *The sociology of childhood* (3rd ed.). Sage/Pine Forge Press.

De La Ville, V.-I. (2007). The consequences and contradictions of child and teen consumption in contemporary practice. *Society and Business Review, 2*(1), 7–14. https://doi.org/10.1108/17465680710725245

De La Ville, V.-I. (2014). Young people as company stakeholders? Moving beyond CSR… *Young Consumers, 15*(1), 3–16. https://doi.org/10.1108/YC-03-2013-00363

De La Ville, V.-I., & Durup, L. (2009). Achieving a global reach on children's cultural markets: Managing the stakes of inter-textuality in digital cultures. In R. Willett, M. Robinson, & J. Marsh (Eds.), *Play, creativity and digital cultures* (pp. 36–53). Routledge.

De Singly, F. (2006). *Les adonaissants*. Armand Colin.

Devinney, T. M., Auger, P., & Eckhardt, G. M. (2010). *The myth of the ethical consumer*. Cambridge University Press.

Evrard, Y., & Busson, A. (Eds.). (2015). *Le management des industries culturelles et créatives*. Vuibert.

Garnier, P. (1995). *Ce dont les enfants sont capables : marcher, travailler, nager, XVIIIe, XIXe, XXe siècles*. Métailié.

Garnier, P. (2015). L'"agency" des enfants : projet scientifique et politique des "childhood studies". *Éducation et sociétés, 36*, 159–173.

Hesmondhalgh, D. (2012). *The cultural industries* (3rd revised edition). Sage.

Itō, M. (2007). Technologies of the childhood imagination: Yu-gi-oh!, media mixes, and everyday cultural production. In J. Karaganis (Ed.). *Structures of participation in digital culture* (pp. 88–111). Social Science Research Council.

James, A. (2009). Agency. In J. Qvortrup, W. A. Corsaro, & M.-S. Honig (Eds.), *The Palgrave handbook of childhood studies* (pp. 34–45). Palgrave Macmillan.

James, A., & Prout, A. (1997). *Constructing and reconstructing childhood: contemporary issues in the sociological study of childhood*. Routledge.

Jenkins, H. (2006). *Convergence culture: where old and new media collide*. New York University Press.

Jenkins, H., Ito, M., & Boyd, D. (2015). *Participatory culture in a networked era: a conversation on youth, learning, commerce and politics*. Polity Press.

Johansson, B. (2004). *Beyond the competent child*. Exploring contemporary childhoods in the Nordic Welfare Societies. Roskilde University Press.

Johnson, D. (2013). *Media franchising: Creative license and collaboration in the culture industries*. New York University Press.

Khaire, M. (2017). *Culture and commerce: The value of entrepreneurship in creative industries*. Stanford University Press.

Kline, S., Dyer-Withford, N., & De Peuter, G. (2003). *Digital play: The interaction of technology culture and marketing*. McGill-Queen's University Press.

Livingstone, S., & Third, A. (2017). Children and young people's rights in the digital age: An emerging agenda. *New Media & Society, 19*(5), 657–670. https://doi.org/10.1177/1461444816686318

Martel, F. (2011). *Mainstream : enquête sur la guerre globale de la culture et des médias*. Flammarion.

Martens L. (2018). *Childhood and markets. Infants, parents and the business of child caring*. Palgrave Macmillan.

Mayall, B. (2002). *Towards a sociology for childhood: Thinking from children's lives*. Open University Press.

McNeal, J. U. (1992). *Kids as customers: A handbook of marketing to children*. Macmillan.

Poirier, C. (2014). Culture et créativité au regard de l'économie. Propositions de cadrage. Actes du colloque "Injonction de créativité et création sous contrainte" 82e Congrès de l'ACFAS, Montréal, mai 2014, 9–16. https://

crea2s.hypotheses.org/files/2017/10/2014_ACTES_Cr%C3%A9ativi-t%C3%A9_ACFAS_Montr%C3%A9al.pdf.

Polanyi, K. (1944). *The great transformation: The political and economic origins of our time*. Beacon Press.

Qvortrup, J., Corsaro, W., & Honig, M. (2009). *The Palgrave handbook of childhood studies*. Palgrave Macmillan.

Robertson, T. S., & Feldman, S. (1976). Children as consumers: The need for multi-theoretical perspectives. *Advances in Consumer Research, 3*(1), 508–512.

Ruckenstein, M. (2011). Children in creationist capitalism. *Information, Communication & Society, 14*(7), 1060–1076. https://doi.org/10.1080/1369118X.2011.565781

Sirota, R. (Ed.). (2006). *Éléments pour une sociologie de l'enfance*. Presses universitaires de Rennes.

Steinberg, S. R. (Ed.). (2011). *Kinderculture: The corporate construction of childhood* (3rd ed.). Westview Press.

Steinberg, M. (2012). *Anime's media mix: Franchising toys and characters in Japan*. University of Minnesota Press.

Stiegler, B. (2008). *Prendre soin de la jeunesse et des générations*. Flammarion.

Warde, A. (2017). *Consumption: a sociological analysis*. Palgrave Macmillan.

Zelizer, V. A. (1985). *Pricing priceless child: The changing social value of children*. Basic Books.

Part 1

Children as prosumers: Moving borders around children's social value and emerging ethical issues

Valérie-Inés de La Ville

The transformation of cultural practices, underpinned by technological innovations and new forms of appropriation and circulation of cultural goods, has given rise to the figure of the "Prosumer" (McLuhan and Nevitt, 1972; Toffler, 1990). The seminal works introducing this concept depict a consumer who, far from being passive and dominated by a cultural offer imposed on him or her, is part of a culture of participation by actively producing cultural content for his or her peers. This merging of the roles of consumer and producer of cultural content is the work of individuals who are able both to develop a critical spirit and to contribute their creativity as consumers, because they are fully aware of how to exploit the possibilities that technological advances offer them to produce and disseminate cultural content. Transposed to children, various questions are raised by this figure of the creative consumer, who invests in crowdsourcing activities proposed by innovation-related marketing schemes, such as campaigns to improve packaging, create brand slogans, create new scenarios for television series, suggest plots for video games, create stories on social networking sites, etc.

Through their media cultural practices, children and adolescents appear to be enthusiastic participants in all these activities that combine an affective dimension, characterizing the sharing of leisure time with parents, schoolmates or family members, and a techno-economic dimension, brought in by corporations that offer new platforms and widgets to disseminate user-generated content. Nevertheless, the "child prosumer" is not a self-evident category or an ontological essence, but remains a disputed figure within public debate and a topic of social controversies that reflect the competing values and moral projects that are assigned to childhood as social and power relationships evolve through time. Thus, the social positioning of the "child prosumer" within this participatory culture paradigm needs to be investigated in depth with the aim of clarifying the underpinnings of the continuous social valuation process through which children's production and consumption practices are permanently assessed and reassessed (Bühler-Niederberger and Hungerland, 2002). The persona of the "child prosumer" is an ongoing, dynamic process through which the changing social status of the child and its agency in commercial realms are negotiated among many representatives of children's interests (De La Ville, 2007).

The four chapters collected in this part of the book shed light on key emerging and disputed moral issues linked to children's and adolescents' prosuming practices within cultural and creative industries. The discussions about the social value of the "child-prosumer" make apparent the tensions between evaluative market moralities applied to young consumers and the moral imperatives embedded in childhood. Assessing the social value of the child-prosumer is a moving ground where moral entrepreneurs as well as public policies endlessly confront the economic and emotional values that consubstantially define childhood in Western mass market-mediated societies (Zelizer, 2012).

1. The changing shape of children's social valuation in cultural industries

Based on his long experience as a pioneer exploring the links between the playful practices of children and youth and the progressive sophistication of marketing strategies in the toy, television (Kline, 1993) and video game sectors (Kline et al., 2003), Steve Kline offers us a longitudinal analysis of the ethical storms that have punctuated the youth-oriented cultural industries since the mid-19th century. With his singular style, always precise, rigorous and imbued with an unparalleled erudition on the subject, he distinguishes three moral doctrines that have contributed to the erosion of the figure of *pater familias* as an anchor for public debate on the educational needs of the child. This contribution extends his remarkable analysis of the "paradox of immaturity" that has structured the public debate on child education since the 17th century and, in modern times, that of socialization and child participation in the commercial realms (Kline, 2006). This paradox remains at the very heart of the public debate in the threefold periodization he establishes to analyze the structural changes in children's socialization process in digitally and commercially mediated cultural industries aimed at children: *The ethos of preparation* mobilizes the figure of an impulsive child, characterized by lax morals, who needs to admire heroes who are law-abiding, rational and capable of controlling their emotions… in order to educate him or her in his or her duties as a future citizen. Professionals in children's publishing, cinema and video games have endeavored to take care of this "*walled garden*" in which a child's imagination can unfold within a safe universe. *The ethos of protection* refers to the State's obligation to ensure the continuous improvement of the child's well-being and his or her emotional, material and educational security. *The ethos of caring duty* extends moral responsibility beyond the family circle, particularly to the various adults who contribute to a child's upbringing, including youth marketing professionals. The duty of these educators is to keep children away from bad influences and forms of exploitation they may undergo as a result of the growing influence of the mass media on their daily lives and leisure time. The self-regulation of the cultural industries with regard to advertising practices for children on television and in the cinema was a first important step forward, but its impact is moderate due to the pervasiveness of online activities that capture children's attention and even instrumentalize them as influencers. Thus, the progressive shift of the public debate on educational issues around the notions of "*Literacy*", then "*Media literacy*", later "*Advertising literacy*", and today "*Data literacy*", reveals that the "paradox of immaturity" of the child's participation in the digitally mediated global cultural industries is constantly being updated according to emerging issues. To justify the ethical choices they make to capture a youth target, cultural industry professionals face a complex web of paradoxes and controversies linked to the confrontation of these three moral doctrines, the implications of which they do not always fully appreciate and which they struggle to disentangle.

With this overall historical framework in mind, the following three empirical studies analyze emerging moral tensions linked to structural evolutions of cultural industries aimed at young people. Conducted in three different contexts – a content-sharing platform, the commercial rhetoric of a marketing consultancy firm and a crowdsourcing campaign – each of them explores the particular ways in which the appreciation of children's place and their activities in market-mediated cultural activities is played out.

2. Emerging ethical issues in the social valuation of the child prosumer

The platforms that underpin the creative activities of "prosumers" in the cultural industries are part of an attention economy whose main aim is to capture the present moment. The legal challenges posed by the activity of the YouTube platform, and more specifically by its YouTube Kids service, are analyzed in detail by Esther Martinez Pastor, Patricia Núñez and Florence Chérigny. Their research puts into perspective the recent court decisions that have been taken to regulate the advertising activity of YouTube, involving child prosumers who publish on the platform the content they have created to share their interests with their peers. This case study highlights the platform's cruel lack of proactivity in terms of social responsibility towards its younger audiences. On the one hand, videos produced by children often include brand-sponsored content, such as a product received for free that the child stages in his or her video, or the obligation to follow a specific script in return for payment in order to enhance the value of the product. This new form of persuasive communication that relies on – but also constrains – the creativity of child prosumers constitutes a new type of advertising message that, for many years, has been neither regulated nor self-regulated by YouTube managers, who regularly claim that the platform has no editorial responsibility for the content that is posted on it. It was under the combined pressure of complaints from parents' associations and the withdrawal of reputation-conscious advertisers that in 2019 YouTube withdrew the comments on videos posted by children or in which children were portrayed. Indeed, to avoid their reputation being endangered, brands, as well as agencies promoting the work of young influencers, are increasingly aware of the need for self-regulatory codes to emerge in order to classify as advertising part of the content created by child prosumers. On the other hand, the issue of capturing data about the cultural practices of children and minors is becoming central for cultural industries targeting youth. The personalization of advertising messages made possible by the processing of young Internet users' browsing data raises a new issue: do children understand the use that media and brands make of their personal data to offer them personalized advertising and influence their tastes and cultural practices? This research is in line with Stephen Kline's analysis by stressing that, given the importance of platforms in children's creative practices, it is necessary to pursue a demanding dialogue between the State, the families and caregivers in the broad sense including brands and platforms, in order to establish the principles of an education focused on "data literacy" and "privacy education" in order to accompany the young apprentice-prosumers. Such a research program calls for in-depth interdisciplinary work, as has already been pointed out by various researchers (Hudders et al., 2017; Verdoodt and Lievens, 2017).

Natalie Coulter and Grace Lao offer a critical reflection on how marketing consultancies instrumentalize children's creative capacities and the emotional bond that unites them to several characters and cultural worlds that target them as an audience. In order to show and promote the added value of their services to media groups targeting youth audiences, marketing professionals highlight the figure of the "superfan". This young consumer, who is passionate about a given fictional universe, will produce additional cultural content: organize a themed birthday party, publish a series of videos about the characters, and feed a Facebook page or an Instagram account to comment on the latest news about the tie-ins aimed at expanding the global reach of the fictional universe, and so on. The "superfan" is thus constructed by professionals in the marketing of children's cultures as an emblematic figure of participation based on a particularly strong emotional bond with a cultural universe and its characters. The creativity of these secondary productions constitutes a free promotional lever to widen the audience of the commercially exploited intellectual property. This culture of participation (Jenkins, Ito and Boyd, 2015), which is taking shape thanks to technological developments on the Web, is generating creative appropriation by audiences, who are acting as promotional relays to extend the commercial reach of the intellectual property. Youth marketing professionals value this investment by the "child prosumer" in a cultural universe that he or she helps to complete, transform and nourish with his or her creativity, as a real work of commercial promotion whose main advantage is that it is free. The child "user-generated content" (UGC) constitutes a participatory production that creates a subsequent advertising market, an audience that can be monetized: "In all these situations, the consumer produces voluntarily and for no pay immaterial goods that create value for the company" (Dujarier, 2014, p. 10). From a critical Marxian-inspired perspective, the authors consider that children appear in the discourse of youth marketing professionals as "alienated proletarians" (Stiegler, 2008) through a participatory market system that exploits their creativity to conquer new audiences. In the words of Shirley Steinberg (2011), this "structuralist" posture is only one side of a more complex phenomenon that should be counterbalanced by a detailed analysis of the empowering dimensions of children's participation in commercial culture: "When children appropriate toys and media productions, they sometimes make meanings that subvert ideological inscriptions, while at other times, their appropriations operate to validate the status quo" (Steinberg, 2011, p. 11). Through their participation in market activities, children have access to resources that nurture the construction of their social identity and the transformation of their status: "The development of the individual by promotion must be grasped from both sides of the promotional sign. It is not enough to look at this question only from the side of reception, that is to look at subjects only as readers/listeners addressed by a certain kind of speech. We must also take account of the way in which the contemporary subject has become implicated in promotional culture as a writer/performer of its texts" (Wernick, 1991, p. 192).

The chapter by Yelyzaveta Hrechaniuk usefully extends this debate by looking at the "*mise en abyme*" between the creativity of cultural industries and children's creativity as illustrated by the children's drawing competition organized by IKEA to launch a range of cuddly toys under the *Sagoskatt* brand in 2017. Drawing on the pragmatic perspective of valuation studies, which aims to explore how a series of values are brought into being, negotiated, assessed, dismissed or reinforced within ongoing social practices, the chapter explores the valuation process of children's productions to select the best drawings sent for this global contest. The corporate commercial communication on social networks enacts children as designers, artists, and lays special emphasis on a masterpiece, an exceptional work, a drawing by Mark, a 7-year-old child, the final winner of the contest in which 70,000 children participated worldwide. This case study analyzes in detail how all the communication about this drawing competition has a dual character, combining both a celebration of cultural values and ideals related to childhood and an advertising or promotional logic to affirm the values carried by the brand. The company's communication on this competition highlights the fact that children's productions undergo a twofold process, on the one hand, of sacralization (Zelizer, 1985) by becoming masterpieces *per se*, emblematic of children's ingenuous creativity and free of market calculations, but also, on the other hand, of instrumentalization, through which they become a flagship action intended to legitimize IKEA's corporate social responsibility policy. Organized by the managers of the Ikea Family loyalty club, the competition not only reaffirms that the brand's mission is to design furniture and objects dedicated to children and the family, but also unites the entire brand community by offering to give its opinion and evaluate children's drawings. Devices for valuing the productions of child prosumers cannot escape promotional culture: "Once we are communicating at all, and especially in public, and therefore, in a medium which is promotional through and through, there is no going outside promotional discourse. (…) there is no *hors-promotion*" (Wernick, 1991, p. 195). Thus, although the Ikea brand values the artistic and creative dimension of the children's productions generated by the competition, it uses them as free promotional material by contractually confiscating the intellectual property rights of children who participate in the competition.

3. The moral vortex of children's social valuation in cultural and creative industries

As the four chapters have clearly outlined, the social valuation of the "child prosumer" is a multi-layered process involving State regulation, collective customs as well as the lay normativities of prosumption, within a broader instituted system of provision (Wheeler, 2019). Quoting Chris Jenks, Stephen Kline reminds us that "(…) the social construction of modern childhood exists not as a sharp divide between adult and child but as a constant ideological struggle over the future of society within the modern matrix of socialization" (Kline, 2006, p. 204). Valuing children's lives within a mass media culture that redesigns the geographies of children's participatory practices confronts adults with a series of ever-emerging ethical issues which are particularly difficult to tackle as they cannot avoid being loaded with emotional dimensions (Zelizer, 2012). Are retailers, marketing consultants (Cook, 2019), consumer advocates, social scientists, parents, educators, brand managers, and State regulators, prepared to deal with unforeseen moral issues emerging from the ever-evolving child prosumption practices? Ultimately, they all are collectively responsible for the future of the childhood they contribute towards delineating, through the moral debates in which they agree to delve.

Specific moralities about the value of children's cultural practices are constituted in and through creative and cultural industries at the crossroads of conflicting knowledge regimes and moral brokers who act on behalf of children, who are key actors of the race to capture and monetize an audience while remaining excluded from contractual relationships. This phenomenon illustrates the particularly sagacious analysis carried out by Andrew Wernick in the early 1990s on the radical transformation brought about by the reconceptualization of the field of culture as a commercial space where cultural productions circulate in competition with one another. From this perspective, no cultural production can avoid being used for promotional purposes: "Promotion in different spheres, then, multiply interconnects – both in terms of the common pool of myths, symbols, tropes and values which it employs and through the way in which each of the objects to which a promotion message is attached is itself a promotional sign, and so on in an endless chain of mutual reference and implication" (Wernick, 1991, p. 187).

The four chapters highlight the role of the creative and cultural industries in the social construction of the "child prosumer persona", whose main social value consists of actively building audiences worth monetizing… Their reflections outline how the balance of power between a variety of knowledge holders and moral brokers evolves through time and transforms the agency of the "child prosumer" to place it at the cornerstone of creationist capitalism (Ruckenstein, 2011). All chapters reveal the endless confrontation of irreconcilable rearing ideals and normative requirements as well as the enduring presence of mythical structures about childhood that create unexpected and unintended moral issues contributing to a permanent redefinition of the social valuation of childhood in rough and controversial relationships between markets and other social or cultural institutions: "Global circulation of the belief that 'real' childhood is organized by a combination of toys, fun, games, fantasy and controlled adventure, appropriately packaged for 'age' and 'stage', is essential to market expansion not in the sense that cultural construction precedes the market, but in the sense that this version of childhood is constituted through the market. The two are inseparable" (Langer 2004, p. 256). Both the social valuation of the child prosumer and the moral economies of prosumption in the creative and cultural industries have a profound effect on children's lives and identities. They also delineate the future of childhood, with its specific temporality in children's eyes: "And if there is one point, moral, or insight that I would have you take from this (book)[2] it is, *The future of childhood is the present*" (Corsaro, 2011, p. 367).

References

Bühler-Niedberger, D., & Hungerland, B. (2002). Children's social value: The sociology of their assessment process. In F. Mouritsen & J. Qvortrup (Eds.), *Childhood and children's culture* (pp. 172–188). University Press of Southern Denmark.

Cook, D. T. (2019). Children's market researchers as moral brokers. *Journal of Cultural Economy, 12*(1), 70–82. https://doi.org/10.1080/17530350.2018.1514316

Corsaro, W. A. (2011). *The sociology of childhood* (3rd ed.). Sage/Pine Forge Press.

De La Ville, V.-I. (2007). The consequences and contradictions of child and teen consumption in contemporary practice. *Society and Business Review, 2*(1), 7–14. https://doi.org/10.1108/17465680710725245

De La Ville, V.-I. (2014). Young people as company stakeholders? Moving beyond CSR… *Young Consumers, 15*(1), 3–16. https://doi.org/10.1108/YC-03-2013-00363

Dujarier, M.-A. (2016). The three sociological types of consumer work. *Journal of Consumer Culture, 16*(2), 555–571. https://doi.org/10.1177/1469540514528198

Hudders, L., Pauw, P. D., Cauberghe, V., Panic, K., Zarouali, B., & Rozendaal, E. (2017). Shedding new light on how advertising literacy can affect children's processing of embedded advertising formats: A future research agenda. *Journal of Advertising, 46*(2), 333–349. https://doi.org/10.1080/00913367.2016.1269303

Jenkins, H., Itō, M., & Boyd, D. (2015). *Participatory culture in a networked era: A conversation on youth, learning, commerce, and politics*. Polity Press.

Jenkins, H., Ito, M., & Boyd, D. (2017). *Culture participative : une conversation sur la jeunesse, l'éducation et l'action dans un monde connecté*. C & F Éditions.

---

[2] The word "book" is our addition

Kline, S. (1993). *Out of the garden: Toys, TV, and children's culture in the age of marketing*. Verso.

Kline, S. (2006). A becoming subject: Consumer socialization in the mediated marketplace. In F. Trentmann (Ed.), *The making of the consumer: Knowledge, power and identity in the modern world* (pp. 199–221). Berg.

Kline, S., Dyer-Witheford, N., & De Peuter, G. (2003). *Digital play: The interaction of technology, culture, and marketing*. McGill-Queen's University Press.

Langer, B. (2004). The business of branded enchantment ambivalence and disjuncture in the global children's culture industry. *Journal of Consumer Culture, 4*(2), 251–277. https://doi.org/10.1177/1469540504043685

McLuhan, M., & Nevitt, B. (1972). *Take today; the executive as dropout*. Harcourt Brace Jovanovich.

Steinberg, S. R. (Ed.). (2011). *Kinderculture: The corporate construction of childhood* (3rd ed.). Westview Press.

Stiegler, B. (2008). *Prendre soin*. Tome 1. *De la jeunesse et des générations*. Flammarion.

Toffler, A. (1980). *Third wave*. HarperCollins.

Verdoodt, V., & Lievens, E. (2018). Targeting children with personalized advertising: How to reconcile the best interests of children and advertisers. In G. Vermeulen & E. Lievens (Eds.), *Data protection and privacy under pressure: Transatlantic tensions, EU surveillance, and big data* (pp. 313–341). Maklu.

Wernick, A. (1991). *Promotional culture: Advertising, ideology and symbolic expression*. Sage Publications.

Wheeler, K. (2019). Moral economies of consumption. *Journal of Consumer Culture, 19*(2), 271–288.

Zelizer, V. A. (1985). *Pricing the priceless child: The changing social value of children*. Basic Books.

Zelizer, V. A. (2012). A grown-up priceless child. In B. Sandin, A. Sparrman, & J. Sjöberg (Eds.), *Situating child consumption: Rethinking values and notions of children, childhood and consumption* (pp. 71–79). Nordic Academic Press.

1

Forecasting through the rear-view mirror: Ethical storm clouds over children's cultural industries

Stephen Kline

On the 4th of September, 2019 Google's subsidiary *YouTube* was fined $170 million by the US Federal Trade Commission (FTC) because they had been collecting data to target ads to children without parents' consent. Citing the Children's Online Privacy Protection Act (COPPA) of 1998, FTC Chairman Joe Simons condemned this violation pointing to the FTC's rule-making in 1999 intended to protect the "privacy" of children who surf the Internet. "Given this rule there is no excuse for *YouTube's* violations of the law" he concluded (BBC News September 4, 2019). Although it is not the first violation of children's privacy to be heard by the FTC, the size of the fine provides a reminder that that the ethical issues underwriting the protection of children in the digitally mediated market have not been diminished by the rapid expansion of children's digital cultural industries. It has also highlighted the need to once again revisit the ethical frameworks applied by cultural industries for communicating with children.

Indeed, the promotional mist that has shrouded the 21st Century growth in digital communication industries seems to now be lifting, exposing on-line children's cultural industries to increasing scrutiny. Although the ethical issues underwriting child protection have been argued throughout the last 200 years, many working in children's emerging cultural industries have been ignoring the ethical frameworks guiding the adult world's interactions with children (CBS News August 25). With this in mind the CCFC (Campaign for a Commercial Free Childhood), the leading US children's advocacy group, pointed to the many unresolved problems associated with online marketing to kids[1]. Its TV advocacy campaign proclaimed a troubling example:

> Social media influencers whose sponsored content sells little kids on everything from toy brands to cereal companies. This kind of advertising is illegal on children's television, but not on the internet, it seems that anything goes. How did we get to this media moment – and how can we move away from it?[2]

Good Questions! Despite the constant pressure of child advocates, many in contemporary children's cultural industries remain narrowly focused on the business of making and marketing specific cultural products for children. Until they are called into court (as so recently happened to *YouTube*, *Facebook* and others on issues of privacy), those working in the children's cultural industries rarely reflect upon the two hundred years struggle over these ethical doctrines guiding modernity. With storm clouds hovering over the future, this essay sets out to clarify these emerging ethical debates that have so galvanized public scrutiny of the expansion of child-oriented cultural industries over the last hundred years. In it, I attempt to both trace the legacy of concerns – about quality, violence, addiction and sexuality commercialism and privacy in children's culture – underwriting the regimes of (self)-censorship prescribed for the cultural industries, as well as identify the new challenges that the increasing commercialization of the internet has presented for educational approaches to protection of children's innocence (Kline, 2010).

In this essay, I focus on the three historical moral doctrines which eroded the legal force of "paterfamilias" in the public debates about children's unique status at the dawn of modernity. The first was *the ethos of preparation*: Valorized as future citizen-workers, children needed to be educated as literate, numerate and morally self-regulating individuals. The second was *the ethos of protection*, that asserted the State's responsibility for ensuring children's well-being and safety. The third, and perhaps most controversial was *a societal duty of care* which implied that not just the father, but all those who interacted with children, had responsibility for protecting them from malign influences and exploitation. Guided

1 Campaign for Commercial Free Childhood. (2019, Sept. 6). Our Impact: CCFC Gets Big YouTube Changes. https://commercialfreechildhood.org/our-impact-ccfc-gets-big-youtube-changes/.

2 Campaign for Commercial Free Childhood. (2020). https://www.commondreams.org/organization/campaign-commercial-free-childhood? (accessed 21 July 2020).

by this tripartite moral framework, modernizing States formulated an elaborate institutional framework for preparing and protecting children until adulthood (Kline, 2005). They invested in children's education but also constructed a regulatory cordon sanitaire around their preparation as competent citizens by measures which protected children from moral, psychological and health hazards in *currated sanctuaries* in which children could learn (public schooling) and play (playgrounds) sanctified in 1989 by the UN treaty on Children's Rights. But as children's cultural industries expanded from books and comics, to film and TV, and now to video games and websites, these emerging moral doctrines also galvanized public controversy in the cultural sector. It is easy to forecast that the digital cultural industries will increasingly find themselves caught up in the paradoxical implications of these moral doctrines as well as the limited policy frameworks that have been proffered to protect children's rights.

This historical review is intended to remind both industry and policy makers that each innovation in communication with children – from public libraries to online social media – precipitated not only new approaches to promoting children's well-being through education (e.g. the literary cannon, media literacy and pro-social advertising) but also forged a re-articulation of the ethical principles protecting them from harm and exploitation. Although this is a potted history, I outline three broad phases in the articulation of the duty of care defined with the elaboration of the legal mandate of "*in loco parentis*" which accompanied innovations in publishing (children's books and comics); the commercialization of TV (direct to child advertising); and now the expansion of on-line digital entertainment (privacy and trans-mediated marketing) demanded reworking of these moral doctrines. I do this arguing that privacy concerns are just the tip of the iceberg in the emerging world of online children's entertainment. As the CCFC foretells, the innovations in children's digital cultural industries– from gamification of food marketing to sponsored influencers in social media – is likely to renew public debates about whether, what and how online cultural industries get to communicate with children.

1. The censoring of modern childhood: The ethos of curation

Cultural historians have noted "modern childhood" is a unique ideological construct which after the reformation supplants the Roman legacy of paterfamilias and its assumption of absolute (and sometimes brutal) paternal control of the life of a child (De Mause, 1974). The modern conception of childhood was grounded in the moral percept of innocence that deemed young children were incapable of distinguishing right from wrong. They therefore had to be cared for, educated and protected from harm until they are deemed to be rational and self-regulating citizens withstanding in the courts. Fueling the 19th Centuries' growing interest in children's unique experiences, Charles Dickens' novels brought attention to the ethical issues problematizing childhood innocence in an industrializing society. How can we hold children culpable for their antisocial behavior, if their immaturity means they are incapable of a guilty mind? To what extent is the State responsible for protecting children from abusive adults not only their own parents or mandated caregivers (orphanages and workhouses) but in the workplace? And to what degree should the modern State take on some of the parental responsibility of caring for and preparing children as future citizen-workers?

These questions helped bring children's lives and experiences to the center of the public debates about the socialization of children in industrial democracies. In the early 19th Century mounting public opprobrium for the abuses of children in mines, factories and mills underwrote a public controversy about the protection of children from exploitation by industrial capitalism (Ariès, 1962). The paradoxical mandate for preparing and protecting children resulted in a Royal Commission in the UK which invoked the doctrine of innocence to sanction child labor for children under the age of 9, while limiting that of 9–11 year olds to 8 hours and those from 11–18 to a maximum of 12 hours per day. It is worth noting here that the State's interest in child protection vied openly with the property rights of poor parents who depended on that income to provide care for their families – thus challenging the principle of *paterfamilias*. It is also worth noting that denied the right to work in the industrializing workplace, modern children were then mandated to attend State schools in order to educate them as literate and law abiding citizens – thus also eroding their parents' sole control over their moral and behavioral training.

No longer exclusively the property and responsibility of the parent, these "becoming" citizens were in need of moral guidance and education, but also protection from malign influences who would exploit or abuse them – at least until they can become capable of distinguishing right from wrong (Kline, 2005). As public debate about child labor, family brutality, universal literacy, temperance and public recreation grew, the socialization of the child became a site of conflict as the desire to protect the "innocent" child vied with anxieties about the means of curbing the antisocial impulses and moral laxity of children. On the one hand the child was constructed as an innocent precursor to the civilized and responsible self; on the other was the State's need to protect them in their own interest against all who would exploit or harm them – even from their own parents.

Confronting this moral conundrum, enlightenment thinkers from Locke to Rousseau had long advocated mass education as the appropriate means of cultivating rational and self-regulating future citizens. Although parental responsibility for care and moral education continues as a central tenet of childrearing, no longer bound by Latin laws of paterfamilias, the common law notion of *in loco parentis* increasingly meant that responsibility for the modern child's moral and intellectual guidance extended to all that would communicate with them. Yet as Chris Jenks (1997) suggested, the social construction of modern childhood emerged not as a sharp dividing line between child and adult, but rather through an ideological struggle waged over the adult world's interactions with children. So too, throughout the modernizing period, the exceptional status of children as "becoming subjects" has placed competing ethical demands – to promote their well-being while protecting them from harm – on all those who would communicate with children whether parents, schools or businesses (Kline, 2008). Public schooling was therefore the first cultural institution to work through the paradoxical exigencies of modern childhood: on the one hand educators had to cultivate an informed and self-regulating moral individual through a mandated curriculum defining rational citizenship; on the other, they had to control antisocial behavior while protecting "innocent" children from harm and brutality. As developing subjectivities children also required moral guidance and education until they are capable of making independent choices – the preparation mandate. But as developmentally incomplete subjects, the modern State was also mandated to protect them from abuse and exploitation while under public care.

In the 20th century, professionals specialized in thinking about children's well-being – especially educators, health professionals and psychologists – played an increasing role in reframing the public discussions of the developmentally appropriate secular curriculum which has legitimized public schooling today. Historians of education have documented the expanding role that teachers, health professionals and psychologists played in the framing the new framework for the cognitive and social development of the vulnerable child. Developmentalism, or a graduated process of cognitive learning through stages of moral, social and intellectual growth has been not only the guiding principle underwriting the secular curriculum of schooling[3] but also the broader public debates about maturation and well-being of children in the modern world. The tension between preparation and protection mandates was resolved within public educational institutions by articulating a professionally moderated secular curriculum that educated children until adulthood.

The modern State invested in children's public education to foster their development as competent citizens. There were two aspects to educators' curatorial thinking about cultural resources suitable for childhood development: within the sanctuary of public school, the choice of reading material was guided by the notion of stage based maturation rooted in a sophisticated rationale for conceptual, moral and practical competences like literacy, numeracy and informed choice. But less understood is the ways, in the name of protecting them from moral harm and dangerous radical ideas, that public education also laid the heavy hand of censorship on the shoulders of educators in the 19th century. In the interest of children's moral development, modern children needed to be exposed to developmentally appropriate knowledge and increasingly complex moral dilemmas, but also protected from dangerous and age inappropriate ideas that could "corrupt the youth" (i.e. the charge that condemned Socrates) or disrupt the normal course of maturation. This task fell to curriculum administrators who adjudicated and willingly banned books that they deemed inappropriate for children's reading – mostly for exposing children to bad role models, sexuality, profanity or dangerous political and religious ideas

3 In education, a curriculum is broadly defined as the totality of student experiences that occur in the educational process. The term often refers specifically to a planned sequence of instruction, or to a view of the student's experiences in terms of the educator's or school's instructional goals (Wikipedia).

2. Libraries and books: The specter of censorship

From the early 20th century on public libraries also had to resolve the tension between preparation and protection. Librarians advocated reading as the golden road to literacy by advising parents about the suitability of literary works specially written for children. They did so by articulating a code for parental control of children's entertainment conceiving of libraries as a professionally moderated cultural sanctuary – a ring-fenced garden – full of developmentally appropriate experiences in which children were allowed to develop at their own pace, protected from not only from the worlds brutalizing realities but also from moral corruption. So the task of thinking about a developmentally appropriate entertainment reading and imaginative experiences fell mostly on the shoulders of librarians (toy librarians in France) – the first cultural custodians to articulate the principles upon which to decide children's access to the growing range of cultural products for children. The principles they adopted have survived and been revived in various self-regulatory codes developed in the cultural industry (see Fig. 1). Indeed, the much celebrated growth of the children's book industry in the early 20th century was facilitated by a consensus among educators and librarians about a children's literary cannon – the imaginative tales of adventure featuring positive role models could inspire children; but also disciplined by the beliefs that profanity, gratuitous violence and sexualized social themes could prove disturbing especially to young children who needed to be protected from the harsher realities of life until they were emotionally mature (Fort Lewis College, 2013).

Children's publishers were really the first cultural industry to navigate the emerging dilemma facing all cultural industries: selling books meant providing children with a literature that they wanted to read but also one that librarians, teachers and most of all parents were willing to buy for children. In the name of providing positive templates for children's healthy maturation they explored the potential of adventure and fantasy to expand the horizon of children's imagination while taking a cue from librarians they also reminded authors to buffer children from darker emotions, moral depravity, sexualized themes and brutalizing realism. The flourishing of children's fiction and toy industries in early 20th century gives testimony to benefits of the professionally curated "walled garden" concept developed by librarians for fictional works.

Fig. 1: Librarian's code for censoring children's books

Racial Issues: About and/or encouraging racism towards one or more group of people.
Encouragement of "Damaging" Lifestyles: Content of book encourages lifestyle choices that are not of the norm or could be considered dangerous or damaging. This could include drug use, co-habitation without marriage, or homosexuality.
Blasphemous Dialog: The author of the book uses words such as "God" or "Jesus" as profanity. This could also include any use of profanity or swear words within the text that any reader might find offensive.
Sexual Situations or Dialog: Many books with content that include sexual situations or dialog are banned or censored.
Violence or Negativity: Books with content that include violence are often banned or censored. Some books have also been deemed too negative or depressing and have been banned or censored as well.
Presence of Witchcraft: Books that include magic or witchcraft themes. A common example of these types of books are J. K. Rowling's Harry Potter Series.
Religious Affiliations (unpopular religions): Books have been banned or censored due to an unpopular religious views or opinions in the content of the book. This is most commonly related to satanic or witchcraft themes found in the book. Although, many books have also been banned or censored for any religious views in general that might not coincide with the public view.
Political Bias: Most commonly occurs when books support or examine extreme political parties/philosophies such as: fascism, communism, anarchism, etc.
Age Inappropriate: These books have been banned or censored due to their content and the age level at which they are aimed. In some cases, children's books are viewed to have "inappropriate" themes for the age level at which they are written for.

Source: Fort Lewis College Website (2013). Common reasons for banning books, Fort Lewis College, Banned Books, Censorship & Free Speech, John F. Reed Library.

Yet this curatorial model was agitated by the growing popularity of pulp fiction and comic books made for kids. So it was that the comic book industry was buffeted by the growing concerns about the banality and violence in children's popular entertainments. The key difference between books and comics was the later sector's adoption of the business model of mass publishing (pioneered by the penny newspaper) which reduced the purchase price with an advertising subsidy while scaling up print runs with cheaper paper and printing methods. The low cost of comics meant that unlike books, comics could be bought by children themselves, without the assumed approval of parents. Seeking the child's repeated purchase at a price equivalent to a candy bar, comic book writers experimented with new templates for children's visual story telling which accentuated adventure, humor and simplicity of action over internal subjective experiences. Dick Tracy, Superman, Tarzan and Donald Duck defined a popular literary cannon that seemed to have lost the charm of Winnie the Pooh and the depth of Huckleberry Finn. From the 1930s on, moral crusaders asserted that comics corrupted youth, hurt their ability to read and appreciate art, and even made them delinquents (Tilley, 2012). Building on the self-regulatory regime developed by the movie industry, the Association of Comics Magazine Publishers (ACMP) developed a set of story-telling guidelines that they hoped could put aside parents' concerns about what their children would find in the comics by binding children's popular cultural productions by a similar set of criteria for dealing problematic contents ranging from nudity, excessive violence and emotionally disturbing ideas of an extreme nature. Facing calls for an outright ban on comics in the 1950s, when Dr. Wertheim's book The Seduction of the Innocents (1954) became a best seller, the industry acceded to a regime of self-regulation administered by the Comic Book Authority (see Fig. 2).

Given children's growing access to new media like comics, radio and the cinema, the benefits self-censorship was realized in the early adoption of a code by the Motion Picture Producers and Distributers of America. With the advent of talking motion pictures apprehension about this emerging cultural industry grew. In 1930, MPPDA, the industry association developed a new code for cinematic works "cooperating with educators… and leaders in the field of child education" which implicitly recognized the role of censorship in works that could be accessed by child audiences. The principle of the code stated: "Motion picture producers recognize the high trust and confidence which have been placed in them by the people of the world, and they recognize their responsibility to the public because of that trust." The code mentioned specifically provisions for the representation of "crime; sex; vulgarity; obscenity; profanity; nudity; religion and nationalism; and repellant subjects (including cruelty to children)". So too, the idea of self-censorship afforded a resolution for the expansion of the entertainment industries generally in the 1950s including radio, movies, comics and TV afternoon and prime time day parts.

But straight jacketed by the sanitization of narrative expected of films made for mass audiences, US film producers found them challenged by more adult oriented films from abroad. To protect less mature audiences,

Fig. 2: The comic book code

Crimes shall never be presented in such a way as to create sympathy for the criminal, to promote distrust of the forces of law and justice, or to inspire others with a desire to imitate criminals.

If crime is depicted it shall be as a sordid and unpleasant activity.

Policemen, judges, government officials, and respected institutions shall never be presented in such a way as to create disrespect for established authority.

Criminals shall not be presented so as to be rendered glamorous or to occupy a position which creates a desire for emulation.

In every instance good shall triumph over evil and the criminal punished for his misdeeds.

Scenes of excessive violence shall be prohibited. Scenes of brutal torture, excessive and unnecessary knife and gunplay, physical agony, the gory and gruesome crime shall be eliminated.

No comic magazine shall use the words "horror" or "terror" in its title.

All scenes of horror, excessive bloodshed, gory or gruesome crimes, depravity, lust, sadism, masochism shall not be permitted.

All lurid, unsavory, gruesome illustrations shall be eliminated.

Inclusion of stories dealing with evil shall be used or shall be published only where the intent is to illustrate a moral issue and in no case shall evil be presented alluringly, nor so as to injure the sensibilities of the reader.

Scenes dealing with, or instruments associated with walking dead, torture, vampires and vampirism, ghouls, cannibalism, and werewolfism are prohibited.

Profanity, obscenity, smut, vulgarity, or words or symbols which have acquired undesirable meanings are forbidden.

Nudity in any form is prohibited, as is indecent or undue exposure.

Suggestive and salacious illustration or suggestive posture is unacceptable.

Females shall be drawn realistically without exaggeration of any physical qualities.

Illicit sex relations are neither to be hinted at nor portrayed. Rape scenes, as well as sexual abnormalities, are unacceptable.

Seduction and rape shall never be shown or suggested.

Sex perversion or any inference to same is strictly forbidden.

Nudity with meretricious purpose and salacious postures shall not be permitted in the advertising of any product; clothed figures shall never be presented in such a way as to be offensive or contrary to good taste or morals.

Source: https://en.wikipedia.org/wiki/Comics_Code_Authority

the MPAA came up with a revised regulatory scheme: The MPAA film rating system was intended to maintain the regimes of censorship for child audiences based on maturity gradation: the MPAA film rating system went into effect on November 1, 1968, with four ratings: *G* for general audiences, *M* for mature content, *R* for restricted (under 17 not admitted without an adult), and *X* for sexually explicit content. In 1972, *G* was changed to the current *PG*, for "parental guidance suggested." In 1984, in response to public complaints regarding the severity of horror elements in PG-rated titles the *PG-13* rating was created as a middle tier between *PG* and *R*. These codes were enforceable at the point of sale, both at the cinema, as well as the rental store[4].

Celebrated originally as an extension of mass education, the rise of the computer gaming in the 1980s as an expanding sector of the entertainment market, like films, calls to protect young computer gamers from adult content including sexual stereotyping, about graphic violence and about morally hazardous role models grew raucous (Kline et al., 2003; Kline, 2005b). But attempts to regulate children's computer game play ran up against the same self-regulatory arguments pioneered by the film industry, resulting in the same comprise: a "rating systems" and guidelines. As the alternative to censorship, industry proponents argued that parents should be the arbiters of children's exposure to popular entertainment. It should not be the bureaucratic State, but parents who should make informed choices about the exposure to cultural content. The industry therefore happily proffered an age-appropriate rating system that warned and advised parents about the nature of the content of the game, seemingly respecting the rights of parents to have the final say in the determination of their own children's graduated exposure to mature themes and adult ideologies in popular culture. The industry's innovation was to add descriptors to the classification system (E; 10+; Teen; M 17+; A 18+) affording parents more flexibility in making decisions about content. But unlike the film industry PG ratings, the video game code (ESRB) was largely intended to prevent enforcement of code through regulatory mechanisms at point of sale – especially by teen and youth.

The cracks were widening in the cordon sanitaire thrown by regulators around children's access and exposure to popular culture when this regulatory model was itself undermined by the shift of gaming into

4 https://en.wikipedia.org/wiki/Motion_Picture_Production_Code.

the on-line space. The 1990s witnessed great innovation in the gaming industries with the first virtual playgrounds – multiuser gaming sites and fantasy role play which migrated online. MMORPG's like WOW and EverQuest, however popular, were incapable of ascertaining the age of the players, because it was impossible to filter players IP's using age-related categories to regulate children's violent play on-line. The codes and guidelines developed by the industry *de facto* became impossible to enforce in the on-line world. So the shift to on-line gaming made it much harder for parents to control their young children's access to mature themes and graphic violence despite the industry's codes which supposedly empowered them (Kline and Guo, 2007b).

These content cum quality codes seem oddly quaint now, as does the idea of censorship for any but the youngest audience. But it should also be noted that popular culture codes certified a shift in public anxieties: mild violence (cartoon and fantasy) and suggestive themes are considered acceptable for audiences 10 and over. In retrospect it can also be noted that it is the comic book that began the creative literary innovations that underwrote this gradual erosion of standards for film, TV and Video Games. Their effect was to build a child and teen fascination with adventure fantasy: indeed, as indicated by the 22.5 billion dollars gross box office from Marvel properties in 2018, the comic book proved a profound innovation in story telling that ultimately undermined the role of librarians in the protection of children from graphic violence, sexualized themes and morally ambiguous fiction. And the comic book's successor – the video games industry is on course to generate just shy of $135 billion in 2018[5].

3. Commercialization of TV culture: The ethos of limited exposure

After WWII, a gradual rethinking of child socialization occurred which Llyod DeMause called the "helping" approach to childrearing (De Mause, 1974). Surrounded by playgrounds and devoted to their comics, cartoons and toys, children's freedom to explore and assess entertainment for themselves was increasingly considered as essential to their

5 https://www.gamesindustry.biz/articles/2018-12-18-global-games-market-value-rose-to-usd134-9bn-in-2018.

healthy maturation, as was parental love and recognition of their accomplishments. Unrestricted leisure and free play were no longer perceived as "devils work" in need of "referees" but now seen as necessary conditions for promoting rational, autonomous and self-expressive individuals. By granting children safe environments and supporting their formation of peer relations and cultural tastes, parents were encouraging children's development according to their own needs and timing. Yet the moral paradox at the heart of this emerging framework of socialization assumed the continuation of the custodial model for the cultural industries – and their willingness to distinguish children's cultural needs from all others.

TV was introduced in the post WWII period into this perfect storm of *laissez faire* parenting, mass media innovation and commercialization which began to agitate the post-war matrix of socialization (Kline, 1992) with consequences for the ethical debates about the responsibilities of the cultural industries for both the promotion and protection of children. Launched amid much progressive chatter about enhancing mass education the rapid diffusion of commercial TV in the 1950s did much to augment the critiques of popular culture generated around comic books. The success of Disney's bringing to life on the screen the magic kingdom of classic folk tales and animal stories with a touch of humor demonstrated the commercial potential of TV for kids. The self-regulatory guidelines for the curation of young children's cultural content was implicitly transferred to TV in these productions – profanity and sexuality should be limited, banality and graphic violence only marginally tolerated if in comedic form in programming for family viewing and after school. Yet as children abandoned the streets and parks to sit in front of the television for up to three hours each day watching cowboys, superheroes and cartoon shows in prime time, the content of child-oriented production became roundly questioned by concerned parents. However, much they appreciated this baby-sitting service, it was hard for parents steeped in the values of America's progressive era, to see mindless cartoons, violence and sitcoms as morally uplifting. As Spigel (1998) noted, children's enthusiasm for TV was increasingly contested as educators claimed that commercial TV was less a magic kingdom of delightful folk tales, than a vast wasteland cultivating an aggressive and poorly educated generation of young couch potatoes.

Three features of this new medium were to especially worry the professional guardians of children's cultural enclaves. The first was the mass reach into modern households that resulted in many children viewing up to three hours of TV daily on their own, beyond the supervision of their parents. Parents worried not only about their children's exposure to mature contents, but their diminishing control over their children's moral and psychological maturation.

> Worse still, parents may not even know how and where their children have acquired this information. With the mass commercial dissemination of ideas, the parent is so to speak left out of the mediation loop, and the child becomes the direct addressee of the message. Perhaps for this reason, the history of children's involvement with mass media have been marked by a deep concern on the part of adult groups to monitor their entertainment and survey their pleasures. (Spigel, 1998, p. 114)

The second was the cartoonish visual storytelling which proved so accessible and attractive to very young audiences that began to worry educators that children's fascination with banal entertainment was distracting children from reading and schooling. Without the guiding hand of parents and teachers, would the immature child have the knowledge and perspective necessary to discriminate between the banal and the civilized in commercialized popular culture available to them in the mediated marketplace? The third was the commercial business model in which the networks prospered by giving kids what they most wanted – banal and violent cartoons sponsored by food and toy manufacturers. Watching TV for three hours a day, exposed children to 20,000 ads per year – a persuasive effort that rivaled and potentially undermined educators and parents' values. Parents began to see that the invisible hand of marketing was also leaving smudgy fingerprints on the screen: the cereals it promoted were too sweet and the toys were too war-line for many parents (Kline, 1993). In short, like it or not, children's marketers had become a major factor in children's learning in front of the TV. Educators began to formulate a precautionary curriculum for media literacy which could serve as the antidote to an onslaught mediated popular culture (Kline, 2018).

Moreover, from the 1960s on, research into the effects of TV began to undergird the ethical debates with notions of children at risk. Studies began to reveal that when left to their own devices, children did not just view the mandated "educational programming" of Mr. Rogers Neighborhood and Sesame Street – even young children watched adult programs too. The entertainment industry's self-censorship wasn't going to save the TV generation from violence and moral extremities. More importantly, the studies of the behavioral consequences of TV viewing began to demonstrate that the harm of too much watching was not just a moral hazard based on extreme content and banality: Heavy viewers' reading and school achievement were being impacted too. Moreover, even comic violence provided young children with role models that resulted in aggressive behavior (NIMH, 1982). So, throughout the waning 20th century the TV industries claims of contributing to children's education while protecting them from the harm looked increasingly wrong-headed. Pulling these concerns together, Neil Postman's laments proclaimed that mass media made kids grow up too soon by violating the developmentally appropriate norms prescribed by child professionals (Postman, 1982).

The cracks in the walled garden metaphor continued to grow as the power of marketers to target young consumers in mass media became equally obvious. Pestered to buy Coon Skin Hats, Frosted Flakes, G.I. Joes and Barbies advertised on TV, parents also became alarmed by the marketers growing influence on their children's preferences for food and toys. The debate about children's TV in the USA therefore shifted from FCC, where the question of quality programming was deliberated, to the Federal Trade Commission (FTC), where the profusion of cereal, snack food and toy ads which punctuated children's entertainment were considered. Although the regulation of misleading advertising dated from 1926, the parental advocates concerns were less focused on the false claims and exaggerations that could be found in children's advertising, than the limited ability of children to understand marketer's persuasive intent.

The body of research that flowed from this debate highlighted both limited parental control of children's TV viewing as well as their unique vulnerability to persuasion rather than the practices of commercial communication. During the 1970s, as child targeted advertising moved front and center in the debates about protecting the TV generation, the ethical questions surrounding when children acquired the capacity for rational choice supplanted the debates about the failure of the industry to enforce content and quality walls around the cultural industries. Could ads have an undue influence on children because of their developmental immaturity? Based on the mounting furor about kids' vulnerability, the FCC in 1974 limited the amount of advertising to 9.5 minutes and called for separation of programming and advertising content based on children's developmental limitations as prudent. But these regulations quickly proved insufficient. Research into children's understanding of

TV found that until they are teens, they cannot be deemed capable of "rational consumer choice" because they cannot recognize ads as such, are unable to make complex product comparisons, and fail to recognize or filter the persuasive techniques used by advertisers (Ward, 1972). In the schools, ever mindful of their duty to protect children from popular culture, teachers began to include "advertising" literacy as part of a protectionist curriculum for popular culture.

The debate grew even more rancorous when in ACT (Action for Children's Television) called on the FCC for a ban on advertising to kids altogether based on a growing body of research which showed that children under eight years of age lacked any understanding of the persuasive intent of TV advertising. In 1978 the FTC imposed strict regulatory guidelines on marketing to children *in children's viewing slots* which included an hourly quota, "bumpers" that separated advertisements from programming, limits on the use of popular TV characters in ads and, cautions about unrealistic claims. Although this regulatory strategy didn't raise issues of freedom of expression, it might have been a mistake. Yet as Jeffery et al. (1982) noted, the industry mobilized against the ban claiming "Advertisers assert that they are helping to teach children appropriate consumer behavior, that children's food preferences are shaped most strongly by parents not advertisers, and that deciding what a child watches on TV is a parental function in which there is no need for federal regulation." As John (1999) later noted, the 10 years of struggle over children's advertising at the FTC proved of little consequence when Ronald Reagan appointed a neo-conservative to the FTC in 1981 who despite the evidence, de-regulated children's commercial TV in the interests of commercial free speech.

Deregulation not only unleashed a wave of innovation in children's commercialized TV programming but the casting aside of the FTC's protectionist concerns about children's vulnerability to commercial persuasion also transformed US TV into a cultural laboratory for experimentation in synergistic brand promotion. *Out of the Garden* (Kline, 1993) recounts the effects of this decimation of the self-regulatory regime for children's commercial TV which produced an astonishing boom in both animated TV production and toy markets. Gone were live action dramas, nature shows and goofy hosted comedic specials of the 1960s replaced by program length licensed toy promotions which saturated children's specialty channels with 30 minute action adventure animations starring brand characters – GI Joe, Transformers, Inhumanoids, Barbie and the Rockers and Gobots – punctuated by ads for these same battle weary action toys. Not surprising that this change in children's programming reignited the age-old debates about gratuitous violence and gender representation in after school and Saturday morning time slots. But the consequences of these innovations in branding spread far beyond the toy market's rapid expansion. During the 1990s the emergent possibilities of animated storytelling highlighted the potential of synergistic marketing approaches that integrated brand properties throughout screen media right up to point of sale. The strategy of brand character promotion went far beyond the design of toy ads: product design and packaging, product placements, cross-promotion, filmic tie-ins, and celebrity endorsements became the integrative elements in the global promotion of children's products in the mediated market. Through licensing deals and cross promotion brand promotions extended across children's culture: Transformer Lunch Boxes, G.I. Joe pajama's and Barbie cereals were an indication that the traditional demarcation between product, programming content and advertising were getting much harder for young children to understand.

Moreover, these character marketing strategies spread quickly from toy marketing to foods where the twin notions of brand affect and synergy sparked further cross-marketing innovations bridging the key sectors underwriting children's TV production: Toys were given away with Happy Meals, while playful fun became the dominate value in food branding. As Kline and Botterill (2012) noted in a study of food branding on TV that character advertising, product placements, celebrity endorsements and cross-marketing deals all undermined not only the distinction between ads and programs, but more fundamentally between the imaginary and the real. One example they mention is a Captain Crunch Choco Donuts cereal ad. It opens with a scene of real children in a supermarket dismayed to find the shelves empty of their favorite cereal. They are deeply disgruntled until Captain Crunch sails into the store on his animated ship inviting the children power-lick the chocolate decks clean which they do with a big slurp of their animated tongues. The last shot shows them at home as their still oversized tongues lick their breakfasted lips as the announcer reminds viewers that Choco Donuts "are part of a balanced chocolatey breakfast."

With ads like this it is easy to see why children's ability to critically understand the persuasive intent of marketing was further diminished by the unfettering of fun and fantasy in the promotional world. In the absence of regulatory restraint and parental approval, media educators once again sought to defend children from unscrupulous marketers by teaching them the competences they needed in a consumer society (Kline, 2007). The first was an expanded understanding of *media literacy* which included a broader range of critical attitudes and cognitive skills required for children to understand themselves as targeted audiences in a market economy. The second was *advertising literacy*, which set out to strengthen the child's ability to recognize advertising techniques in their various forms in order to critically interpret the product claims made in branded promotions (Kline, 2010). Hardly surprising that 20 years after deregulation of TV, the World Health Organization's report on population weight gains of the child population *reignited the ethical debates about food advertising targeting children.* Media critics and health advocates held the food advertisers responsible for the changing weight status of the child population the globesity crisis also exposed new limitations in the ethical framework for protecting child audiences from "systemic risks" that not only took advantage of their unique vulnerability to persuasion but also because food marketing caused demonstrable harm (Kline, 2011). As anxiety about child obesity grew, so too did the calls to policy makers to ban ads because of the unhealthy bias found in children's food advertising on TV.

Although there are several reasons that population weight gain is associated with heavy TV watching, the one that got singled out was their exposure to the TV diet – the constant barrage of high salt and sugary fast foods that are marketed on children's time TV. This critique is in some ways new for it not only highlights the important shift from moral arguments about children's ability to recognize ads to an empirical *harm done to their health* but also to the difficulties of regulating any systemic bias in food advertising (Kline, 2011). Protectionist debates fought over globesity reframed the regulatory regimes of children's time TV – invoking bans on food advertising to children (UK), stricter codes on visual representation and limits on verbal health claims. It also opened up the scope of topics included in regulatory regimes by noting the marketing synergies achieved in the screen-based entertainment system which included social media and promotional websites (Kline and Botterill, 2008). But it was already clear that bans on food ads would be ineffective: Firstly, because children who also watched prime time programs were still exposed to food marketing messages, and secondly because children were migrating on line where they were exposed to not only violent games but the proliferation of food promotion – even in child targeted infotainment on line. Tracking these changes in marketing strategy did help refocus media educators' thinking about the "firewall's available for protecting children" in the face of expanding commercial culture online. To counter this problem, educators and children's advocates also began to articulate a new precautionary digital media literacy (Hobbs, 2004) that recognized both the lack of consent and new forms of commercial exposure being experienced in the trans-mediated marketplace which uses edutainment sites to gather personal information on line for targeting children.

4. Back to the future: The ethos of privacy

The commercialization of the internet in 1994 at first provided meager offerings for younger children other than a few experimental on-line play spaces (usually university developed) and infotainment sites (dictionaries, language learning etc.). But soon building on community bulletin boards – the precursors to social media empires like *MySpace* and later *YouTube* and *Facebook* – some chat rooms for children began to appear. Recognizing the importance of parental acceptance of on-line educational resources, a few entrepreneurs launched child-oriented virtual worlds modeled on the walled garden principle. Generally speaking these virtual worlds were conceived and promoted as child-friendly multiuser chat and play spaces – walled gardens – where the moderator's role was to discipline speech (profanity), to keep out suspected child molesters; and to banish bullies and other forms of harassment. Using a subscription business model which required parental knowledge, the gatekeeper was assumed to be the parent who gave consent to kids' access based on subscriptions (Dewey, 2014).

Yet surrounding these child-friendly virtual gardens was a rapidly changing digital infrastructure offering infotainments ranging from global weather reports to porn sites. And concerns about these supposedly safe enclaves for young viewers grew louder as children began to plug their TV sets into their video game consoles. At the forefront of on-line innovation was the gaming industry whose popular adventure, sports and MMORP games (*Ultima, Starcraft, Everquest*) attracted ever more teen gamers online (Kline et al., 2003). Because of IP anonymity, online gaming sites could not distinguish whether the player was an adult or child – despite age related ESRB ratings. Advocacy groups and researchers sounded the alarm bells about younger children playing them too: horrified by the graphic violence of shooters and the prevalence of pornography online, advocates called for safeguards against the mature content they were exposed to on their computers (Kline and Guo, 2007a).

Rather than regulate violent content online however, the US Federal Trade Commission (FTC) proposed COPPA (Children's Online Privacy Protection Act of 1998) intending to "Protect kids who surf the internet." In April 20, 1999 the FTC issued rules that demanded that operators of commercial websites and online services *directed to children under 13* that if they collect, use, or disclose personal information from children, they must obtain the consent of parents. The Chairman of the FTC Robert Pitofski proclaimed that "This proposed rule aims to achieve that goal by *putting parents in control of personal information that is collected from their children on the Web."* Although the rule highlights privacy as a key ethical concern, it is worth noting that COPPA has no age appropriate content codes, nor does it distinguish infotainment from branded persuasion. Its focus is only to provide support for the parents control of the exposure of children under 13 to inappropriate content online.

In addition to its limited scope, the proposed rule also stated the FTC's willingness "to accommodate varied business practices and the fast pace of technological change." Hardly surprising as Chung and Grimes (2006) point out in their critique of the COPPA, although website privacy policies required parental consent, the question of what is done with metadata remained unclear: "One of the most important shortcomings of the act is its narrow definition of privacy and what constitutes personal information. For instance, the COPPA laws apply only to personal information obtained from a child in identifiable form" (Chung and Grimes, 2006). They give the example of Neopets.com, where children are awarded "Neopoints" (the currency required to purchase food and items for the virtual pets in the game) for completing surveys on various topics including product preferences (that can be advertised on the sites). In order to play with Neopets, a young user's parents must agree to relinquish their personal information for commercial use. But did parents' consent to Neopets use of surveys to target their children with advertising? Clearly the certifying of parental approval does not prevent online brands from gathering and selling meta-data collected and stored in aggregate form based on navigation of the site or as kids respond to questionnaires embedded in the site.

Although the FTC anticipated that innovation in children's online entertainment industries would continue to define the future of the internet in the 21st century they did not understand how better targeting of young audiences would extend problems created by commercialization of the internet. So they should hardly have been surprised to hear that by 2018 YouTube was bragging to Mattel that its channel was the leader in reaching children aged 6–11, even when compared with top TV channels, by gathering better audience data. In the wake of limited regulation, educators and advocates have been attempting to integrate privacy concerns into digital media literacy programs by incorporated privacy rights into the badges certifying informed consent online (Smith et al., 2017).

5. Back to the future II: The emerging ethos of commercial trans-mediation

YouTube was not the first to use meta-data for researching and targeting the youngest netizens. Building on the popularity of simple games like Pokemon and Barbie, and guided by the commercial success of websites like Neopets and Webkinz, children's growing interest in playing simple computer games online was abundantly evident: A 2007 study (Casual Games Market Report, 2007) revealed 200 million regular users of all ages each month. It must be said that many of these first young children's game sites were careful to maintain a sanitized child friendly look and feel of adventure games – mostly they were age appropriate and non-violent. Parents generally welcomed them into children's lives because they appeared to offer harmless play and distraction. Indeed, the appearance of this benign digital entertainment space for kids' exploration and play may have accelerated the migration of child audiences to online advertainment. An NPD study showed that almost 80 % of children aged six to eleven that went online sought out digital games (Lee et al., 2009).

The developments of a loyal fan base in turn inspired other marketers to leverage the growing popularity of online gaming by integrating the internet into their marketing strategies which used their online presence as an integral part of brand strategy (Dahl et al., 2009). As Grimes (2011) later pointed out, the youthful audience was built by marketer's diligent exploration of the numerous ways that gaming could provide leverage for the commercialization of the internet. As Grimes said: "To paraphrase an executive of MindCandy, creators of virtual pet Moshi Monsters, online game sites are 'not only an additional revenue source, but (something that) allows for a deeper connection with children and their everyday play experiences'. By enabling a coordinated commercial construction of the design, rule systems and action opportunities that make up the play space, virtual worlds technologies offer the promise of much greater control over the contents and themes of play itself" (Grimes, 2011, p. 4). As Kline and Botterill (2011) have similarly noted many children's marketers were experimenting with innovative ways of managing audience flow across the trans-mediated screen culture: In their study of TV cross marketing of brand characters they point to a Kinder Egg ad on TV which depicts a rosy checked cherub of 7 who returns from a family shopping expedition proudly proclaiming to his mother how his recently purchased chocolate egg contained a secret code for playing a computer game that he loved. Pretty soon the son and mom are enjoying quality time together playing video games game whose premise is collecting eggs together. Such appeals in TV ads demonstrate only one of the important ways that a trans-mediated promotional strategy configured around brand affect marketing was re-orchestrating children's screen culture they argue. And nowhere was this erosion of the distinction between playful content and brand advertising more in evidence than online. While television viewing continued to preoccupy health advocates concerns about children's excessive screen time, thanks to marketers' growing exploration of trans-media marketing synergies mobile media, video games and online social media got more critical attention (Common Sense Media, 2014; Panic et al., 2013).

The children's food industry has indeed proven to be especially enthusiastic about building successful games capable of attracting over one million children every month (Harris et al., 2012). Indeed, early in the 21st Century compounding the preponderance of unhealthy products sold on children's time TV, UK Food Commission (2005) also documented 41 non-broadcast food marketing techniques used in the UK claiming: "Marketing campaigns aimed at children and young people move smoothly between different formats, perhaps combining product placement in blockbuster films; which in turn feature characters who will appear on food products and in interactive games; backed by websites offering music downloads and movie clips, containing yet more inducements to buy" (2005, p. 3). Cereal, fast food and snack product logos not only proliferated online, but these branded social media sites wove games and infotainment into branded web-destinations where young children could play games, compete for points, buy virtual goods, share their creations and view short cartoons (Alvy and Calvert, 2008; An and Stern, 2011).

Advergaming, is the term often used to describe this new form of extended product placement built around games that are specifically built around the product, or brand character: On these sites, brand promotion plays a central role in play action (Culp et al., 2010; Hofmeister-Tóth and Nagy, 2011). One early review of the advergame market for children's cereal identified 15 cereal company-sponsored websites for children owned by General Mills, Kellogg's and Post (Harris et al., 2012). Club Kelloggs[6] for example offers a child-oriented website which features multiple games including Froot Loops (12 games), Rice Krispies (4), Frosted Flakes (1), Eggo (3), and Corn Pops (1). Children who sign up as a member (with parental permission of course) can earn badges and awards, as well as track and share high scores with others. But these are promotional sites: in these connected branded virtual spaces, animated brand avatars provide the point of entry into a broader brand universe characterized by a panoply of playful contests, exploration, stylization questionnaires and consumer preferences were included in the fun. They also provide ways of targeting young consumers: Kraft Foods' Postopia.com site for example encourages players to earn "Postokens" by submitting a "code" found on the inside of specially marked boxes of child-oriented Post cereal brands – including Fruity Pebbles, Alpha-Bits, and Oreo O's.

A 2015 study by the Casual Games Association found that 44 % of children play online every day, while 41 % play at least a few times a week. Indeed, the gamification of children's food marketing has contributed to the significant boom in on-line promotional spending. Tony the Tiger, Toucan Sam and a vast array of other brand characters became the face of many of the games targeting kids under 12. Harris et al. also found that the advertainment websites achieved the highest number of child visitors in 2011 belonged to Kellogg's, led by FrootLoops.com (161,900 unique child visitors per month), AppleJacks (116,200) and CornPops.com (59,500). This was followed by three General Mills sites that averaged between 29,300 to 52,300 unique monthly visitors (Harris

---

6 http://www.clubkelloggs.ca/.

et al., 2012). While a TV commercial exposes the brand for 15 or 30 seconds, children play these branded games on average for 43 minutes at a time. Moreover, while visiting these advergaming sites children are not only exposed to brand messages repeatedly but asked to give up personal data that is useful to marketers for both knowing their preferences and targeting them. Moreover by integrating consumer research protocols within the game play elements of the game or with consumer incentives to buy the very products being promoted on the site, advergaming sites provide a continuous stream of personal information about user preferences and other useful market-research data to brand managers.

Courtney Chu's (Chu, 2018) recent survey of children's food advergaming web sites documents the dramatic growth in food branding online targeting kids under 13. By embedding repeated brand exposure in games, some even purport to have an educational rationale. Yet as she notes, it is not the content of these casual game sites that seems problematic, so much as the new forms of commercialization underwriting online playtime: with simple themes, easy to understand game mechanics and interruptible game flow they are intended to both strengthen brand affect and provide data on child audiences below the radar of parental concerns. Nor is digital literacy programs of much use in young children. In a small experimental exposure study of 18 children aged 4 to 8 who regularly surf the internet she found only one eight years old who was able to identify on-line games as promotions for a food brand. Her research also confirmed that advocates concerns about food branding online are not constrained to the limitations of privacy rules in guarding against data mining and targeting of young children on-line but must address children's capacity to recognized the intent of the immersive branded advergaming directed at young children who lack the ability to distinguish commercial intent in a branded online environment.

Coda: Déjà vu all over again

In the 21st century, privacy has blended with commercialization to broaden efforts at defining ethical frameworks for children in digital communication policy. Editing my essay in the shadow of the Covid-19 pandemic I couldn't help but notice that most countries that have implemented smart phone apps for contact-tracing have privileged the principle of "informed consent" to confront the violations of privacy built into the infrastructure of digital communication technology. Yet there remains a profound tension between the public interest in health and safety and the private individual interest in privacy because metadata are constantly available for mining – by corporations, by governments, and by hackers with corrupt intent. Given the pressing health crisis of this pandemic the ethos of informed consent may offer an acceptable compromise: but when it comes to children who have been spending more time at home on line, the concerns about informed consent in a digitally connected market democracy what informed consent means remain unresolved.

The changes taking place in marketing to children under 13 online during the 21st century have complexified the prior ethical debates about children's vulnerability to inappropriate content and corporate branding strategies that targets them – but not negated them: firstly because digital media have changed children's media use patterns especially during the pandemic; secondly because data scrapping and targeting takes place without comprehensive parental consent; and thirdly because synergistic brand promotion and product placement in movies, infotainment, advergaming and TV are subverting children's ability to distinguish entertainment from commerce. It seems that it took twenty years for the FTC to realize that advertising to children has moved online: With no regulation of online commercialism beyond parental agreement, marketers ability to address child audiences in ways that took advantage of their limited ability to identify commercial speech has been dramatically enhanced. So the problem of figuring out how children can be protected from exploitation and harm in commercialized on-line entertainment remains. The UK's CAP code provides a preliminary ethical guideline to address these very issues stating:

The CAP Code rules on the recognition of advertising require that marketing communications must be obviously identifiable as such. This guidance identifies situations where marketing communications directed at under-12s are likely to require "enhanced" disclosure to ensure recognition. It provides marketers with advice on how to comply with the Code.

Unfortunately, it appears that few online marketers are paying attention…

References

Alvy, L. M., & Calvert, S. L. (2008). Food marketing on popular children's web sites: a content analysis. *Journal of the American Dietetic Association, 108*(4), 710–713. http://doi.org/10.1016/j.jada.2008.01.006

An, S., & Stern, S. (2011). Mitigating the effects of advergames on children. *Journal of Advertising, 40*(1), 43–56. http://doi.org/10.2753/JOA0091-3367400103

Ariès, P. (1962). *Centuries of childhood: A social history of family life*. Vintage Books.

Balfour Jeffrey, D., McLellarn, R. W., & Fox, D. T. (1982). The development of children's eating habits: The role of television commercials. *Health Education Quarterly, 9*(2–3), 78–93. https://doi.org/10.1177/109019818200900208

Batchelor, J. (2018). *Global games market value rising to $134.9bn in 2018*. GamesIndustry.Biz. https://www.gamesindustry.biz/articles/2018-12-18-global-games-market-value-rose-to-usd134-9bn-in-2018.

Butler University, Libraries and Center for Academic Technology. *Banned books: Reasons for banning books*. http://libguides.butler.edu/banned-books?p=217686.

Campaign for Commercial Free Childhood. (2019, Sept. 6). Our impact: CCFC gets big YouTube changes. *Campaign for Commercial Free Childhood*. https://commercialfreechildhood.org/our-impact-ccfc-gets-big-youtube-changes/.

Casual Games Association. (2015). https://www.statista.com/statistics/694723/frequency-children-us-play-favorite-gaming-apps/.

Chu, C. H. (2018). *The issues at play: Examining the learning potential in advergames and nutritional games for children* (Thesis M.A., Communication, Art & Technology: School of Communication, Simon Fraser University). http://summit.sfu.ca/system/files/iritems1/17910/etd10582_CChu.pdf.

Chung, G., & Grimes, S. M. (2005). Data mining the kids: Surveillance and market research strategies in children's online games. *Canadian Journal of Communication, 30*(4), 527–548. https://doi.org/10.22230/cjc.2005v30n4a1525

Committee of Advertising Practice. (2017). *Recognition of advertising: online marketing to children under 12 Advertising Guidance* (p. 9). Committee of Advertising Practice. https://www.asa.org.uk/asset/27DBEBF0-6EEB-4E49-A44173CC8A9F5451.2F38244B-29EA-4830-85B5A5D65E-4CA6C6/.

Culp, J., Bell, R. A., & Cassady, D. (2010). Characteristics of food industry web sites and "advergames" targeting children. *Journal of Nutrition Education and Behavior, 42*(3), 197–201. http://doi.org/10.1016/j.jneb.2009.07.008

Dahl, S., Eagle, L., & Báez, C. (2009). Analyzing advergames: Active diversions or actually deception. An exploratory study of online advergames content. *Young Consumers, 10*(1), 46–59. http://doi.org/10.1108/17473610910940783

DeMause, L. (Ed.). (1974). *The history of childhood.* Rowman & Littlefield.

Dewey, C. (2014). A complete history of the rise and fall and reincarnation of the beloved 90s chat room. *Washington Post*, Oct. 30.

Federal Trade Commission & Gruenwald Henderson, J. (2019, September 4). *Google and YouTube will pay record $170 million for alleged violations of children's privacy law.* Federal Trade Commission. https://www.ftc.gov/news-events/press-releases/2019/09/google-youtube-will-pay-record-170-million-alleged-violations.

Fort Lewis College Website. (2013). Common reasons for banning books, Fort Lewis College, John F. Reed Library. *Banned Books, Censorship & Free Speech.* November 15.

Grimes, S. M. (2010). *The digital child at play: How technological, political and commercial rule systems shape children's play in virtual worlds* (Thesis Ph.D Communication, Art & Technology: School of Communication, Simon Fraser University). https://summit.sfu.ca/item/11270.

Harris, J. L., Speers, S. E., Schwartz, M. B., & Brownell, K. D. (2012). US Food company branded advergames on the Internet: Children's exposure and effects on snack consumption. *Journal of Children and Media, 6*(1), 51–68. http://doi.org/10.1080/17482798.2011.633405

Hobbs, R. (2004). A review of school-based initiatives in media literacy education. *American Behavioral Scientist, 48*(1), 42–59. http://doi.org/10.1177/0002764204267250

Hofmeister-Tóth, Á., & Nagy, P. (2011). The content analysis of advergames in Hungary. *Qualitative Market Research: An International Journal, 14*(3), 289–303. http://doi.org/10.1108/13522751111137514

Jenks, C. (1996). *Childhood.* Routledge.

John, D. R. (1999). Consumer socialization of children: A retrospective look at twenty-five years of research. *Journal of Consumer Research, 26*(3), 183–213. http://doi.org/10.1086/209559

Kline, S. (1993). *Out of the garden: Toys, tv, and children's culture in the age of marketing.* Verso.

Kline, S. (2005). Is it time to rethink media panics? In J. Qvortrup (Ed.), *Studies in modern childhood: Society, agency, culture* (pp. 78–98). Palgrave Macmillan UK. https://doi.org/10.1057/9780230504929

Kline, S. (2007a) When it comes to consumer socialization, are children victims, empowered consumers or consumers-in-Training?, In S. Mazzarella (Ed.). *20 questions about youth and the media* (pp. 281–290). Peter Lang.

Kline, S. (2007b). Digital disturbances: On the promotion, panic, and politics of video game violence. In D. Taras, M. Bakardjieva, & F. Pannekoek (Eds.), *How Canadians communicate. II: Media, globalization, and identity* (pp. 167–194). University of Calgary Press.

Kline, S. (2010). Children as competent consumers. In D. Marshall (Ed.), *Understanding children as consumers.* Sage.

Kline, S. (2011). *Globesity, food marketing and family lifestyles.* Palgrave Basingstoke.

Kline, S. (2015). From media analysis to risk reduction pedagogy: Rethinking literacy in Canada. In A. Lee, Z. Kai, & K. Chan (Ed.), Proceedings of Fourth International Conference on Media Literacy *Multidisciplinary Approaches to Media Literacy: Research and Practice*, CUC/ HK Baptist University.

Kline, S., & Botterill, J. (2008). Targeting, synergy and flow in the mediated marketing of playthings. In G. Brougère (Ed.), *La Ronde des jeux et des jouets.* Autrement.

Kline, S., & Botterill, J. (2011). From counting calories to fun food: Regulating the TV diet in the age of obesity. In J. Finn (Ed.), *Images in action: Readings in visual communication and culture.* Oxford University Press.

Kline, S., Dyer-Witheford, N., & De Peuter, G. (2003). *Digital play: The interaction of technology, culture, and marketing.* McGill-Queen's University Press.

Lee, M., Choi, Y., Quilliam, E. T., & Cole, R. T. (2009). Playing with food: Content analysis of food advergames. *Journal of Consumer Affairs, 43*(1), 129–154. http://doi.org/10.1111/j.1745-6606.2008.01130.x

Moore, E. S., & Rideout, V. J. (2007). The online marketing of food to children: Is it just fun and games? *Journal of Public Policy & Marketing, 26*(2), 202–220. https://doi.org/10.1509/jppm.26.2.202.

National Institute of Mental Health (U.S.). (Ed.). (1982). *Television and behavior: Ten years of scientific progress and implications for the eighties: Vol. 1 Summary report.* U.S. Department of Health and Human Services, Public Health Service, Alcohol, Drug Abuse, and Mental Health Administration, National Institute of Mental Health.

Novacic, I. (2019). « It's kinda crazy »: Kid influencers make big money on social media, and few rules apply. *CBS NEWS.* (Aug. 23) https://www.cbsnews.com/news/kid-influencers-instagram-youtube-few-rules-big-money-cbsn-originals/.

Orciari, M. (2013). Foods advertised on popular children's websites do not meet nutrition standards. *YaleNews.* (Jul. 8) https://news.yale.edu/2013/07/08/foods-advertised-popular-childrens-websites-do-not-meet-nutrition-standards.

Panic, K., Cauberghe, V., & De Pelsmacker, P. (2013). Comparing TV ads and advergames targeting children: The impact of persuasion knowledge on behavioral responses. *Journal of Advertising, 42*(2–3), 264–273. http://doi.org/10.1080/00913367.2013.774605

Postman, N. (1982). *The disappearance of childhood.* Delacorte Press.

Press, *A.* (2019). YouTube fined $170m for collecting children's personal data. *The Guardian.* (Sept. 4). https://www.theguardian.com/technology/2019/sep/04/youtube-kids-fine-personal-data-collection-children-.

Rideout, V. J. (2014). Advertising to children and teens: Current practices: A common sense research brief. In S. Pai (Ed.), *Common sense media.* https://www.commonsensemedia.org/file/csm-advertisingresearchbrief-20141pdf/download.

Smith, K. L., Shade, L. R., & Shepherd, T. (2017). Open privacy badges for digital policy literacy. *International Journal of Communication, 11*(0), 2784–2805.

Spigel, L. (1998). Seducing the Innocent: Childhood and television in postwar America. In H. Jenkins (Ed.), *The children's culture reader* (pp. 110–135). New York University Press.

The International Association of Consumer Food Organization. (2003). *Broadcasting bad health: Why food marketing to children needs to be controlled* (p. 29). International Association of Consumer Food Organizations. http://www.foodcomm.org.uk/pdfs/Broadcasting_bad_health.pdf.

Tilley, C. L. (2012). Seducing the innocent: Fredric Wertham and the falsifications that helped condemn comics. *Information & Culture: A Journal of History, 47*(4), 383–413. https://doi.org/10.1353/lac.2012.0024

Ward, S. (1972). Children's reactions to commercials. *Journal of Advertising Research, 12*(2), 37–45.

Codes available at:

Children's Literature: Fort Lewis College Website. (2013). Common reasons for banning books, Fort Lewis College, John F. Reed Library. *Banned Books, Censorship & Free Speech.* November 15, 2013.

Comic Code: http://cbldf.org/resources/history-of-comics-censorship/history-of-comics-censorship-part-1/.

MPPC. https://en.wikipedia.org/wiki/Motion_Picture_Production_Code.

2

Entertainment or advertising? YouTube channels displaying content created by kids

Esther Martínez Pastor, Patricia Núñez, and Florence Chérigny

The content that children watch is increasingly fragmented, and the constant emergence of new social networks and devices accentuates this phenomenon. Within this ecosystem, companies have implemented new strategies to reach young audiences and brands develop 360-degree marketing strategies that integrate both offline and online campaigns. Creating entertaining content through videos allows brands to achieve a child friendlier presence and closer connection to the audiences, thus creating an affinity to the brand that would not otherwise be possible (Large, 2014). Influencers participate in these modalities, enhancing a branded communication that flows from the influencers' YouTube channels, through television shows and ends in real life with commercial events in retail outlets. Influencers are recognized experts in connecting with their young audiences in a more credible way than classical advertising campaigns, since the content they produce seems less branded and more authentic to their followers.

This new type of marketing is not only more personalized; it is also integrated into the content children are used to consuming from diverse platforms. In this context, brands create stories and establish authentic and genuine relationships with their audiences. Minors are the core target of these innovative branding strategies, since they hang out on online media, and prefer to access content – be it television programs or Netflix series – online, instead of watching conventional television (Montgomery, 2011). The Ofcom study (2019) states that children aged between 8 and 11 prefer to watch YouTube (49 %) compared to television (14 %), while for adolescents aged 12 to 15 years old the percentages are 49 % compared to 16 %, respectively.

Since 2017, children have entered digital media on a large scale as content creators (Ofcom, 2019): EvanTubeHD was the pioneer in 2011 in the United States, followed by other child content creators. Among them, Ryan, who started his channel "Ryan Toys Review" in 2015 by the age of 5, achieved a revenue of 22 million dollars in 2018 and 26 million dollars in 2019 (Hale, 2019). Furthermore, beyond his role as an expert influencer for young child audiences, he recently launched his own brand in collaboration with Wal-Mart (Berg, 2018).

Children aged under 12 increasingly enjoy the entertainment content that young influencers upload to the YouTube platform (McRoberts et al., 2016; Yarosh et al., 2016) as they are attracted by the stories that child influencers create with toys and brands. They imitate their preferred influencers by buying the products which the latter mention on their channels to enact creative game-playing (Brown and Hayes, 2008, p. 32). Through the videos they publish, children content creators have more power to influence purchases than any advertising campaign (Ramos Serrano and Herrero-Díaz, 2016; Tur-Viñes et al., 2019). The huge impact these young influencers have on their fans explains why brands collaborate with kid influencers to have their products mentioned in the videos they create.

The types of advertising formats that children prefer are emotional, surprising and interactive entertainment messages (Ipsos/Google, 2012) such as subscriptions, unboxing, sponsorships, promoted content, affiliate links, "see more" links and product tests (McReynolds et al., 2015; Wu, 2016; IAB, 2017)[1]. Influencer videos that take the form of tutorials, product reviews or entertainment content are often a new form of paid advertising with very little regulation or oversight. As marketing and entertainment strategies increasingly intertwine, it is quite difficult for young audiences to distinguish between entertainment content and

1 Unboxing is unpacking a toy and telling the audience what it contains. Sponsorship implies that a brand sponsors a video. Promoted content is the creation of a paid content promoting the brand. Affiliate links are links that refer to a site where you can buy the products shown in the video. A 'see more' link redirects the audience to a website to obtain further information on everything that the box contains. Product testing consists of videos where the products given by brands are used and showcased.

commercial content. A series of research works (Burgess, 2012; Blades et al., 2013; Chester, 2015; García et al., 2015; Campbell, 2016; Craig and Cunningham, 2017; Martínez-Pastor, 2019) emphasize the importance of distinguishing advertising produced by minors, as well as advertising spaces used by minors, from the advertising content which they consume. They all question whether a minor should be allowed to post content on social networks or advertise content on the channels they create on YouTube, even with the consent of their parents or legal guardians.

Following this rationale, this chapter develops a comparative approach to the regulations relating to YouTube content creators who are minors and to the social actors who participate in that ecosystem in Europe and in the United States. This approach will successively study the aspects that fall under consumer law and concern misleading advertising (I), then those that fall under personal data law and concern targeted advertising (II).

1. Aspects relating to misleading advertising under consumer law

Here we will examine the regulations in force in the United States and Europe (1.1), the self-regulatory effort put in place by the stakeholders (1.2) and the litigation relating to misleading advertising (1.3).

1.1. Youth influencer videos and the regulation of advertising to minors

Both the European and the United States regulations consider that minors must always be informed of what they are watching and must not be misled by covert advertising, or content disguised as entertainment. All advertising content must be clearly identified as such, and differentiated from other kinds of content (Lievens, 2010; McLaughlin, 2013; Staksrud, 2013). Children should not be tricked into thinking that their favorite YouTuber sincerely enjoys a new toy, when the YouTuber has an advertising contract with a brand to promote the toy in the videos he produces. Video-sharing platforms are not always compliant with these contractual rules, which apply in conventional media such as television. Consequently, some initiatives emerged to attempt to regulate this nascent online market and protect children, in Europe and in United States[2].

In Europe, consumers are protected from misleading advertising both through the *Unfair Commercial Practices Directive* and in the recent *Audiovisual Media Services Directive*. Article 6 of the *Unfair Commercial Practices Directive* states:

> a commercial practice shall be regarded as misleading if it contains false information, and is therefore untruthful or in any way, including overall presentation, deceives or is likely to deceive the average consumer, even if the information is factually correct, in relation to one or more of the following elements, and in either case, causes or is likely to cause him to take a transactional decision that he would not have taken otherwise.

Advertising is misleading when the context does not overtly situate its persuasive goal and when consumers get confused by the nature and the presentation of the message. Advertising must be understood to be content with a clear persuasive purpose, even if the brand which promotes the content does not clearly appear. In this respect, the *Audiovisual Media Services Directive* (2018) prohibits surreptitious advertising and makes it obligatory for all commercial communications to be readily recognizable for all consumers (Art. 9.1). Thus, "Member States shall ensure that video-sharing platform providers clearly inform users where programmes and user-generated videos contain audiovisual commercial communications" (Art. 28b) through regulation and self-regulation of media.

Many European countries have developed self-regulation codes for the advertising sector, with special reference to children[3]. In addition, the Directive prohibits advertising from inciting minors to purchase based on their inexperience or credulity, or from directly encouraging

---

2 Examples include the EU directives on advertising, reports from the European Advertising Standards Alliance (EASA) and the Advertising Standards Authority (ASA) in the United Kingdom, as well as reports from the IAB in Spain (IAB, 2015), and different guides have been drawn up by the Federal Trade Commission (FTC) in The United States of America.

3 These countries are, for example, the United Kingdom (Influencer's Guide to making clear that ads are ads), France (Part of *Recommandation Communication publicitaire digitale*), Belgium (Belgian Advertising Council Recommendations on Online Influencers), Germany (*Leitfaden zur Kennzeichnung von Werbung auf Instagram*), Ireland (ASAI Guidance Note), Sweden (The Swedish Consumer Agency Guidance on marketing in blogs and other social media), the Netherlands (Part of SRC, the Dutch Advertising Code), among others.

them to persuade their parents or others to buy the advertised goods or services, exploiting the special trust minors place in parents, teachers or other persons, or unreasonably showing minors in dangerous situations (Art. 9.1.g). As regards content creation, this Directive defines the contractual parties involved in this ecosystem, including the video-sharing platform provider, video-sharing platform service and "user-generated" videos, and their responsibilities.

This Directive leaves each Member State to ensure that video-sharing platform providers, such as YouTube, meet the regulations relating to minors both as regards content (violence, hatred or pornography) and regarding any advertising reaching them, which may impair their physical, mental or moral development (Art. 28b and Art. 6a.1). However, these platforms still refuse to accept any liability related to user-generated content, i.e. the videos uploaded by their users... Platforms argue that, even though they have their own and third-party control measures, they cannot monitor the ever-increasing content that is uploaded, and they assert that, if a video is reported for justified reasons, it is withdrawn within hours. The debate is going on as contenders consider that platforms should be the ones primarily responsible for all the content they disseminate, as is the case in other media such as television.

1.2. Videos by young influencers and the rules of self-regulation of advertising practices

In Europe, the European Advertising Standards Alliance (EASA), which consists of both European national self-regulatory organizations, and the leading advertising industry associations, prepared the *Best Practice Recommendation on Influencer Marketing* (2018) in which it recommends EU country self-regulatory associations to regulate influencers' advertising content. This code of best practices stresses that all advertising content must be immediately and clearly identifiable as such for the target audience. It suggests using labels or hashtags that indicate it is marketing content, or inserting warnings expressly stating "these products have been sent for free to give a review" or "the trip was sponsored by" whenever the intent is to advertise (advertising agreement, gifts and compensation in kind). Both the influencer and the sponsoring brand are responsible for complying with these obligations.

Within the framework of the *Audiovisual Media Services Directive*, the United Kingdom protects minors by the *Advertising Code* (Section 5)

(ASA), and the *Guidance on Recognition of Advertising: Online Marketing to Children under 12* (ASA, 2017). These codes warn that marketing communications directed at children should not contain anything that could result in physical, mental or moral harm, or in dangerous situations without adult supervision, and should not encourage children to copy practices that may be unsafe for a child, or exploit their credulity, loyalty, vulnerability, and lack of experience. In addition, the *Guidance on Recognition of Advertising: Online Marketing to Children under 12* (ASA, 2017) and *Advertising Guidance Note on Child Brand Ambassadors* (ASA, 2019), warn of the need to identify and differentiate between entertainment and advertising content and gives the definition of "highly immersive" marketing communication features: "prolonged or in-depth interactivity, principally, game-play or narrative such as that of a story in audiovisual content (…) The usual separations between advertising and other content – spatial and/or thematic – are absent"[4]. In this case, advertisers are asked to make their communications identifiable to children by using markers such as "#ad" or "advertisement." IAB Spain has launched legal guidelines aimed at advertising professionals and parents who are content creators, to advise them on legal issues relating to advertising on sharing platforms.

Along the same lines, the United States, through the Federal Trade Commission (FTC) prepared the guidelines entitled *Endorsement Guides: What People Are Asking* (2015) and *Guides Concerning the Use of Endorsements and Testimonials in Advertising* (2009). These suggest that kid YouTubers should clearly indicate the advertising content in their videos with a text that states: "This product has been sent to me by…"; "Company X gave me [name of product], and I think it's great", "Paid ad", "Ad", or similar.

1.3. Complaints and request about deceptive practices of influencer marketing

At the current time, complaints have been filed in the United States and in Europe both about kid YouTuber content creator channels and about YouTube as a video-sharing platform, despite the limitations stated

4 ASA 2019 – Advertising Guidance on Recognition of advertising: online marketing to children under 12.

by the regulations and the warnings by self-regulation associations to clearly indicate advertising content.

One of the first complaints was filed with the FTC by different organizations to protect children in 2015[5] and 2016[6]. In both cases, they appeal to the FTC, in accordance with Article 5 of the *Federal Trade Commission Act*, which prohibits unfair advertising acts or practices, to investigate YouTube for the misleading advertising in toy videos directed at children and other sectors. The complaint focuses on the Google platform, brands and child YouTuber channels that are accused of displaying disguised advertising among the entertainment content they broadcast. It states that it is time for the FTC to take swift and decisive action, to protect children from a practice that is prohibited in children's television. The Center for Digital Democracy, taking action together with Campaign for a Commercial-Free Childhood and Public Citizen, explained:

> Corporate predators are using young Internet influencers, admired by kids, to hawk their wares to children, even to young children (…). The marketers and the advertising platforms enabling and promoting this activity should be ashamed. But since they're not, we need the FTC to act to end their outrageous practice.

In 2017, the Children's Advertising Review Unit (CARU) examined the YouTube Channel "Ryan Toys Review", and made a series of recommendations: "Recommends More Prominent Disclosures of Ad Content", that promotional content be better identified. The channel responded: "We will implement procedures to enhance disclosures of connections to brand marketers in accordance with CARU's voluntary guidelines in this continually expanding field" (CARU, 2017). Along the same lines, "Truth in Advertising" filed a complaint with the FTC against the RyanToysReview channel (Truth in Advertising, 2019) calling for the need to identify entertainment content, as the channel's content was "a mash-up of personal vlog and 'unboxing' videos, a blend of innocent childhood antics and relentless, often overwhelming consumerism" (The

---

5 "Request for Investigation into Google's Unfair and Deceptive Practices in Connection with its YouTube Kids App" (Campaign for a Commercial-Free Childhood et al., 2015).

6 "Complaint, Request for Investigation and Request for Policy Guidance on the Deceptive Practice of Influencer Marketing Directed to Children" (The Center for Digital Democracy, Campaign for a Commercial-Free Childhood and Public Citizen, 2016).

Verge, 2016). "Unfortunately, it is often difficult to discern the innocent (or sometimes not so innocent) antics in Ryan ToysReview videos from the sponsored content. And for preschoolers, it is impossible to discern the difference" (Truth in Advertising, 2019, p. 1). In addition, many videos starring Ryan do not clearly indicate the appropriate age for use. The complaint is still awaiting a response.

Many associations in several countries put legal pressure on the parties involved in the advertising ecosystem in order to protect young children[7].

2. Aspects related to targeted advertising with regard to personal data law

The particularity of online advertising lies in the extreme personalization that certain targeted advertising models achieve, offering each individual specially chosen ads. Carrying out this profiling requires the collection of large amounts of personal data since the more detailed a profile is, the higher its market value. But the activity of collecting personal data from minors is a regulated activity (2.1), which has given rise to a dispute directly challenging YouTube's practices (2.2), leading the company to reconsider the conditions of its self-regulation (2.3).

2.1. Videos of young influencers and the regulation of personal data

Unlike the United States, which regulates personal data sector by sector, and has chosen to devote a special text to the protection of minors online (the COPPA law), the European Union has chosen a text that is intended to apply to all processing of personal data of people of all ages (the GDPR), with special treatment for the personal data of minors.

---

7 In Spain, the *Consejo Audiovisual de Publicidad de Cataluña* (CAC, 2019) reported 59 YouTuber videos, starring children and teenagers, with 43 million views, for surreptitious advertising aimed at children and teenagers. It urged the platform to adopt measures to identify commercial content in a manner that is understandable for children.

2.1.1. In the United States: The Children's Online Privacy Protection Act

In the United States, The Children's Online Privacy Protection Act (COPPA) is the primary legislation regulating the personal data of minors[8]. Passed in 1998, this US federal law came into force in April 2000 to regulate the collection of personal data from children under the age of thirteen on the Internet.

The COPPA Act applies to any online service provider, such as a website or mobile application, that targets minors under the age of thirteen or whose service they use. Although COPPA in theory only targets children of US nationality, simple economic logic leads all operators in the world with content aimed at this population to have to comply with the law. Furthermore, the FTC has indicated that US-based online service providers must comply with the law, even if they only collect data from foreign children. For these two reasons, the law is therefore global in scope.

Thus, before collecting any information from a minor, the Internet operator is obliged to seek the prior consent of a parent duly identified as such. After collection, it is also obliged to transmit, at the request of a parent, all the data it has collected on the child. The consent of the parent is revocable at any time and the operator must, at the request of a parent, delete the collected data. A principle of proportionality is also laid down between the data collected and the service provided, as well as reasonable security measures to protect the data.

COPPA set at thirteen years the age at which a minor can act alone and give his consent without the approval of his legal representatives, even though in practice it may seem doubtful that a minor over thirteen years of age would be able to grasp all the consequences of using online services that would collect his data. The issue was also raised that a minor under thirteen years old may usurp an identity enabling him/her to circumvent the COPPA. To resolve this difficulty, the FTC proposed

---

8 The following are considered as personal data: the name, postal and email addresses, telephone number, as well as in general any information which makes it possible to identify or contact the child. However, the COPPA also covers information relating to interests and navigation habits collected with the help of cookies, when these are linked to data which allow a child to be identified.

that the parent send an email to the service provider or send answers to an online quiz that could not be resolved by a minor.

The notion of "verifiable parental consent" has also been the subject of much criticism because of its imprecision. The FTC has explained that reasonable efforts must be made to collect and verify such consent. But while platforms are not theoretically allowed to collect the personal data of a 13-year-old without parental consent, in practice, it is well known that children use their parents' accounts to watch videos without being monitored. Furthermore, it is also established that, despite the creation of its children's channel "YouTube Kids" in 2015, many parents have continued to use general YouTube as their children's babysitter, with YouTube continuing to offer *de facto* very popular content geared towards children under the age of thirteen.

The notion of "content aimed at children under 13" has also been criticized for its vagueness. While the FTC provides some answers by indicating that it takes into account, among other things, the use of colors, drawings, etc., it remains complicated to distinguish between content for children and content for an older audience. The criterion of 'actual knowledge' of the presence of minors on the platform could have led to awkward situations where services were not initially designed for a young audience. Nevertheless, YouTube was fined $170 million by the FTC on September 4, 2019, demonstrating that the FTC does not use a restrictive definition of the concept. Indeed, in the United States, only the FTC has the power to take legal action or to sanction, through negotiated agreements, platforms that violate the provisions of COPPA. Negotiated agreements are often binding on companies that must comply with a set of criteria to become "COPPA compliant".

In addition, there is another body of rules of direct interest to YouTube advertising activities, which is less well known because it is more recent and deserves to be mentioned: the California Consumer Privacy Act, (CCPA) promulgated by the State of California on 28 June 2018 and in force since 1 January 2020. The CCPA requires any company operating in the State to inform consumers about the personal data it collects about them and how it is used, and prohibits companies from selling the personal data of consumers aged 13 to 16 without their consent. The sharing of data of minors under 13 years of age requires the consent of parents or a legal guardian.

While the CCPA has often been seen as being in line with the general personal data protection regime (GDPR) adopted in Europe on 27 April 2016, in reality the CCPA is a lighter and much more liberal version of it. On the one hand, because it is aimed only at consumers and only for-profit companies operating in California, with revenues in excess of $25 million annually, or which hold information on at least 50,000 consumers, or which generate more than 50 % of their revenues through the sale of corporate data, whereas the GDPR provides protection for users regardless of the context in which their data are used. On the other hand, because the penalties provided for by the CCPA are much lower than those of the GDPR (up to $7500 compared to 20 million euros). Finally, the text provides for consumers to be remunerated in exchange for their personal data, whereas this monetization of personal data is not contemplated by the GDPR.

2.1.2. In Europe: Specific rules for minors within the GDPR

In Europe, Regulation 2016/679 of 27 April 2016 on the protection of natural persons with regard to the processing of personal data and on the free movement of such data, known as the "GDPR," is the reference text. It takes into account the need to protect minors on the Internet, no longer through a specific text such as COPPA, but through specific provisions for them within a general legal regime. The GDPR highlights the vulnerability of "children", a term used within the Regulation, and considers that children "merit specific protection with regard to their personal data, as they may be less aware of the risks, consequences and safeguards concerned and their rights in relation to the processing of personal data". However, unlike the United States, the European Union has chosen a text that is intended to apply to all processing of personal data of people of all ages. However, when the data processed concerns a minor, this general regime is subject to adjustments. On the one hand, Article 6 of the GDPR provides that processing is lawful if it is necessary for the purposes of the legitimate interests pursued by the controller or by a third party, "except where such interests are overridden by the interests or fundamental rights and freedoms of the data subject which require protection of personal data, in particular where the data subject is a child". Therefore, the vulnerability of minors presupposes that, when a balance is made between their interests and the legitimate interests of the controller, it is always the interests of the minors that prevail. On the other hand, Article 8 of the GDPR lays down specific conditions regarding the consent of the minor in the context of data processing by information society services, and only for such processing. According to this article, "the processing of the personal data of a child shall be lawful where the child is at least 16 years old." Thus, as a matter of principle, minors over the age of 16 may register alone on a platform such as YouTube or a social network, their consent being considered sufficiently informed. Conversely, minors under 16 years of age need parental consent when registering. However, the GDPR underlines that Member States may provide through national legal provisions for a different age allowing a minor child to give consent without parental authorization, provided that this age is not lower than 13 years. In France, for example, for the sake of consistency with other texts, it was decided that the age of digital majority would be set at 15 years.

Where the minor's consent cannot be obtained and parental authorization is required, information society services professionals must endeavor to "make reasonable efforts to verify [...] that consent is given or authorised by the holder of parental responsibility over the child, taking into consideration available technology" (Art. 8(2) of the GDPR). The problem of the effectiveness of this provision has raised the question of how to ensure whether or not the child is of the age of digital majority on the Internet.

Furthermore, Recital 58 of the GDPR states, "Given that children merit specific protection, any information and communication, where processing is addressed to a child, should be in such a clear and plain language that the child can easily understand." This obligation of transparency of the controller is repeated in Article 12 of the GDPR. Finally, the right to erasure of one's data is guaranteed for minors, whatever their age, as Article 17 of the GDPR emphasizes that children benefit from this right to be forgotten. The fact that the data subject was a minor at the time of the collection and initial processing of the data is thus sufficient in itself to invoke the right to be forgotten.

Fines for failure to comply with the provisions of the GDPR can amount to 4 % of a company's turnover. For the time being, as far as minors are concerned, no decision seems to have been taken under Article 8. The decision of the French personal data regulator (CNIL), imposing a penalty of 50 million euros against Google on January 21, 2019, in application of the GDPR for lack of transparency, unsatisfactory provision of information and lack of valid consent for the personalization of advertising, did not explicitly take into consideration the processing of data of minors implemented by YouTube.

2.2. YouTube practices challenged by the FTC

In April 2018, an alert was issued by 23 digital rights and child protection organizations, accusing YouTube of collecting personal information (location, device used, phone numbers) from underage children without the parents' knowledge and then using such information to post targeted advertising, in violation of the COPPA law. The complaint filed by the associations with the FTC stated, for example, that the search for "children's videos" on YouTube returned 243 million results.

After a thorough investigation of YouTube's behavioral advertising practices, the FTC and the Attorney General of the State of New York, on behalf of all citizens of the State of New York, filed a Complaint for Permanent Injunction, Civil Penalties of New York against Google and YouTube in the Federal Court for the District of Columbia. In September 2019, the President of the FTC announced a settlement agreement with Google and its subsidiary YouTube providing for a penalty of $170 million, with $136 million paid to the FTC as a civil penalty and $34 million paid to New York State as compensation. In addition, the parties agreed that Google and YouTube would be subject to various obligations: no longer to use or benefit in any way from data collected illegally in the past, to develop a mechanism to systematically identify every publication targeting children under 13 years of age, and to provide special annual training for their employees to ensure a more uniform application of the obligations.

Was it a good settlement? Views are divided. According to the FTC president, the settlement affirmed that protecting children's personal data is and will remain a priority for the federal agency, with the penalty representing an amount three times greater than the largest privacy violation penalty imposed on Google in the past, and an amount 30 times greater than any other amount received by the FTC in enforcing COPPA. Commissioner Simons publicly warned: "Finally, to the business community at large, let me be clear: the FTC takes its obligation to enforce COPPA seriously. If companies violate COPPA, the FTC will take aggressive action, require corrective measures and use its authority to seek substantial civil penalty".

On the other hand, Commissioner Rohit Chopra publicly denounced the inadequacy of the agreed penalty and the four-month period given to Google and YouTube to continue to accumulate data and benefit from the data already collected: "Despite this specific authority, the Commission repeats many of the same mistakes from the flawed Facebook settlement: no individual accountability, insufficient remedies to address the company's financial incentives, and a fine that still allows the company to profit from its lawbreaking. The terms of the settlement were not even significant enough to make Google issue a warning to its investors." The Commissioner considered that the FTC took a different course of action depending on its target, noting that the penalties imposed on small companies were much more severe than those involving powerful players. The amount of the penalty imposed does indeed appear to be ineffective in light of Google's financial strength and the seriousness of the observed behavior. However, the bad reputation of Google and YouTube resulting from the publicity given to this penalty may prove to be a greater deterrent than the amount of the penalty. In order to assess the real impact of this decision, it remains to be seen whether it will be likely to effectively stop the unlawful conduct in the future. In this respect, the new rules put into force by YouTube, under the self-regulation arrangements, should be examined.

2.3. A form of "forced self-regulation" imposed on YouTube by the FTC

As a result of the agreement negotiated with the FTC, YouTube has adopted new rules to comply with the U.S. Trade Commissioner's guidance and to comply with existing U.S. online child protection laws. YouTube said it would now "treat personal information from anyone watching children's content on the platform as coming from a child, regardless of the age of the user".[9] The collection of personal information and its use on videos that target children under 13 will be restricted, resulting in a partial demonetization of those videos and disrupting the business model of YouTube and YouTubers.

The main changes made by YouTube concern certain features that will no longer be available for content aimed at children, such as personalized

---

9 https://youtube.googleblog.com/2020/01/better-protecting-kids-privacy-on-YouTube.html.

advertising that is displayed according to users' profiles. YouTube ads on children's videos will still be included, but they will be less personalized. These ads will be based on the context of the video and not on the use of minors' personal information. There will also be no more "super chat" where juniors could make donations or the "merch shelf" (a small horizontal drop-down menu with products to buy). Comments, notifications, playlist options or live chat will also be banned from children's videos. Finally, YouTube channels for children will no longer be able to share stories, or post notifications, and the "community" tab will disappear.

It remains to be determined which videos "aimed at children" are affected by these new rules. When asked about the criteria, YouTube explained that the targeted videos will have topics, characters and themes that are child-centered. Channels containing nursery rhymes or featuring children seem to be at the heart of the target. On the other hand, gaming or animation videos should not fall within these criteria.

However, since YouTube still refuses to be considered as a form of media, it will not put in place measures to determine what is – or is not – children's content. Creators themselves will have to specify whether their videos were made for children because, depending on the platform, they are in the best position to determine their target audience. A metric has been built into YouTube Studio to make it easier for them to identify the audience for their content. In addition, YouTube will continue to use the learning machine to identify new content for children. But creators will also be able to change their audience designation if they think that YouTube has misjudged one of their videos. The platform will only change this setting if it detects abuse or a mistake, which ultimately leaves room for a certain margin of error.

As soon as the FTC reached an agreement with YouTube, many content creators were explicitly concerned about the impact this decision would have on their business and alerted the public to the risks of their videos being demonetized. Famous YouTubers rose up in protest, believing that compliance could mean the demise of their channel altogether. The issue of demonetization was just as important for the platform itself! Indeed, the interests of creators and YouTube converge to exploit the image of minors within the framework of a business model largely based on advertising integrated into videos that are particularly popular when they feature children, a model which is shaken up by the FTC's decision.

In light of the risks associated with potential litigation by the FTC, and to avoid escalating penalties, YouTube could have chosen to move all children's videos to its YouTube Kids dedicated site, created in 2015, which is not supposed to collect advertising data, and which presents itself as a safer space for children. However, the price to pay was probably too high, because children's videos are among the most popular with all audiences and generate significant advertising revenue, which would not be the case on YouTube Kids. The FTC's decision therefore calls into question YouTube's business model, which has already been disrupted in recent years by a succession of scandals involving violent, inappropriate content or pedophile networks, resulting in advertiser withdrawals and lost revenue.

Recently, some semi-professional publishers seem to prefer to distribute their videos on other platforms, such as Netflix or Amazon, believing that YouTube is too risky an investment. The company is thus caught between economic ambitions that invite it to continue to feed the public's appetite for the videos of young influencers and economic ambitions that dissuade it from pursuing this path because of the flight of advertisers and creators to other platforms deemed more virtuous. The changes made by YouTube at the beginning of 2020, following the agreement negotiated with the FTC, are the result of a compromise that could be challenged in the future by ethical considerations related to the status of child influencers, which seem strangely absent from concerns for the moment.

2.4. From child participation to child labor

Regulations have always had a traditional understanding of children as subjects who must be protected (Christensen and Prout, 2002) because they are sensitive, inexperienced and credulous. Thus, it is important that the content they watch conforms with current legal regulations and the self-regulatory codes established by the advertising sector. However, this paternalist perspective of understanding minors and the consequential need to protect them is contradictory to the current practice of minors on the Internet who play an increasingly role as social influencers and participatory actors (Christensen and Prout, 2002). Minors are subjects who have their own experiences and knowledge and participate in networks by creating their own content and consuming their own experiences. From a legal perspective, participation is promulgated by the

Convention on the Rights of the Child, which emphasizes that participation should always be supervised by the adults who are the guardians of the minor. Thus, the law should be more explicit and clearly indicate the age at which minors can make their decisions for themselves.

The videos of young influencers have raised important questions about the interests of the children they portray, particularly in the United States where some very disturbing abuses have been identified (Holcombe, 2019)[10]. Increasingly, psychologists and child welfare officials are concerned about the exposure of young children on social platforms. Indeed, there is concern that parents who choose to expose their children may do so as part of "a narcissistic quest of their own, but using children as alibis" (Haza, 2019) or for profit, which may not be in the best interests of the child. Can a child build up a healthy self when he or she sees his or her intimate life constantly exposed, sometimes from the cradle on, to millions of people? Should we be concerned about the child's ability to deal with early media exposure or to live in fear of a possible future bad buzz that would damage his or her reputation? Can the child build up proper self-esteem in the face of the outpouring of criticism or even hatred that his or her online activity may provoke? From a legal point of view, these questions are a reminder of the respect for the right to image and privacy in principle owed to the child.

Sometimes, the child's involvement is such that it no longer seems to be a play activity or a leisure activity which has been freely consented to. The child's participation is forced, especially when the tight schedule of publishing videos, which does not include scenes cut or re-done several times, becomes a full-time activity. It is then feared that the minor may sacrifice his or her childhood to produce ever more content, entertain ever more fans, maintain a lucrative business which is similar to concealed labor, and become an influencer realizing parental desires, without benefiting from the protection that would be due to him or her under labor law, company law or even family law. From an economic point

---

10 Some examples of this abuse: participation in cheese challenges, which involved throwing slices of cheese into the face of a young child; challenges involving spending twenty-four hours in a box, or only eating yellow or black food for twenty-four hours. One family mother, whose channel generated more than 250 million views, starved and pepper-sprayed her children when they refused to take part in the production of videos.

of view, the status of the income generated by these lucrative programs involving the child needs to be clarified.

This is why some have argued in the United States for the California Child Actor's Bill, which protects child actors, to be applied to child influencers. As early as 2018, Democrat Kansen Chu, a member of the California State Assembly, introduced an amendment to the California Child Actor's Bill to cover "the employment of a minor in advertising on social networks", which has not been acted upon. French parliamentarians have taken into account the need to legislate on the status of child influencers by unanimously adopting on first reading, before the National Assembly, on 12 February 2020, a bill whose purpose is "to set up a legal framework, which will be internationally pioneering, for the production of these videos which will ensure that the interests of the child prevail".

This proposal, which aims to regulate the commercial exploitation of the image of children under the age of sixteen on online platforms, extends the prior individual authorization regime applicable to children employed in the entertainment, advertising and fashion sector to children whose image is broadcast for profit on video-sharing platforms and whose activity falls within the legal framework of an employment relationship. Where the activity does not, strictly speaking, fall within the framework of an employment relationship, the proposed law creates an *ad hoc* legal framework by introducing a declaration regime which must lead to the application of protective measures, both in terms of hours and remuneration, and by subjecting the platforms to several obligations. The law introduces a fine of €75,000 for video-sharing platform services which do not comply with these obligations.

Anticipating this change in the regulatory framework, the *Fédération française des industries jouet puériculture* (French federation of toy and childcare industries) has set up a charter of best practices for working with underage influencers, a first in Europe. At the same time, the French personal data protection authority, the CNIL, decided in November 2019 to carry out an experiment specifically focused on the YouTube service, which underlines the need to strengthen media literacy on the one hand, and relations between public authorities and platforms on the other, in order to improve the transparency of algorithms and ensure that users are clearly informed of the recommendations made to them. On 21 April 2020, the CNIL also launched a public consultation on the rights of minors in the digital environment.

The playbor of the child influencer

The case of YouTube illustrates the transformations brought about by the emergence of a new phase of "media capitalism" (Jeanneret, 2014). The violence of this economic model, which is based on *playbor* – a word made up of play and labor – appears doubly aggressive. On the one hand, YouTube's strategy of mobilizing "crowds" has led the company to massively accept contributors' productions featuring children in conditions that are sometimes degrading for the latter, without any real ethical considerations. By hiding behind its status as a platform that does not coordinate anything, YouTube has allowed a social phenomenon to flourish which, combined with the use of advertising according to the traditional logic of multifaceted economic models, focuses on the added value of the child, but which does not have the child as its primary beneficiary. Staged and merchandised, the child appears as an object of investment (investment by his/her family, investment by partner brands, etc.), entertainment and added value provided by a highly remunerative advertising revenue.

Based on a system of targeted promotional videos whose ethics and legal regularity are questionable from the point of view of consumer law and personal data law, the practice of child influencers questions not only the status of the child actor and that of the child consumer, but also that of the child content producer and that of the child data producer. At the center of the system, the child influencer often appears reduced to the status of a consumer rather than a creative individual, staging an act of tele-shopping recommendations: a child unpacking toys in unboxing videos, a child tasting fatty, salty or sugary foods, a child praising make-up products or women's lingerie, reinforcing gender stereotypes, and so on. This advertising operation finds its target, thanks to a recommendation algorithm that resonates perfectly with the fascination of the very young for repetition. It feeds a system where the child spectator-consumer finds himself a passive data producer self-feeding the advertising he consumes, without even being aware of being exposed to this advertising hype. Media capitalism overvalues the act of consumption and celebrates the merchandising of the individual. Of course, with YouTube Kids, Google offers an alternative. But this alternative seems, as it stands, confined to the very limited status of an offer "for conscience's sake" that has not found its audience. The stakes are elsewhere.

It was only under pressure from the FTC's decisions that YouTube agreed to modify its terms and conditions of use to improve the protection of children, with regard to both misleading advertising and targeted advertising. Major advertisers (Disney, Epic Games, Nestlé, etc.) abruptly withdrew their ads, forcing YouTube to announce an improvement in its algorithm to remove pedophiliac comments from videos that attract sexual predators. This is a sign that everyone in their respective role (parents, citizens, brands, professional federations, regulatory authorities, legislators, etc.) can be part of a change to ensure the protection of children.

References

Advertising Standards Authority (ASA). *Advertising code.* Retrieved from: https://cutt.ly/Xrcqqh8.

Advertising Standards Authority (ASA). (2017). *Guidance on Recognition of advertising online marketing to children under 12.* Retrieved from: https://cutt.ly/3rcqoQL.

Advertising Standards Authority (ASA, 2019). *Advertising guidance note on child brand ambassadors.* Retrieved from: https://cutt.ly/urcqyDK.

Alexandre, O. (2015). YouTube ou l'imaginaire sous contrôle: Voyage dans les images formatées et monétisées des Youtubers. *Revue du Crieur, 1*(1), 122–127. doi:10.3917/crieu.001.0122

Balleys, C. (2018). Comment les adolescents construisent leur identité avec YouTube et les médias sociaux. *Nectart, 1*(6), 124–133. doi:10.3917/nect.006.0124

Blades, M., Oates, C., & Li, S. (2013). Children's recognition of advertisements on television and on Web pages. *Appetite, 62*, 190–191. doi:10.1016/j.appet.2012.04.002

Bullich, V. (2015a). La propriété artistique comme régulation de la *trivialité. Communication & langages, 3*(185), 67–88. Retrieved from: https://www.cairn.info/revue-communication-et-langages1-2015-3-page-67.htm.

Bullich, V. (2015b). Régulation des pratiques amateurs et accompagnement de la professionnalisation : la stratégie de YouTube dans la course aux contenus exclusifs. *Les Enjeux de l'information et de la communication, 3B*(16). Retrieved from: https://lesenjeux.univ-grenoble-alpes.fr/.

Burgess, J. (2012). YouTube and the formalisation of amateur media. In D. Hunter, R. Lobato, M. Richardson, & J. Thomas (Eds.), *Amateur media: Social, cultural and legal perspectives* (pp. 53–58). Routledge.

Campaign for a Commercial Free Childhood and Center for Digital Democracy. (2015a). *Request for investigation into Google's unfair and deceptive practices in connection with its YouTube Kids app*. Retrieved from: https://cutt.ly/Wrl4HJF.

Campaign for a Commercial Free Childhood and others. (2015b). Request for investigation into Google's unfair and deceptive practices in connection with its YouTube Kids App. Retrieved from: https://cutt.ly/UrcqlqC.

Campbell, A. (2017). Rethinking children's advertising policies for the digital age. *Georgetown Law Faculty Publications and Other Works, 1945*. Retrieved from: https://cutt.ly/yrl4B56.

Children's Advertising Review Unit (CARU). (2017). *CARU examines YouTube channel 'Ryan Toys Review*. Recommends More Prominent Disclosures of Ad Content. Retrieved from: https://cutt.ly/Xrz6vnD.

Christensen, P., & Proud, A. (2002). Working with ethical Symmetry in social research with children. *Childhood, 9*(4), 477–497.

CNIL. (2019). Capacité à informer des algorithmes de recommandation. Une expérience sur le service YouTube. Retrieved from: https://cutt.ly/Wuvrze6.

Consejo Audiovisual de Publicidad de Cataluña (CAC). (2019). *Presencia de contenidos publicitarios en canales de youtubers infantiles y adolescentes*. Retrieved from: https://cutt.ly/KrzqSTg.

Corsaro, W. A. (1997). *The sociology of childhood*. Pine Forge Press.

Craig, D., & Cunningham, S. (2017). Toy unboxing: Living in a (n unregulated) material world. *Media International Australia, 163*(1), 77–86. doi:10.1177/1329878x17693700

Defy Media (2016). *Acumen report Youth Video Diet*. Retrieved from: https://goo.gl/JtXjKi.

European Advertising Standards Alliance (EASA). (2018). *Best practice recommendation on influencer marketing*. Retrieved from: https://cutt.ly/Orx62qU.

European Union (EU). (2000). Directive 2000/31/EC of the European Parliament and of the Council of 8 June 2000 on certain legal aspects of information society services, in particular electronic commerce, in the Internal

Market (Directive on electronic commerce). Retrieved from: https://cutt.ly/Jrl4M3W.

Federal Trade Commission (FTC). (1998). *Children's online privacy protection rule (COPPA).* Retrieved from: https://cutt.ly/Srl4AJo.

Federal Trade Commission. (2009). *Concerning the use of endorsement and testimonials in advertising.* Retrieved from: https://cutt.ly/UrcqQt0.

Federal Trade Commission (FTC). (2015). *Endorsement guides: What people are asking.* Retrieved from: https://cutt.ly/krcqnPv.

Federal Trade Commission (FTC). (2019). Complaint for permanent injunction, civil penalties, and other equitable relief (Case No.: 1:19-cv-2642). Retrieved from: https://cutt.ly/Trl4O5A.

Fédération française des industries Jouet Puériculture (FJP). (2020). *Charte Kid'influenceurs.* Retrieved from: https://cutt.ly/IuvrDFk.

Ghÿsselinckx, D. (2019). Dans le cadre d'un placement de produit réalisé sur YouTube, quel est le moyen de divulgation le plus efficace pour optimiser la compréhension des enfants âgés entre 8 et 12 ans? Louvain School of Management, Université catholique de Louvain. Retrieved from: http://hdl.handle.net/2078.1/thesis:20660.

Google. (2017a). *Creator academy.* Retrieved from: https://creatoracademy.YouTube.com.

Google. (2017b). *Paid product placements and endorsements.* Retrieved from: https://goo.gl/9B2b87.

Hale, J. (2020). Ryan's world has spawned 1,000 products in 75,000 stores, will rake in $150 million this year. *TuberFilter.* Retrieved from: https://cutt.ly/auvr4Qj.

Haza, M. (2016). Paroles d'expert: Marion HAZA et les enfants stars sur YouTube. *Observatoire de la Parentalité & de l'Éducation numérique.* Retrieved from: https://cutt.ly/8uvtujd.

Holcombe, M. (2019). What happens when parents abuse and exploit children for internet fame. *CNN.* Retrieved from: https://cutt.ly/Cuvtatb.

Holloway, D., Green, L., & Livingstone, S. (2013). Zero to eight: Young children and their Internet use. *London School of Economics (LSE).* London, United Kingdom: EU Kids Online. Retrieved from: http://eprints.lse.ac.uk/52630/1/Zerotoeight.pdf.

IAB Spain. (2015). *Guía Legal Menores y Publicidad Content.* Retrieved from: https://cutt.ly/Orl47GM.

IAB Spain. (2017). *Guía Legal: Marketing de Influencers.* Retrieved from: https://iabspain.es/estudio/guia-legal-marketing-de-influencers/.

IAB Spain. (2018). *Guía legal: niños influencers.* Retrieved from: https://iabspain.es/estudio/guia-legal-ninos-influencers/.

International Chamber of Commerce (ICC). (2016). *Statement on code interpretation – ICC reference guide on advertising to children.* Retrieved from: https://cutt.ly/yrl4446.

IPSOS/GOOGLE (2012). *Teens & Twenty-Somethings Research Study.* Retrieved from: https://www.thinkwithgoogle.com/marketing-strategies/video/media-habits-of-teens-and-twenty-somethings-2012/ Janneret, Y. (2014). *Critique de la trivialité. Les médiations de la communication, enjeu de pouvoir.* Éditions Non Standard.

Katz, J., & Fener, V. (2019). Is a YouTube COPPAcalypse coming? FTC rules could start demonetizing creators in 2020. *Tubefilter.* Retrieved from: https://cutt.ly/DrxeOsM.

Lange, P. (2014*). Kids on YouTube: Technical identities and digital literacies.* Left Coast Press.

Lievens, E. (2010). *Protecting children in the digital era: The use of alternative regulatory instruments.* Martinus Nijhoff.

Lievens, E., Dumortier, J., & Ryan, P. (2006). The co-protection of minors in new media: A European approach to co-regulation. *Journal of Juvenile Law & Policy, 10,* 97.

Martínez-Pastor, E. (2019). Menores youtubers en el ecosistema publicitario de los juguetes: límites normativos. Youtuber minors in the advertising ecosystem of toys: normative limits. *Espacios, 40*(7), 5–15.

McLaughlin, S. (2013). Regulation and legislation. In B. O'Neill, E. Staksrud, & S. McLaughlin (Eds.), *Towards a better Internet for children? Policy pillars, players and paradoxes* (pp. 77–91). Nordicom.

McReynolds, E., Hubbard, S., Lau, T., Saraf, A., Cakmak, M., & Roesner, F. (2017). Toys that listen: A study of parents, children, and Internet-connected toys. In Proceedings of the 2017 CHI Conference on Human Factors in Computing Systems. *Association for Computing Machinery,* 5197–5207. doi: 10.1145/3025453.3025735

Mcroberts, S., Bonsignore, E., Peyton, T., & Yarosh, S. (2016). Do it for the viewers!: Audience engagement behaviors of young YouTubers. [Conference Paper]. In Proceedings of the The 15th International Conference on Interaction Design and Children (IDC '16). *Association for Computing Machinery*, 334–343. doi: 10.1145/2930674.2930676

Montgomery, K. (2011). Safeguards for youth in the digital marketing ecosystem. In Dorothy G. Singer & Jerome L. Singer (Eds.), *Handbook of children and the media* (pp. 631–633). Sage Publications.

Ofcom. (2016). *Children and parents: Media use and attitudes report.* Retrieved from: https://cutt.ly/Orl7wbF.

Ofcom. (2019). *Children and parents: Media use and attitudes report 2018.* Retrieved from: https://cutt.ly/puvtQLh.

Popper, B. (2016). YouTube's biggest star is a 5-year-old that makes millions opening toys: Blurring the line between playtime and business. *The Verge.* Retrieved from: https://cutt.ly/EuvtG2x.

Ramos Serrano, M., & Herrero-Díaz, P. (2016). Unboxing and brand: YouTubers phenomenon through the case study of Evantubehd. *Prisma Social*, 90–120. Retrieved from: https://cutt.ly/vrl4N8T.

Staksrud, E. (2013). *Children in the online world: Risk, regulation, rights.* PhD thesis, Ashgate.

The Center for Digital Democracy, Campaign for a Commercial-Free Childhood and Public Citizen. (2016). Complaint, request for investigation, and request for policy guidance on the deceptive practice of influencer marketing directed to children. Retrieved from: https://cutt.ly/7rcqV4C.

Truth in Advertising (2019). *Ryan ToysReview's deceptive native advertising.* Retrieved from: https://bit.ly/2NeKfVt.

Tur-Viñes, V., Núñez-Gómez, P., & Martínez-Pastor, E. (2019). YouTube, menores y cultura colaborativa. Revisión bibliográfica de la investigación académica, *Historia y Comunicación Social*, *24*(1), 331–351.

Wu, K. (2016). YouTube marketing: Legality of sponsorship and endorsements. *Journal of Law, Business, and Ethics*, *22*, 59–91. Retrieved from: https://cutt.ly/duvt0OY.

Yarosh, S., Bonsignore, E., Mcroberts, S., & Peyton, T. (2016). YouthTube: Youth video authorship on YouTube and vine. *In Proceedings of the 2016 ACM Conference on Computer Supported Cooperative Work.* Retrieved from: https://cutt.ly/drl7eHx.

YouTube. (2019a). *More updates on our actions related to the safety of minors on YouTube.* Retrieved from: https://cutt.ly/yrxquAW.

YouTube. (2019b). Novedades importantes para todos los creadores : cumplimiento de la COPPA. Retrieved from: https://cutt.ly/srxepng.

YouTube. (2019c). Próximos cambios en el contenido dirigido a niños en YouTube.com. Retrieved from: https://cutt.ly/wrxeo1h.

YouTube elimina los comentarios en los vídeos de menores. (2019). *El Mundo.* Retrieved from: https://cutt.ly/grxqkwI.

3

Superfans and evangelizers: Young people's creative entanglements with promotional culture

NATALIE COULTER AND MARY GRACE LAO

> "Get your superfans to evangelize your IP (Intellectual Property) they do the work for free." (Insight Kids, 2017)

Every year the trade publication KidScreen holds its annual conference, the KidScreen Summit, in Miami, Florida. The Summit touts itself to be the "world's leading conference on the business of kid's entertainment" with 2000 delegates from around the world. At the 2017 conference in Miami, youth marketing gurus from Insight Kids, urged the audience to "get your superfans to evangelize your IP (Intellectual Property), they do the work for free". The audience of media professionals nodded in agreement and leaned in towards the speakers to find out how to engage the "superfan". As scholars of young people's cultures, it was not a surprise that media companies think of children as superfans who will promote media properties, for free, and yet, it was quite shocking to hear it stated so boldly, without any reflection.

These bold statements made by one of the top children's market research companies in the world, reveal the radical shifts currently taking place in the production ecologies of children's media (Potter and Steemers, 2017). Young people's creative labor is becoming entangled with the promotional activities of the children's media and entertainment industry, as children's media and entertainment companies groom children to be product evangelizers and pint-sized marketers for their intellectual properties. Despite these major shifts, there has been very little attention given by academics to the creative work of young people in the marketing and promotion of the intellectual properties of children's media. These corporate strategies to harness the creative labor of young people are alarming and warrant serious academic consideration. It is urgent that a study exploring the children's media and entertainment industry's harnessing of children's creative labor is completed. This work underpins much large discussions of children's labor and work in the digital age and questions the rights children have over their own creative labors.

The goal of this paper is to explore the implications of how children's media and entertainment companies utilize these marketing tactics in promoting an intellectual property. In seeking to understand children's entanglements in the ecologies of marketing and promoting IPs, this paper will seek wider clarity on the commercial epistemologies that ideologically define childhood through the logics of the marketplace. Our analysis is grounded in a political economic approach.

Using the above quote from Insight Kids as an entry point into an assessment of young people's creative labor in the promotional practices of the children's media and entertainment industry in the attention economy, we frame our arguments around three key phrases in the quote stated at the beginning of this paper; "superfan", "work for free", and evangelize. First, we will unpack what is meant by superfan to explore the commercial epistemologies of the industry's making meaning. Second, we think through the term "work for free" as a form of immaterial labor, and finally we address how evangelization affectively entangles young people in the colonial projects of consumer capitalism.

This paper is part of a larger project that is a political economic analysis of the entanglements of young people's creative labor in the promotional ecologies of the children's media and entertainment industry. For this larger project we accessed the industry materials of the children's entertainment industry starting with the trade publications such as *Kidscreen* (children's media industry), attended the 2017 *Kidscreen* conference and reviewed the corporate literature such as annual reports, corporate websites, and business case studies, of key market research companies that specialize in children's media.

1. Superfan

Getting superfans to evangelize an intellectual property reveals much about the current state of children's media. Firstly, it reveals how much children's media has become a vehicle to sell merchandise. Children's media is no longer simply content, instead it has become an intellectual property designed to move licensed products and experiences. Mattel, for example, at the Kidscreen Summit declared itself to be a content company, in that they make content that by extension sells toys. Barbie™ has traditional media, such as movies, and TV shows, but it also has a blog, a YouTube channel, a website with games, a chat room and apps, all designed to drive the audience to purchase Barbie toys and merchandise. This of course is nothing new. Since the 1980s in what Englehardt (1986) called the "Strawberry Shortcake strategy", children's media has been designed to push merchandised product. But it has taken on a new form within the convergence culture of the past two decades as intellectual properties have become transmedia texts that replicate across multiple platforms often by harnessing the creative powers of fans (see Jenkins and Deuze, 2008).

The formation of character merchandising as a central to the business model of the media entertainment companies arose two decades earlier in Japan with the development of anime with the iconic weekly animated TV show *Tetsuwan Atomu* (Astro Boy 1963–1966). Marc Steinberg's 2012 book *Anime's Media Mix: Franchising Toys and Characters in Japan*, situates Astro Boy at the center of a shift in Japanese media ecology where merchandising moved to the core of the business as both a means generate value and to promote a franchise.

It was not until the 1980s that the shift in the corporate strategies of children's media and entertainment companies from the main product being the media content itself and instead becoming about character licencing occurred in North America driven by changes in broadcasting policy. As a result, children's television shows essentially became 22-minute advertisements for media companies to promote their intellectual properties to niched segments of the child consumers. In the United States, under the direction of the neoliberal administration of President Ronald Reagan who contended that the government shouldn't operate as national nannies, the government offloaded the responsibility of regulating children's media onto the free market. In the 1980s Congress stripped the Federal Trade Commission (FTC) of many of its duties to regulate the media as the FCC (Federal Communication Commission) relaxed many of its policies that regulated children's advertising and completely deregulated the limits on the amount of commercial minutes permitted during children's television shows (Kunkel, 2001, p. 385).

In this deregulated space, the promotion of intellectual properties and its accompanying merchandised products could now occur within the content of a television show. Taking advantage of these new opportunities the children's media industry alongside the toy industry began to develop intellectual properties that could be both a 22 minute television show, and be a toy line with many different characters that could be sold in the toy stores, something that would not have been allowed under the old regulations. Shows such as The Smurfs (1981–1990), He-Man (1983–1985) and The Transformers (1984–1987) all became television shows that peddled toys built on the characters of the shows, and with the magic of character licensing these intellectual properties adorned a wide range of consumer products including clothing, bedding, furniture, school supplies.

Since the 1980s children's media business model moved away from simply being about creating content that could amass large audiences and instead focused on creating opportunities to develop lucrative licensing opportunities (Englehardt, 1986; Kline, 1993; Seiter, 1993). This centering of intellectual properties in the business objective has taken a new turn in the past decade alongside the radical shifts in the mediascape to a convergence culture where intellectual properties circulate across multiple media platforms courting media audiences to migrate with them while these same audiences have new tools to actively engage with the intellectual properties. In this new space the child's affective engagement with an intellectual property is no longer simply as a consumer/audience but is instead as a potential promotional force as young people's creative and emotional labor is harnessed to disseminate, aggregate and promote media IP's.

Insight Kids, headed by Sarah Chumsky, is a market research company based in New York and part of a larger agency called Insight Strategy Group a subsidiary of MarketCast Group which claims it is a "leading provider of marketing research services and data analytics, servicing the global entertainment industry" (MarketCast Group, 2019, "About MarketCast Group", para. 2). In 2017 Insight Kids released its latest market research study called FanPrint™. According to Insight Kids website, FanPrint™ is a large qualitative and quantitative research study that looked at 2000 children and 39 IPs to explore two questions, first "what drives kids to Ips", and second, "what are the underlying qualities that help kids connect to IPs" (Chumsky, 2017). Based on this research the company developed (and trademarked) the FanPrint™ algorithm, which Insight Kids claims to parce out the difference between those who "kinda like" an intellectual property and superfans who "can't live without" an intellectual property. Knowing this difference could "make or break" a company's success in the "crowded industry" (Chumsky, 2017).

Insight Kids claims to be able to assist media creators in "beefing up" their engagement with fans and determining what will drive superfandom for each media product. The secret in their approach, according to Insight Kids, is that it determines the relationships of fandom to stages of child development. This allows CME companies to position their media product "naturally " to kids as they do "the work of growing up" (Insight, 2017, "Spark their imagination", para. 2). The FanPrint™ algorithm ties fandom to children's development, which means, as the company notes "child-targeted brands have an opportunity to play a major role in childhood" (Chumsky, 2017).

"So how do you turn a casual fan into a Superfan?" Insight Kids asks on its website. "Give kids what they need developmentally. Our survey of 2000 kids revealed that kids become Superfans of the IPs that help them with their most important task – the work of growing up. Within that, fandom does a particularly good job of helping kids grow as individuals" (Insight, 2017, para. 3).

Not only does this statement reveal the current workings of the media marketplace, but it also reveals the epistemological framings of childhood. Insight Kids is not simply articulating theories of child development but is actually defining stages of "growing up" as opportunities for fan development; framing stages of childhood according to the logics and needs of Insight Kids to harness children's fandom into the promotional services of the children's media and entertainment industry. In doing so Insight Kids acts as a "moral broker" softening the moral tensions between understanding the child as an economic actor and seeing the child as needing "commercial deference" by blurring the boundaries between markets and culture (Cook, 2019). These tensions trace back to the mid-1960s when marketing consultants such as James McNeal began to acknowledge the complex ways that children are a consumer market. McNeal's later work famously defined children as three markets, a current market purchasing to their own desires, as a future market of consumers to be cultivated and as an influential market shaping families' purchasing decisions (McNeal, 1998, 2007). By the mid-1970s once children had gained visibility in the marketplace, research began to focus on the socialization of young people as consumers establishing a new body of research on how children grow and develop as consumers (John, 1999). In the 1990s the field began to adopt complex, qualitative ethnographic research methodologies that prioritized children's perspectives and voices heightening the tensions between conceptualizing the child as a market actor with a pecuniary value to be researched in order to meet a commercial goal, versus ontologically framing the child as a sentimental, agentive being with the right to offer opinions and preferences on messages made for their consumption (Cook, 2019). In this tension, market researchers with their knowledge about children, become moral brokers trading in definitions of the child between the commercial spheres of their clients, and the moral sphere of the child (Cook, 2019).

Insight Kids is part of what Daniel Cook has called the commercial epistemologies of childhood in which the industries in the knowledge ecology of childhood and children's consumer culture, such as market research firms like Insight Kids create value by defining and construct cultural categories of childhood according to the logics of the marketplace (2011). Cook argues that "commercial epistemologies are ways of 'knowing' about children and childhood that arise from the interested positions of those whose livelihoods revolve around ascertaining the marketability of goods and ideas" (Cook, 2011, p. 258). Cook puts the term "knowing" in quote marks to trouble the word, to know something, is of course, ideological. The "knowing" of children is a process that both describes and constructs the child simultaneously (Cochoy, 1998). This known child is not an embodied child, but an imagined child that is a "figment of the commercial imagination" produced to meet the demands of the cultural industries of children (advertising, marketing, media, retail, and technology) as these industries research, target, and trade their knowledge of children and youth and vie for children's attention in the marketplace (Cook, 2004, p. 7).

Drawing upon the theoretical frames of posthumanism and new materialism, recent scholarship in the field of children's studies, acknowledges the networks, flows and assemblages "within and through which a particular form of childhood or child is produced" (Prout, 2011, p. 10). The purpose of this paper is to illustrate how the children's market research industry, and in particular Insight Kids is an actor in the networks and flows of the framing of the child. The imagined child of Insight Kids is an example of the conceptual and material forces that constitute the child, in ways that are always relational, fluid and in process (Murris, 2017).

The center piece of the Insight Kids "knowing" the child consumer is the concept of the superfan. Baked into the definition of the superfan is that the fan's passions have a promotional value for the IP as the superfan will extol the merits of an intellectual property. The superfan's interactions with the marketplace of the intellectual property is more than simply being a consumer of the merchandise and media, the superfan is also a promoter of the intellectual property as an "evangelizer". Insight Kids defines the superfans as someone who "will not only hyper-engage and buy everything they can, but they will also shout your merits from the rooftops" (as quoted in Chumsky, 2017, para. 3). The impetus here is clear, superfans, according to the logics of the children's market researchers, are both potential consumers and promoters.

The superfan, as described by Insight kids, has the power to persuade their passions for the intellectual property to others. Media brands, according to Insight Kids, need to find ways to leverage the superfan's passion for the intellectual property and circulate this passion to their friends, who are new audiences that can be brought to the intellectual properties. Insight Kids states this blatantly, "Our research shows that 69 % of Superfans talk to friends or family members about their fandom at least once a week" the company tells prospective clients of its market research (Insight, 2017, para. 2). The superfan, like other forms of promotional performers – micro celebrities and social media influencers for example – bring their own audiences to a media property (see Abidin, 2017; Khamis et al., 2017). Henry Jenkins work on the affective economies of fan culture, suggest that "the ideal consumer, is active, emotionally engaged and socially networked" (Jenkins, 2006, p. 20). The superfan is just this, active, emotionally engaged and socially networked as they shout an IP's merits from the rooftops, to paraphrase Chumsky. As such their creative labors and passions are deeply entangled in the promotional ecologies of children's media industry.

2. "Work for free"

The second statement that we wish to unpack here is "work for free". Clearly part of the attraction as outlined by Digital Kids, is kids as superfans, do the work for free. The statement reveals a shift in the labor of marketing as young people's creative fandoms are entangled in the marketplace, that superfans do the work for free. Having audiences produce value for media properties is not a new phenomenon as Dallas Smythe argued in 1977. Smythe argued that the audience was a commodity, and that the audience performed labor and produced value through the practices of media consumption. The media's main role is not to create or disseminate content but to deliver audiences to advertisers. Thus, the product of the media industry is the audience, as it is the audience that is being sold that is the core of the media's business model (1977). What Smythe was arguing was that audiences perform unpaid labor time that media companies exploit when they sell audiences to advertisers. Smythe's work was instrumental in understanding how media industries are productive for capitalism and bound up in the processes of commodification

Smythe's work set the stage for rethinking digital labor in the context of digital capitalism and has provided a basis from which to read the audience/follower/ as engaged in a form of labor practice (see Fuchs, 2014). Audience labor has been defined as "user generated content" where users freely create content for internet platforms through comments and engagements (Hesmodhalgh, 2010). It has also been framed as "free labor," a term that acknowledges the complexity of knowledge production that is both "enjoyed and exploited" (Terranova, 2004). Some conceive of audience labor as immaterial labor, noting the emotional work involved in producing cultural meanings of media texts (Cote and Pybus, 2011), while others emphasize the perpetual production of data that can be instantaneously harvested (Kennedy 2006; Andrejevic, 2007; Fuchs, 2012). At the core of these arguments are reflections on how the value of cultural commodities are created by those that use, follow, or fan over them – a value that is never compensated as work. The superfan's work for free is just this, the creation of value for a cultural commodity, in this case a media property, in a way that is recognized as work but not compensated as work.

The superfan that Insight Kids calls upon to "do the work for free" is not necessarily online. The superfan evangelizes in both digital and non-digital spaces. At the 2017 Kidscreen Summit, Insight Kids used the example of a birthday party for a seven-year-old girl who is a fan of Harry Potter. While she had read all of the books, seen the movies and had been to The Wizarding World of Harry Potter™ in Orlando Florida, her friends at the party had various levels of knowledge of Harry Potter, many with no introduction to the intellectual property. But by the end of the Harry Potter birthday party, the friends had all played quidditch and tried Butter Beer. As Chumsky states, with this new introduction to the world of Harry Potter, "after this birthday party they were able to have this shared experience and were able to evangelize this brand to their other friends at school" (Mattias and Chumsky, 2017). The birthday party is a moment of work as Insight Kids tells its audience of children's entertainment and media professionals, where the work of marketing is being done by the superfan, for free.

The superfans described by Insight Kids are part of the affective structures of neoliberal capitalism. In expressing their fandom and passion for an intellectual property, the superfan circulates the affective value of media texts (Hills, 2014, p. 6). For many scholars of fan studies, this affective labor of promoting, circulating and sometimes repurposing media properties is theorized as a form uncompensated digital labor through the production of value through the flows and circulations of networked content (Terranova, 2000; De Kosnik, 2012). But superfandom as affective labor is in both the circulation of passions for media properties, but also in attaching meaning to the subjective formations of being a fan.

Superfandom, can be read through the lens of what Lazzarto terms immaterial labor, a series of affective activities that are not normally recognized as "work" and function as a means to produce subjects (Lazzarato, 1996). In other words, immaterial labor are the "kinds of activities involved in defining and fixing cultural and artistic standards, fashions, tastes and consumer norms, and, more strategically, public opinion" (Lazzarato, 1996, para. 2) For Lazzarto it is immaterial labor that "produces the cultural content of a commodity" (para. 2). While it is tricky to define the amusement practices of a seven years old girl at her birthday party as labor, the birthday girl is producing value for cultural commodity. Her passion for Harry Potter is being "harnessed as work", in what the autonomist Marxist call the social factory where work processes have moved from the factory to society "setting in motion a truly complex machine" as Terranova eloquently states (2000, p. 33).

The complex machine illuminated by Insight Kids is a form of marketing where the right kinds of children (those deemed to be superfans) are lured into the promotional activities of intellectual properties "for free". New work in the field of marketing by such scholars as Minna

Ruckenstien and Julia Granroth (2019) argue that marketing is collapsing in on itself, as we are so hyper-marketed to, in such niched ways, that marketing itself begins to become invisible, and undiscernible from all other cultural content. Where marketing becomes increasingly indiscernible from the fabric of everyday life (Zwick and Bradshaw, 2016). Marketing itself becomes invisible because marketers focus on fandom as part of a child's developmental milestones and appears as a rite of passage rather than a purposeful marketing effort to push a product on the consumer. For Baudrillard (1998), this gives the appearance of an intimate relationship between the person and a commodity where none exists. The harnessing of the passions of young people to promote media properties exemplifies this collapse as the boundaries between content, marketing and fandom, are increasingly blurred.

In the birthday party, for example, Harry Potter superfandom becomes associated with the celebration of a child's birthday, the developmental milestone, through Harry Potter-themed birthday cakes and games, the cultural traditions associated with birthdays. The birthday party becomes a marketing moment of superfandom that reproduces the affective passions of the Harry Potter franchise. With Sara Ahmed's (2005) affective economies in mind, the superfan's affective labor entices their friends to connect through and around the Harry Potter franchise. The Harry Potter birthday party reveals the affective entanglements of young people with the material objects and assemblages of fan cultures as a conceptual and material force (Murris, 2017). As Steinberg notes, the purpose of transmediated moments of material engagements with IP's is to support the collective life of the IP. Therefore, "each instance of consumption" Steinberg argues "must be regarded as a form of production that further develops the entire media franchise and the consumer desire that supports it" (2012, p. 141).

3. Evangelize

The final phrase in the quote that we wish to draw attention to, is the term "evangelize". According to the Oxford English Dictionary, evangelize means to "convert, or to seek to covert someone". To evangelize is to persuade with passion, faith and a deep belief in the object of conversion. Thus to "evangelize an IP", a superfan needs to have an intense emotional belief in the value of the intellectual property and to be able to mobilize this emotion as they proselytize the intellectual property to others. The superfan's passion, faith and deep belief of the intellectual property has the ability to persuade others to also have similar passions.

Insight Kids is not the only marketing research firm to use such religious terms in describing the superfan. As Alison Hulme, a research analyst writes in Marketing Week "superfans also persuade. They are zealous connectors with a strong desire to convert others and can sometimes stir up the frenzied worship of a brand. They convert brand awareness into something tangible by convincing people to act who otherwise may not have done. Acting as kind of online missionaries, they turn friends into sales – so an evangelical superfan is a seriously valuable asset" (2010, para. 5)

The religious connotations in Hulme's quote reveal the affective expectations of the superfan as a colonial enterprise. The terms "evangelization", "conversion" and "missionaries" are deeply rooted in in an imperial discourse of colonization. Insight Kids, like Hulme, draws upon the colonial metaphor of missionary work by using the term evangelize. The work that is being done "for free" by superfans is the emotional labor of arousing passion for an intellectual property and proselytizing that passion to their networks.

The colonial imperative of children's market research is nothing new. The market segmentation of young people in the past century has been a deeply colonial process. For example, market research companies have even claimed that they have "discovered" a new market of young people, such as the teen market in the 1950s or the tween market in the late 1980s (see Coulter, 2012 and 2014). The settler/colonial conceit that a segment of young people can be "discovered" belies the colonial imperative of market research as process of subjugation that produces the colonized as knowable, coherent and unified (see Bhabha, 2001). Linking back to the earlier discussion of Cook's notion of commercial epistemologies, the act of "knowing" and "discovering" are colonial acts that discursively frame the subject according to the logics and needs of the knower, who in this case are the imperial forces of consumer capitalism. None of this should be too surprising since capitalism works only by finding new markets to colonize (see Williamson, 1986). What is noteworthy here, in the case of Insight Kids strategy, is that children as superfans are entangled in the colonial mission of the evangelization of IPs. As children "evangelize" an IP, the boundaries between promotion and passion collapse. In Steinberg's words, "the work of consuming [is] extended across the child's living space and waking life, which in turn accelerate[s] the environmentalization of media within the lives of these child consumers" (2012, p. 168). The act of marketing is naturalized as an expression of passion and becomes nearly invisible, undiscernible to those who are being proselytized to.

The entanglements of young people into the promotional ecologies of the children's media and entertainment industry is part of the affective structures of neoliberal capitalism. Honing in on the three key terms of the Kids Insight quote, "superfan" "work for free" and "evangelize" opens up an opportunity to explore the entanglements of children's affective passions with the promotional ecologies of the children's media and entertainment companies. The superfan reveals how young people's affective passions are seen as potential resources to be harnessed by the media corporations of children's entertainment; "work for free" exposes how it is a form of immaterial labor that produces value for a media property, and "evangelize" addresses the deeply colonial nature of the commercial epistemologies market research. But these lines of explorations also raise many other issues in terms of thinking about children's labor in digital economies and the rights that young people have to their own digital labor. What happens to our understandings of children, we can ask, when young people are seen as evangelizers for corporate brands, or even more pointedly as "pint sized marketers" as Insight Kids has called them.

We need to ask broader questions about what this means in terms of how we conceptualize young people's creative work and children's rights to their own affective experiences as fans. We also need to ask much broader questions that explore how young people are swept into the colonial projects of market expansion, particularly as the children's media and entertainment industry is becoming increasing globalized with new avenues for media distribution. And how young people negotiate and respond to being part of these expansions. We also need to consider the multiple, intricate and complex ways that CME's take up and implement Insight Kids market research findings, as well as addressing young people's engagements with these new trajectories of promotion. The excited declaration of getting "superfans to evangelize your IP" since they provide free labor is only the tip of a much broader sets of entanglements of young people in the promotional ecologies of children's media and entertainment, that we are only beginning to be able to unentangle.

References

Abidin, C. (2017). #familygoals: Family influencers, calibrated amateurism, and justifying young digital labor. *Social Media + Society, 3*(2), 1–15. https://doi.org/10.1177/2056305117707191

Ahmed, S. (2004). Affective economies. *Social Text, 22*(2), 117–139. https://doi.org/10.1215/01642472-22-2_79-117

Andrejevic, M. (2007). *Ispy: Surveillance and power in the interactive era.* University Press of Kansas.

Baudrillard, J. (1998). *The consumer society: Myths and structures.* Sage Publications.

Bhabha, H. (2001). The other question: Stereotype difference, discrimination and the discourse of colonialism. In S. Seidman & J. C. Alexander (Eds.), *The new social theory reader: Contemporary debates* (pp. 388–401). Routledge.

Chumsky, S. (2017, Apr. 7). Fueling fandom among today's kids. *Kidscreen.* https://webcache.googleusercontent.com/search?q=cache:T_5vD3h-V85YJ:https://kidscreen.com/2017/04/07/fueling-fandom-among-todays-kids/+&cd=1&hl=fr&ct=clnk&gl=fr&client=ms-google-coop.

Cochoy, F. (1998). Another discipline for the market economy: Marketing as a performative knowledge and know-how for capitalism. *The Sociological Review, 46*(S1), 194–221. https://doi.org/10.1111/j.1467-954X.1998.tb03475.x

Cook, D. T. (2012). Commercial epistemologies of childhood: "Fun" and the leveraging of children's subjectivities and desires. In D. Zwick & J. Cayla (Eds.), *Inside marketing: Practices, ideologies, devices* (pp. 257–267). Oxford University Press.

Cook, D. T. (2019). Children's market researchers as moral brokers. *Journal of Cultural Economy, 12*(1), 70–82. https://doi.org/10.1080/17530350.2018.1514316

Coté, M., & Pybus, J. (2011). Learning to immaterial labour 2.0: Facebook and social networks. In M. A. Peters & E. Bulut (Eds.), *Cognitive capitalism, education, and digital labor* (pp. 169–194). Peter Lang.

Coulter, N. (2012). From toddlers to teens: The colonization of childhood the Disney way. *Jeunesse: Young People, Texts, Cultures, 4*(1), 146–158. https://doi.org/10.1353/jeu.2012.0009

Coulter, N. (2014). *Tweening the girl: The crystallization of the tween market* (New edition). Peter Lang.

De Kosnik, A. (2012). Fandom as free labor. In T. Scholz (Ed.), *Digital labor: The Internet as playground and factory* (pp. 98–111). Routledge.

Engelhardt, T. (1986). The shortcake strategy. In T. Gitlin (Ed.), *Watching television: A pantheon guide to popular culture* (pp. 68–110). Pantheon Books.

Fuchs, C. (2012). Dallas Smythe today – The audience commodity, the digital labour debate, Marxist political economy and critical theory. *TripleC: Communication, Capitalism & Critique. Journal for a Global Sustainable Information Society, 10*(2), 692–740. https://doi.org/10.31269/triplec.v10i2.443

Hesmondhalgh, D. (2010). User-generated content, free labour and the cultural industries. *Ephemera: Theory & Politics in Organization, 10*(3/4), 267–284.

Hills, M. (2015). Veronica Mars, fandom, and the 'Affective Economics' of crowdfunding poachers. *New Media & Society, 17*(2), 183–197. https://doi.org/10.1177/1461444814558909

Hulme, A. (2010). The Fan-ship Factor. Understanding the role of the superfan in social media marketing. *Marketing Week*. May 7 Retrieved from: https://www.marketingweek.com/the-fan-ship-factor-understanding-the-role-of-the-superfan-in-social-media-marketing/.

Insight. (2017). *How entertainment brands turn kids into superfans.* June 16, 2017. Retrieved from: https://insightstrategygroup.com/thinking/kids-and-family/how-entertainment-brands-turn-kids-into-superfans.

Jenkins, H. (2006). Fans, bloggers, and gamers: Exploring participatory culture. New York University Press.

Jenkins, H., & Deuze, M. (2008). Editorial: Convergence culture. *Convergence : The International Journal of Research into New Media Technologies, 14*(1), 5–12. https://doi.org/10.1177/1354856507084415

John, D. R. (1999). Consumer socialization of children: A retrospective look at twenty-five years of research. *Journal of Consumer Research, 26*(3), 183–213.

Kennedy, H. (2006). Beyond anonymity, or future directions for internet identity research. *New Media & Society*, 8(6), 859–876.

Khamis, S., Ang, L., & Welling, R. 2017. Self-branding, 'micro-celebrity' and the rise of social media influencers. *Celebrity Studies, 8*(2), 191–208.

Kline, S. (1993). *Out of the garden: Toys, TV and children's culture in the age of marketing.* Verso.

Kunkel, D., & Castonguay, J. (2011). Children and television advertising. In D. G. Singer & J. L. Singer (Eds.), *Handbook of children and the media* (2nd revised edition) (pp. 375–392). Sage Publications.

Lazzarato, Maurizio (1996). Immaterial labor. In P. Virno & M. Hardt (Eds.), *Radical thought in Italy: A potential politics* (pp. 142–157). University of Minnesota Press.

MarketCast Group. (2019). MarketCast Group appoints Graham McKenna to CMO. October 31, 2019.

Matthias, S., & Chumsky, S. (2017). Hot research: How to woo the elusive superfan. Insight Research Group. Presentation. Kidscreen Summit.

McNeal, J. U. (1998). Tapping the three kids' markets. *American Demographics*, 20 (April), 37–41.

McNeal, J. U. (2007). *On becoming a consumer: The development of consumer behavior patterns in childhood.* Butterworth-Heinemann.

Murris, K. (2017). The post-human child: iii. In D. Kennedy & B. Bahler (Eds.), *Philosophy of childhood today: Exploring the boundaries* (pp. 185–197). Lexington Books.

Potter, A., & Steemers, J. (2017). Children's television in transition: Policies, platforms and production. *Media International Australia, 163*(1), 6–12. https://doi.org/10.1177/1329878X17693936

Prout, A. (2011). Taking a step away from modernity: Reconsidering the new sociology of childhood: *Global Studies of Childhood*, 4–14. https://doi.org/10.2304/gsch.2011.1.1.4

Prout, A., & James, A. (1997). A new paradigm for the sociology of childhood. In A. James & A. Prout (Eds.), *Constructing and reconstructing childhood: Contemporary issues in the sociological study of childhood.* Falmer Press.

Ruckenstein, M., & Granroth, J. (2019). Algorithms, advertising and the intimacy of surveillance. *Journal of Cultural Economy, 13*(1), 12–24. https://doi.org/10.1080/17530350.2019.1574866

Seiter, E. (1993). *Sold separately: Children and parents in consumer culture.* Rutgers University Press.

Smythe, D. W. (1977). Communications: Blindspot of Western Marxism. *CTheory, 1*(3), 1–27.

Steinberg, M. (2012). *Anime's media mix: Franchising toys and characters in Japan*. University of Minnesota Press.

Terranova, T. (2000). Free labor: Producing culture for the digital economy. *Social Text, 18*(2), 33–58. https://doi.org/10.1215/01642472-18-2_63-33

Terranova, T. (2004). *Network culture: Politics for the information age.* Pluto Press

Wiliamson, J. (1986). Woman is an island: Femininity and colonization. In T. Modleski (Ed.), *Studies in entertainment: Critical approaches to mass culture. Underlined and Notations* (pp. 99–118). Indiana University Press.

Zwick, D., & Bradshaw, A. (2016). Biopolitical marketing and social media brand communities: *Theory, Culture & Society, 35*(5), 91–115. https://doi.org/10.1177/0263276415625333

4

Masterpiece: Thinking about children and creative industries with values

Yelyzaveta Hrechaniuk

Cultural and creative industries are preoccupied with values. Creativity, innovation, novelty, design – these recognizable buzzwords also capture what is important and valuable in and for the industries. Tensions between these different values, such as "arts" and "commerce", have defined and identified creative industries since the term came into use (Garnham, 2005; Moeran and Strandgaard Pedersen, 2011; O'Connor, 2010). Child studies, which is the field I come from, also takes interest in the valuing and pricing of children and childhood, which often give rise to debates, controversies and moral panics (Lee, 2005; Sparrman, Sandin and Sjöberg, 2012; Zelizer, 1985/1994). This chapter makes a space for these two interests to meet and makes it possible to look into how children matter in and for creative industries.

I explore a collection of Ikea soft toys where each of the toys is based on a child's drawing. Now, Ikea is a furniture and design company and not strictly speaking a creative industry. But given that design, innovation and creativity are central for the company (Inter IKEA Systems B.V., 2017), I decided to use Ikea as an empirical case. The choice is also guided by a broad understanding of the notion of creative industries as those producing commodities and services associated with culture or entertainment (Caves, 2000). Seeing Ikea as a creative industry also allows the concept to be revisited. What happens when the notion of cultural and creative industries is stretched beyond music, film and TV production, publishing and performing arts (Caves, 2000; Moeran and Strandgaard Pedersen, 2011; Negus and Pickering, 2011)?

1. Values in creative industries

The values of creative and cultural products are something that stands out in the literature about creative and cultural industries (Jones et al., 2016; Moeran, 2012; Moeran and Strandgaard Pedersen, 2011; Negus and Pickering, 2011). Drawing largely on organization and business studies, this literature understands value as being socially constructed rather than an inherent capacity of objects. One example is Brian Moeran and Jesper Strandgaard Pedersen's (2011b) study of competitions, fairs, and festivals that in its attention to competitions is relevant to the empirical case analyzed in this chapter. Moeran and Strandgaard Pedersen (2011b) theorize value(s) in terms of social relations and call for scrutinizing production and negotiation of values of cultural products. At the same time, their value theory tends to pre-distinguish valuation and evaluation, economic Value and cultural values. It is emphasized that monetary valuation and non-monetary evaluation are tightly interconnected but they are *theoretically* understood as distinct (see also Jones et al., 2016; Moeran 2012). This approach, however, implies that it is possible to analytically distinguish where valuation ends and evaluation begins. The theory offers a classification of different kinds of values, such as technical/material, social, and utility values, to name a few. It also suggests a mechanism that could account for how various non-monetary values get "exchanged for" (Moeran and Pedersen, 2011b, p. 12) a monetary value. For instance, when cultural products with their aesthetic, material and sentimental values, are assigned a price. According to my understanding, carrying out such structured, sometimes all too detailed, analytical classifications *beforehand* goes against the ambition of these very same theories to account for the "ongoing social construction and negotiation" (Moeran and Pedersen, 2011b, p. 15) of values.

Besides tensions in the understanding of how values are produced, the way the actors producing values are theorized in this approach also invites questions. Value is said to be assigned to cultural products by particular groups of people, often professionals "whose whole lives consist in experiencing and judging values" (Jones et al., 2016, p. 762). The actors in question are, for example, artistic creators, producers, or cultural market intermediaries. But coming from child studies, my first question is perhaps not surprisingly: What about children? The understanding of either economic or non-monetary values that is limited primarily to professional risks excluding not only children but many other groups who are seldom allowed the expert "judge" position. What could their role be in the production of values, especially when children are the ones co-creating cultural products?

2. Valuation studies

The question is then how we can think about values in a more empirically grounded way that takes into consideration what I discuss above. This chapter draws on valuation studies informed by Science and Technology Studies (STS). This emerging field takes a pragmatist stance and suggests exploring how values are enacted in practice (Doganova et al., 2014; Dussauge et al., 2015; Helgesson and Muniesa, 2013; Kjellberg et al., 2013; Muniesa, 2012). In other words, how they are produced, negotiated, assessed, sustained and dismissed (Doganova et al., 2014). This requires digging into the nitty-gritty of social practices, which in this chapter are texts, images and videos, to ask *who* establishes and maintains values, and *how*. The actors in question can be individuals and institutions, as well as mechanisms put in place to assess, rank and evaluate. These are referred to as valuation devices (Dussauge et al., 2015b), and competitions and contests are two prominent examples.

Valuation studies encourages the explanation and exploration of values, rather than using them as taken-for-granted phenomena "with explanatory power" (Dussauge et al., 2015a, p. 2). What valuation studies can bring to studies of creative industries is the open-ended exploratory approach. It suggests that values are produced and sustained *as* economic, non-economic, aesthetic, financial and so on *in practice*. This is instead of studying practices with a ready theoretical classification of values in mind, such as the distinction between economic and non-economic values, art and commerce, valuation and evaluation. The idea is to look at "*all kinds of values*" (Dussauge et al., 2015a, p. 8, italics in the original) as they are performed in social practices. So this approach takes interest in how actors bring values into being (Woolgar and Lezaun, 2013); how borders and overlaps between, say, art and commerce are put into place, sustained and dismantled. By refusing to stabilize the notion of values via defining or typologizing, valuation studies is dedicated to understanding values as precarious, always in the making, and brought into being though the process of valuation.

3. Introducing the case

The soft toy named *Lion* is part of Ikea's limited collection called *Sagoskatt* which was sold worldwide in 2017. *Sagoskatt* visually stands out from Ikea's range of soft toys: the bright-colored quirky monsters, animals with asymmetrical eyes and paws, mashups of several creatures, such as the unicorn dog, look nothing like the realistic stuffed pigs and elephants. The *Sagoskatt* collection is based on children's drawings, chosen through a drawing competition arranged yearly by Ikea where children up to 12 years old are encouraged to submit drawings of their "dream soft toy". The *Lion* is drawn by 7-year-old Mark (a pseudonym) from the United Arab Emirates who became one of 10 winners of Ikea's drawing competition held in 2016. The empirical material I analyze in the chapter consists of several social media posts presenting Mark as the winner of Ikea's drawing competition. Two of them Ikea United Arab Emirates published on their official Facebook account and two more on Instagram and Twitter platforms. One Facebook post includes a photo of Mark with the drawing (IKEA UAE, 2017a) and the other is a 1-minute-long video of the celebration that Ikea organized for Mark and his family in Ikea store (IKEA UAE, 2017b). A few months afterwards Ikea UAE used the same photo in their call for a new round of the drawing competition on their Instagram and Twitter (IKEA UAE, 2017c; IKEA UAE, 2017d). These examples of Ikea's promotion show how Ikea communicates to the public the results of their drawing competition, the upcoming release of the toy collection and the new round of the drawing competition.

In the following analysis I will explore what I call the *masterpiece* value of Mark's drawing brought into being in the material. The aim is to understand how entities such a child's drawing come to count as valuable and to whom. I stay with the borrowed word *masterpiece* as it is the notion used by Ikea themselves. And a richer one for that matter than classifying and labelling it as "exceptionality" or "creativity" value, which could be alternative ways of understanding the case. I argue that while the *masterpiece* value seems to refer solely to the drawing, both this product and the child as its creator are valued by Ikea and the audiences of the promotion materials.

4. Making the masterpiece

Masterpiece. As I was looking through the empirical material, this one word used in a Facebook post published by Ikea UAE caught my attention (IKEA UAE, 2017b). *Masterpiece* refers to a pencil drawing of a yellow-and-orange creature with a long stripy body, two legs and an egg-shaped face framed by a bushy bright-orange circle. Its fluffy orange tail is pointing upwards. A pair of eyes looks from the creature's yellow face directly at the viewer, below them – an orange nose and a curve of a smile. Mark's drawing of a lion is quirky and eye-catching thanks to its bright colors. But a *master-piece*? In the following analysis I take a closer look at the ways in which Mark's drawing comes into being (Woolgar and Lezaun, 2013) as a masterpiece in the text and the video in Ikea's post. Instead of taking at face value the statement that the drawing *is* out-of-the-ordinary or exceptional, I explore how the *masterpiece* is made in practice.

Ikea UAE's Facebook post includes a one-minute video clip and the following text in the caption:

Example 1.

We're so proud that Mark from Dubai was one of the 10 winners in our drawing competition this year. Watch him describe his masterpiece 🦁

The lion head emoji placed next to *masterpiece* playfully specifies that the word refers to the drawing of the lion. Categorizing children's drawings as art is by itself not unusual (Änggård, 2005; Bendroth Karlsson, 2014; Låby, 2018). Child winners of Ikea's competition are called artists and designers throughout the promotional materials for the *Sagoskatt* collection (e.g. IKEA UAE, 2017d). But what is special about *masterpiece* is that it performs the drawing as an exceptional work. Not only does the word connect the drawing to the arts discourse but also to the arts of special skill, craftsmanship and value. As an expression of the highest art form, *masterpiece* produces an order of drawings where some are positioned higher than others.

One of the top 10 winners also does the work of ordering child participants of the drawing competition, and separating the "winners" from the rest. To be sure, drawing activities may well be fun and playful, but Ikea's drawing competition is nevertheless a contest, where children's drawings (and children) are evaluated against one another. To give an idea of the scope of the competition, Ikea reports receiving 70,000 drawings in 2016 (IKEA Sweden, 2017b). With one submission accepted per child (e.g. IKEA Sweden, 2017a), this allows us to assume that the same number of children and families participated. Meaning that Mark's and the rest 9 winning drawings withstood a hard competition. Competitions understood as valuation devices (Dussauge et al., 2015b) order and classify things into "more" and "less" valuable, so displaying competition results is part of performing such an order. *A masterpiece* falls under the "most" valuable.

Note that the caption says *Watch him describe* ***his*** *masterpiece.* The drawing is produced as Mark's own, neither Ikea's, nor anybody else's. Without aiming to establish a definitive ownership, I would like to think out loud and ask: whose is the drawing of the lion?

The video embedded in the post (IKEA UAE, 2017b) shows two events: Mark redrawing the lion and a celebration organized by Ikea in honor of Mark as a winner of the competition. The video opens with a close-up of Mark drawing the lion on a piece of paper. The camera follows the movements of the pen and lingers on the focused expression on Mark's face. When in a few shots the camera zooms out we see that Mark is sitting at a table in a model Ikea children's room, surrounded by Ikea furniture, textiles, picture frames, toys and other products. While drawing, Mark talks about the process of creating the lion:

Example 2.

I took part in the drawing competition and decided to draw a fluffy lion. Its nose was orange and its mane was yellow. Its eyes were black and the tail had orange and yellow. And then I put stripes on it.

Let me pause here and observe that stripes are hardly a common thing for lions to have. In the video this is left without comment. But another "quote" of Mark becomes thought-provoking when put next to this excerpt from the video clip. By quote I refer to a short text describing the drawing that is included in the promotion for the *Sagoskatt* soft toy collection. Under the heading *Designer thoughts* ten such short texts by each of the child winners provide a comment on their drawings. In the quote Mark says (IKEA USA, 2017[1], n.p.):

Example 3.

Even though he's a lion, he has the name "Tiger" since I was in a hurry when I named him.

In Ikea's product index the toy is called *lion* (IKEA Sweden, 2017). Looking at the drawing of a lion named Tiger with this in mind could tell something interesting about how the drawing is valued. First, that children's creations are not easily classifiable: should the plush animal be named according to what it "is" or to what it is called? Then there is an arguable paradox of Ikea enacting the child winners of the competition as *designers*, and their drawings as a *masterpiece*, yet not following through with the design idea completely. To make it clear, my goal here is not to argue how cultural products *should* be valued. I am interested in exploring how they are valued in practice by various actors, which in this case is not free from tensions and negotiations.

5. Prosumption and creative co-production

Finally, there is a legal dimension to the question of "whose" the *masterpiece* is. In Ikea's drawing competition the moment a drawing is submitted, the participant hands over the intellectual property rights, which include copyright and design rights, to the company (IKEA Sweden, 2017a). In this sense as well, Mark's drawing is not entirely "his". At this point the concept of prosumption comes to mind. If prosumption is understood as an intertwinement of consumption and production (Ritzer and Jurgenson, 2010; Ruckenstein, 2011; Ruckenstein, 2015), the *Sagoskatt* toy collection is a clear example. The idea of children as both (co-) producers of soft toys and their target consumers is captured in the tagline used to market the collection: *design for kids, by kids.*

---

1 Not all promotion materials were accessible through Ikea UAE's web page or social media, such as the child winners' quotes. So I complement the analysis with resources from other local Ikea pages: here with a press kit from Ikea USA's web page https://www.ikea.com/ms/en_US/media/pressroom/FY18-Lets-Play/SAGOSKATT_Press-Kit.pdf (accessed 21 April 2020).

To adult consumers Ikea's offer of co-production (Andersson, 2009) is well-known. Similar to the notion of prosumption, co-production here means that in return for low prices consumers do a share of work, such as collecting and assembling the furniture. This relationship is framed in terms of the customers' thrift (Andersson, 2009). But what happens when this is an offer of, say, a creative co-production, where the consumer is free not just to customize the purchased product, such as Nike shoes (Lury, 2004), but design it from scratch? A creative co-production offered to children, and a competitive one for that matter. One could ask whose thrift is at stake in this case, since the child winners of the competition are not paid in monetary terms. This is not to say that they receive nothing in return: the following section of the chapter will focus on a celebration organized for Mark by Ikea. Yet it is not uncommon for children's prosumption to be framed by companies in terms of fun, play and creativity (Ruckenstein, 2011; Sjöberg, 2013), and Ikea's drawing competition is not an exception. This makes it all-important to consider what the stakes are for both children and creative industries in such co-production practices.

6. Making the audiences

If nobody is around to see a masterpiece, is it a masterpiece? Here I will take a closer look at the second part of the video in the Facebook post (IKEA UAE, 2017b) to argue that Mark's drawing is valued not only by Ikea. The audiences on social media who view, share and comment on Ikea UAE's posts also engage in the making of the *masterpiece*. After Mark displays the finished drawing towards the camera, the video jumps to the celebration in honor of him becoming one of the winners of the drawing competition. It is organized by and at Ikea, so we see Mark entering the upper floor of the store with his family. They are greeted by Ikea staff lined up alongside the aisle, clapping, taking photos and popping confetti-filled crackers. The mood appears joyful, the tempo of the video fast-paced. The celebration also involves gifts: in the video Mark is handed two lion-shaped balloons, a large basket, and an oversized Ikea gift card that he and his family are shown holding together with an Ikea employee in the final frame.

As well as a *masterpiece*, the celebration displayed performs Mark's drawing as something exceptional. The drawing helped him win the competition, and that is no ordinary occasion. By organizing a festivity for the competition winner, filming and publishing it online, Ikea also enacts Mark's competition win as a valuable achievement to be recognized. Confetti, balloons, and gifts – this is hardly an everyday occurrence. And the number of invited guests? Unlimited, as the video is openly shared on Ikea UAE's Facebook page. At the time of writing[2], it has 12 thousand views and more than 200 actions, including shares, reactions, and comments. Publishing the video online together with the encouragement *Watch him describe his masterpiece* (Example 1) invites the public to join a festive moment. The moment that could otherwise be a "private" family event shared by Mark, his family and Ikea. Speaking of families, it is perhaps not incidental that Ikea's drawing competitions are managed by the company's membership club called Ikea Family. To submit a drawing, the child's parent or guardian also needs to be a current Ikea Family member or become one (IKEA Sweden, 2017a). Through the video, the audience becomes part of this performed "family", a togetherness. Ikea itself is performed as an engaged child- and family-centered company that highly values children and their creativity.

Let me further build on the idea of the audiences' engagement in valuation. Note *we're so proud* in the video's caption (Example 1). This reinforces the exceptionality of both the drawing and its author, showing that valuations of the two are not easy to tell apart (see also Hrechaniuk, 2019). At the same time, the *we're so proud* statement also performs an intimate bond between the child, the company and the consumer public. *We* is ambiguous: since the caption is posted by Ikea UAE, it appears that the pronoun refers to the company. Yet as the comments section below the post shows, users pick up on the feeling of pride:

Example 4.

User's comment: *Well done mark* [*sic*]*! That makes ur [sic] dad and mom more proud of you!!!*

Ikea UAE: *You're right, we"re* [*sic*] *all proud of Mark* 🙂.

While the Facebook user writes about Mark's parents, Ikea UAE both agrees with the statement and widens the group of people who "are" proud of Mark. In Ikea's response and in the caption (Example 1) *we...*

2 As of June 1, 2020.

all stands for many more people than Mark's parents and Ikea UAE. It enacts a personal and close relationship between Mark, his family, Ikea and the users and potential consumers seeing the post on Facebook, and perhaps especially those buying the *Sagoskatt* toys.

The notion of *proud* referring to the child and the competition win is repeated in another Facebook post by Ikea UAE (IKEA UAE, 2017a). A noteworthy moment of valuation happens in the interplay between the photo of Mark and his drawing and the following caption included in the post:

Example 5.

Congrats Mark for being one of the top 10 winners in our worldwide drawing competition. 🎉🎉 *You made us very proud. We can't wait to see your soft toy come to life next year* 😊😊🎊🎉🎉🎊

The photo shows Mark smiling, facing the camera and holding a large poster with his drawing of the lion and the caption *Fluffy Lion* placed on top of the poster. Below the drawing are the words *Great Drawing, Mark! Store Manager, Ikea Dubai*, a signature in blue ink and Ikea's blue and yellow logo. By stating that the drawing is *great*, accompanied by the official logo and signature, the poster "certifies" the quality of the drawing. By putting this on display, Ikea also performs itself as an organization *in a position* to valuate artistic works and designs. As I mentioned earlier, in the *Sagoskatt* marketing the winning drawings are also referred to as *designs* and child winners are called *artists* and *designers*. This (self-) legitimizes Ikea, a design company, to evaluate children's drawings. Had they been "mere" drawings rather than designs, it would not perhaps be as clear why the furniture and home design company is in a position to decide what is and what is not *great* or a *masterpiece*.

7. Consumption of (values of) children

Looking at displays of the *masterpiece* and *great drawing*, all of which feature Mark, the notion of the consumption *of* children comes to mind (Zelizer, 2012). An addition to consumption by children, for children (e.g. by their parents) and among children, it brings attention to complex cases of consumption. Using the notion of consumption of children

Viviana A. Zelizer (2012) asks how we can understand valuation practices such as surrogacy, black market babies and adoption. These are practices where valuations of children's lives in monetary and non-monetary terms often come in conflict with one another, hence the famous expression "pricing the priceless." Here I am interested in this notion widened to include more intangible ways of consuming children, such as consuming values, ideals and norms (see Sparrman and Sandin, 2012). Not only do Ikea UAE's posts announce Mark's victory in the competition and produce the *masterpiece* value of Mark's drawing, but they also bring into being certain norms and values of children and children's creativity for public consumption.

Yet as I was looking at how the materials analyzed so far appear to center on the "figure of the 'creative child'" (Cook, 2018), something else became visually prominent. The video clip is filled with Ikea products that arguably do not *need* to be in the frame to tell the story of Mark's drawing. Rows of Ikea soft toys in the background, Mark sitting at an Ikea table, drawing with Ikea pens, the party held at the Ikea store (Example 2). The final sentence in Example 5 does the work of announcing that and when the Lion will be manufactured as a soft toy. The posts are as much a celebration of the child winner as they are an advertisement for Ikea's children's section. They are after all promotion materials, and Ikea is a for-profit company, so this is hardly a surprising finding. Neither is my goal to argue what values creative industries "should" promote. The analysis focused rather on the values that they do promote, and the outcomes of this for products co-created by children for other children. Does the lion toy become more precious when it is marketed as a cultural product based on a *masterpiece*?

Concluding thoughts

This chapter explores the *masterpiece* value of a children's drawing. Rather than taking it for granted, the analysis focuses on making values and norms visible (see also Sparrman, 2019) and untangling how this value is accomplished in Ikea's promotion. Through an exploration of values, it shows that valuing children is far from being *only* about children. The term "*masterpiece*" brings into being in a particular way not just the drawing of the lion as exceptional and Mark as its creator, but also Ikea and the audiences engaging with the promotion materials. A togetherness, a "family" uniting all these actors is brought into being through and around Mark's victory in the drawing competition. A togetherness gathered around celebration and the feeling of pride in the child and his drawing. But also with Ikea's brand and products taking center stage. In addition to looking at how values of children are produced and sustained in practice, the chapter asks who is or are the actors producing values, and whose values become important (Dussauge et al., 2015a). Ikea may not *be* a creative industry in a strict definition of the term, but for this chapter what it *does* matters the most. The company has so far organized five international drawing competitions in 2014–2019. They resulted in five *Sagoskatt* collections, that is a total of 40 soft toy characters, sold worldwide in Ikea stores, and the same number of child winners. Thinking with values makes it possible to ask what happens when companies like Ikea define what is important, desirable and valuable for children and families, or when creative industries become self-appointed judges of commodities co-created by children.

Exploring how the *masterpiece* value is made and sustained in practice is itself a challenging enough task. But it has been perhaps even more challenging to grapple with who and what are actually being valued. It is not only that Mark's drawing comes into being as a *masterpiece*, but the child is also produced as exceptional, and his competition win as an occasion worth celebrating. The analysis then suggests that in practice values of children and of their drawings are entangled: masterpieces make artists, and vice versa. In a similar vein it encourages the question: could creative children contribute towards making creative industries into creative industries? The offer of creative co-production makes artists and designers of children but perhaps also a creative industry out of Ikea.

Acknowledgements

I am grateful to Anna Sparrman and Alex Orrmalm for their careful and thoughtful readings of the earlier drafts of this chapter.

References

Andersson, F. (2009). *Performing co-production: On the logic and practice of shopping at IKEA*. Uppsala University, Geografiska regionstudier.

Änggård. E. (2005). *Bildskapande – en del av förskolebarns kamratkulturer* [Making pictures – A part of preschool children's peer cultures]. Linköping University, Department of Thematic Studies.

Bendroth Karlsson, M. (2014). Om barn och bilder – en historisk tillbakablick [About children and images – A historical overview]. In M. Bendroth Karlsson & T. Karlsson Häikiö (Eds.). *Bild, Konst och Medier för Yngre Barn: Kulturella redskap och pedagogiska perspektiv* (pp. 11–21). Studentlitteratur.

Caves, R. E. (2000). *Creative industries: Contracts between art and commerce.* Harvard University Press.

Cook, D. T. (2018). Panaceas of play: Stepping past the creative child. In S. Spyrou, R. Rosen, & D. T. Cook (Eds.), *Reimagining childhood studies* (pp. 123–137). Bloomsbury Academic.

Doganova, L., Giraudeau, M., Helgesson, C.-F., Kjellberg, H., Lee, F., Mallard, A., Mennicken, A., Muniesa, F., Sjögren, E., & Zuiderent-Jerak, T. (2014). Valuation studies and the critique of valuation. *Valuation Studies, 2*(2), 87–96.

Dussauge, I., Helgesson, C.-F., Lee, F., & Woolgar, S. (2015a). On the omnipresence, diversity, and elusiveness of values in the life sciences and medicine. In I. Dussauge, C.-F. Helgesson, & F. Lee (Eds.), *Value practices in the life sciences and medicine* (pp. 1–31). Oxford University Press.

Dussauge, I., Helgesson, C.-F., & Lee, F. (2015b). Valuography: Studying the making of values. In I. Dussauge, C.-F. Helgesson, & F. Lee (Eds.), *Value practices in the life sciences and medicine* (pp. 267–285). Oxford University Press.

Garnham, N. (2005). From cultural to creative industries. *International Journal of Cultural Policy, 11*(1), 15–30.

Helgesson, C.-F., & Muniesa, F. (2013). For what it's worth: An introduction to valuation studies. *Valuation Studies, 1*(1), 1–10.

Hrechaniuk, Y. (2019). Children's creativity. In A. Sparrman (Ed.). *Making culture:* Children's and young people's leisure cultures (pp. 28–32). Kulturanalys Norden.

IKEA Sweden. (2017a). IKEA mjukdjur-teckningstävling 2017. Information och villkor för tävlingen [IKEA soft toy drawing competition 2017. Information and terms and conditions]. https://m.ikea.com/se/sv/pages/avdelning/teckningstavling/ (accessed 9 February 2018, the link is no longer active).

IKEA Sweden. (2017b). *SAGOSKATT* MJUKDJUR [*Sagoskatt* soft toys]. In: IKEA Oktobernyheter 2017. Available at: https://via.tt.se/pressmeddelande/ *Sagoskatt*- mjukdjur-27-oktober-2017? publisherId=2111134&releaseId=3245483 (accessed 29 November 2019, the link is no longer active).

IKEA UAE. (2017a). 6 February. Available at: https://www.facebook.com/IKEAUAE/photos/a. 184985191683383. 1073741829.179158848932684/706620066186557/? type=3&theater (accessed 2 March 2020).

IKEA UAE. (2017b). 27 May. Available at: https://www.facebook.com/IkeaUAE/videos/761016070746956/?v=761016070746956 (accessed 2 March 2020).

IKEA UAE. (2017c). 19 November. Available at: https://www.instagram.com/p/Bbq-LArlyNd/?hl=sv&taken-by=ikeauae (accessed 2 March 2020).

IKEA UAE. (2017d). 19 November. Available at: https://twitter.com/IKEAUAE/status/932168913655422977 (accessed 2 March 2020).

Inter IKEA Systems B.V. (2017). *This is IKEA*®. Available at: https://www.ikea.com/ms/media/pdf/This_is_IKEA_Oct_2017.pdf (accessed 21 April 2020).

Jones, C., Svejenova, S., Strandgaard Pedersen, J., & Townley, B. (2016). Misfits, mavericks and mainstreams: Drivers of innovation in the creative industries. *Organization Studies, 37*(6), 751–768.

Kjellberg, H., Mallard, A., Arjaliès, D.-L., Aspers, P., Beljean, S., Bidet, A., Corsin, A., Didier, E., Fourcade, M., Geiger, S., Hoeyer, K., Lamont, M., MacKenzie, D., Maurer, B., Mouritsen, J., Sjögren, E., Tryggestad, K., Vatin, F., & Woolgar, S. (2013). Valuation studies? Our collective two cents. *Valuation Studies, 1*(1), 11–30.

Lee, N. (2005). *Childhood and human value: Development, separation and separability*. Open University Press.

Lury, C. (2004). *Brands: The logos of the global economy*. Routledge.

Låby, E. (2018). *Vinnande bilder!: Teckningstävlingar för barn 1938–2000* [Winning pictures!: Art competitions for children 1938–2000]. Linköping University, Department of Thematic Studies.

Moeran, B. (2013). *The business of creativity: Toward and anthropology of worth*. Taylor & Francis.

Moeran, B., & Strandgaard Pedersen, J. (2011a). *Negotiating values in the creative industries: Fairs, festivals and competitive events*. Cambridge University Press.

Moeran, B., & Strandgaard Pedersen, J. (2011b). Introduction. In B. Moeran & J. Strandgaard Pedersen (Eds.), *Negotiating values in the creative industries: Fairs, festivals and competitive events* (pp. 1–35). Cambridge University Press.

Muniesa. F. (2012). A flank movement in the understanding of valuation. In L. Adkins & C. Lury (Eds), *Measure and value* (pp. 24–38). Wiley-Blackwell.

Negus, K., & Pickering, M. (2011). Creativity and cultural production. In B. Moeran & A. Alačovska (Eds.), *Creative industries: Critical readings*. Vol. 1. *Concepts* (pp. 249–267). Berg.

O'Connor, J. (2010). *The cultural and creative industries: A literature review*. 2nd ed. Available at: https://www.creativitycultureeducation.org/publication/the-cultural-and-creative-industries-a-literature-review/.

Ritzer, G., & Jurgenson, N. (2010). Production, consumption, prosumption: The nature of capitalism in the age of the digital 'prosumer'. *Journal of Consumer Culture, 10*(1), 13–36.

Ruckenstein, M. (2011). Children in creationist capitalism. *Information, Communication and Society, 14*(7), 1060–1076.

Ruckenstein, M. (2015). Playing Nintendogs: Desire, distributed agency and potentials of prosumption. *Journal of Consumer Culture, 15*(3), 351–370.

Sjöberg, J. (2013). *I marknadens öga: Barn och visuell konsumtion* [In the eye of the market: Children and visual consumption]. Linköping University, Department of Thematic Studies.

Sparrman, A. (2019). Children and young people's leisure culture. In A. Sparrman (Ed.), *Making culture:* Children's and young people's leisure cultures (pp. 7–17). Kulturanalys Norden.

Sparrman, A., & Sandin, B. (2012). Introduction: Situated child consumption. In A. Sparrman, B. Sandin, & J. Sjöberg (Eds.), *Situating child consumption: Rethinking values and notions of children, childhood and consumption* (pp. 9–31). Nordic Academic Press.

Sparrman, A., Sandin, B., & Sjöberg, J. (Eds.). (2012). *Situating child consumption: Rethinking values and notions of children, childhood and consumption*. Nordic Academic Press.

Woolgar, S., & Lezaun, J. (2013). The wrong bin bag: A turn to ontology in science and technology studies?. *Social Studies of Science, 43*(3), 321–340.

Zelizer, V. A. (1985/1994). *Pricing the priceless child: The changing social value of children*. Princeton University Press.

Zelizer, V. A. (2012). A grown-up priceless child. In A. Sparrman, B. Sandin, & J. Sjöberg (Eds.), *Situating child consumption: Rethinking values and notions of children, childhood and consumption* (pp. 71–81). Nordic Academic Press.

Part 2

Insights into the social construction of childhood by cultural and creative industries

Pascale Garnier

As in the case of "children" and "adults", "membership categories" often go by pairs: the meaning of one of these terms cannot be understood without the other and they are associated with different predicates and category-bound activities that are socially controlled (Sacks, 1974). In Western societies this is the result of a long historical process that has been at first analysed by Ariès (1962), as the increasing "segregation" of children outside adults' life, with the new importance of education and the rise of schooling. In her book *Pricing the priceless child*, Zelizer (1985) has pointed out one of the major trends of the social and cultural construction of our modern Western vision of childhood: the withdrawn of children from economic labor and the increasing importance of affection in families' relations between children and adults. Nowadays, this distinction is reinforced by the institutionalization of childhood, in terms of the construction of different age categories defining what is authorized, permitted, advised, forbidden, to avoid, etc., at such or such age. This institutionalization goes with the growing importance of age conventions, in particular age as a number of years that is supposed in the internationalization of the cultural content aimed to children and public regulations, including the definition of childhood as a category shared by everyone under 18 years of age in the United Nations Convention on the rights of the child. The social construction of childhood by cultural and creative industries involves age categories, not only as a normative order distinguishing different audiences and producers, but also as a matter of continuous classification struggles and debates regarding the arbitrariness of the classifications related to age (Garnier, 2014).

A striking example of this kind of game about age limits or borders may be illustrated by YouTube's strategies: initially its access is dedicated to teenagers and adults, but in fact as young children use it frequently without adults' supervision and control, the company has created in 2015 YouTube Kids App targeting very young children and infants (aged 0–5 years), labelled as "digitods" (Holloway et al., 2015). Instead of products aimed for what is called a "family" audience, YouTube Kids App advertises a specific space of consumption based on age differences: "For years, families have come to YouTube, watching countless hours of videos on all kinds of topics. Now, parents can rest a little easier knowing that videos in the YouTube Kids app are narrowed down to content appropriate for kids" (quoted in Burroughs, 2017, p. 4). Construction of infants « as demographic » is important not only for the present, but also for future brands' consumers. It also opens room for "algorithmic infant" understood as a "discursive positioning of the audience through the algorithm", where the algorithm replaces the parent as a curator of consumption choices as parenting (Burroughs, 2017, p. 6). But in fact parenting does not simply disappeared: it stills strongly associated with parental individual responsibilities grounded on age differences, while what we call "family" can be understand as a whole, a domestic unit where its members, younger and older ones, share more or less the same life style.

Age categories are at the heart of constant transactions between the producers of cultural goods and their users, while national and international public policies and regulations seem always to react with delay in order to prevent misuses and to protect children (Pastor et al., in this book). Through the three chapters of this part of the book we will see that age is really a cue for understanding the role of cultural and creative industries in the production of childhood, from the very beginning of babies' life, to the transition to adulthood. And at least, we will have to think about the diversity of children and teenagers: the importance of age categories in the industrial and marketing strategies may hide the social inequalities of cultural consumptions.

1. Between parents and children: Cultural consumptions and productions

From adults' normative viewpoint, cultural and creative industries are sites of troubles and promises that remind us the traditional and dualistic moral representations of childhood: on one side "angels" or vulnerable innocent and on the other side "devils" or powerful agent (Valentine, 1996a). The same tension is underlined in Buckingham's study of *The material child* (2011) between "exploited" or "empowered" young consumers. Between the promises of a new heaven, regarding future educational benefits of digital technology used for children's learning, and moral panics about children's everyday lives, for example, the risk of obesity or negative online experiences, such as aggression or cyberbullying, harmful content, sexting, etc., there is room for the study of the complexity of children's own perspectives and experiences.

This tension is newly and well documented by Valérie-Inés de La Ville's analysis about promotional discourses staging digital parenting using digital innovations in the baby care industries, such as baby's monitoring, apps or connected objects and toys. She shows how the brands' discourses strategies try to provide the parents with a feeling of security and confidence and at the same time to fill their desire to enhance young children's skills and autonomy. She studies the "parents-young child consumer cluster" from different intertwined perspectives: the first one is related to what is defined as "good" parenting; the second one is about the vision of early childhood and what kind of children, this kind of goods is performing; the third one is linked to how the goods aim to strengthen the relationship between parents and their children. Digital parenting labor does not go without children's surveillance, but we cannot forget how parents themselves are under surveillance: brands' strategies are increasingly grounded on big data given by their users, blurring the border between public and private (Smith and Shade, 2018). Thus, the commodification of childhood (Cook, 2004) goes hand in hand with that of parenthood. Parent-child affection, including the importance of emotional labor (Hoschild, 1983), is also translated into goods and services. Managing risk and opportunities balance is a challenge for all parents and more globally it enhances le role of an economy of attention towards children. This extension of children's life's rationalization and accountability can be understood both as an increasing discipline and as productive investment in human capital (Foucault, 2008). New technological commodities do not suppress parental vigilance: they call for a more permanent surveillance on every moment of children's life and requires their parents' presence, even through technological mediation and services. If fathering is more and more promoted, this presence lies massively upon mothers' shoulders.

From the parent-child cluster's consumption to the family's production of cultural goods, the chapter of Stine Liv Johansen about children on YouTube lead us to the other side of families' lives. The author offers a fascinating case study of a girl, becoming a YouTube star with the organization of her family towards an economic business. The importance of girls' video production on YouTube is not new (Banet-Weiser, 2011). What is new is perhaps the success story of peer-to-peer cultural productions that engages a whole family's business. It involves a tension between the girl's everyday life as a child, almost like her followers, and the increasing need of rationalization of family's labor as she's becoming a "celebrity". On the one side her celebrification is based on shared playful practices with her fans, mixing cute and rebellious attitudes. On the other side, building a transmedia franchise of content across different platforms and for different kind of products (board games, books, films, etc.), leads to the beginning of professionalization of family business, with the employment of a management agency and, more recently, the mother's professional shift for the development of this family business. Such as in the case of numerous kids unboxing channels, this kind of little business looks like a "proto-industry featuring professionalising-amateur content creators engaging in content innovation and media entrepreneurship across multiple social media platforms to aggregate global fan communities and incubate their own media brands" (Cunningham, 2017). Like Janus, there is a double face of this YouTuber success' story: culture of participation of young sharing a "digital playground" (Danby et al., 2018) and parents' control and guidance, under the supervision of a professional of media. Far from the celebration of an individual child agency and participation among peer-groups, the chapter shows how this success is rooted in family life. But peers are often aware of this monetization of "celebrity" and additionally, as gender and social class, age plays an important role in peer-to-peer cultural industry: "children construct age identities in their discussions of microcelebrities" (Martinez and Olsson, 2019, p. 49).

2. Transition to adulthood between teenagers

The anthropological approach of the consumption of goods coined by Douglas and Isherwood (1979) underlines the link between moral judgments, cognitive categories and objects: it is through the objects that a culture acquires stability and consistency, that it becomes visible and convincing. Goods also provide a "service of marking": "every good can be perceived as a simple sample, a simple part of a flow of markings which participates in the elaboration of a system of classification" (Douglas and Isherwood, 1979, p. 97). This "service of marking" participates in the definition of one's identity. Objects and practices assign dualistic gender categories to individuals. It is also the case with age categories: sometimes objects are "too small" or "too big" for a certain child; reciprocally, sometimes children are "too young" or "too old" to have such or such stuff. Often at the heart of conflicts and negotiations between parents and children, the objects also act as markers of "normality" in relation to the children's development.

Goods are equally essential in social relationships between peers. Peer groups present strong hierarchies between different ages: "Children do not just learn age concepts, they also develop complex ideas about a global age structure"; in the case of peer groups, the age structure is also a hierarchy, and as such it is "based on a system of inequality" (Passuth, 1987, p. 189). As Passuth points out, children consider age as commensurate to knowledge within the social hierarchy, not as a logical-mathematical number of years. This hierarchy involves power relations marked by tests of strength, but also a moral sense of what is a "legitimate" behaviour at a given age. It appears in children's criticism of other children who supposedly act "too old" or "too young" for their age: "Some age differences are legitimate, while others are illegitimate" (Passuth, 1987, p. 189).

Goods mark also the "rites of passage" during the social life cycle (Van Gennep, 2019), the transitions between different ages, in particular between adolescence and adulthood. This is the case with mas media culture such as TV series aimed at teenagers that are used as transitional objects as it is showed in the chapter of Ève Lamendour, *An expanding luxury land: a journey through the magical world TV series are offering to the teenage audience.* She offers a new and exciting contribution on the evolution of the US TV series since the 1990s, analyzing how they put in stage goods of desire and of distinction. Based on a semiotic theory of reception, Ève Lamendour underlines the importance of fiction for teenagers as an "active way of being in the world." Watching TV series offers different ways of performing one's identity, not only in the present but also in the world that teenagers want to belong in the future. Growing-up is understood as becoming different, not only adult but also belonging to an elite. Grounded on a detailed analysis of the TV series, this chapter underlines a major shift around the 1990s: the decline of the importance of families' bounds and household and the rise of the autonomous high school students. Thus the fiction of the series is also a denial of the classical sociological studies of the role of families' socialization in the reproduction of cultural inequalities (Larreau, 2003). It offers a counter-space where teenagers learn the goods' distinctive values and the behaviors that "naturally" fit with it. It seems that the cultural dimensions of the goods are less important than the economical ones, dealing with standardized luxury productions (such as bags, cloths…), instead of the locally produced goods with high cultural value analysed by Boltanski and Esquerre (2020), in their study of the new trends of capitalism in Europe.

More than a century later, Veblen's ideas (1994) about luxury conspicuous consumption are useful for showing how teenagers represent a kind of "leisure class," outside the economic market as producers but at the center of the market as consumers, subjugated by luxury goods that increasingly permeate the US' TV series there are watching massively every day. It may be perhaps rooted in the historical American ideology of the "self-made man," but in a very different context of brand strategies and their relations to the media mass culture. Thus, the chapter stresses the importance of the cross-references between brands and TV series, notably through the actors who play both in advertisements and in the teenagers' series.

This chapter opens the question of the discrepancy between these fictions and the realities of the teenagers' everyday life. Maybe it can be linked to the expansion of counterfeit luxury goods all around the world. Fake products are increasingly produced as the demand for "real" luxury goods is increasing itself. But both seem to obey to the same demand: "The need for individualism and uniqueness is one of important characteristics of counterfeit consumers" (Pinto da Cunha Brandão and Gadekar, 2020). This is also a paradox of teenagers' demands: to be unique and to look like their peers, to share the same lifestyle and to belong to the same world, even if it is a fictional word.

This question of the gap between a luxury world put into TV fictions and teenagers' realities leads also to wonder about the sociological properties of the real teenagers' audience, in terms of gender, social class, ethnicity, etc. It is not only an empirical question but also a theoretical one. As Bourdieu (1993) said: "youth is just a word", criticizing age as a theoretic and universal category that hides the reality of the inequalities between young people. Open at the end of the 1960s this debate about the relative importance of social class and age categories in cultural studies remains alive. It has been more recently analysed about media and marketing clichés, such as "Y Generation" and "Digital Natives" (Lardellier, 2006 and 2016). Of course we need to analyse how the diversity of teenagers' consumptions depends on economic, social, cultural, families' backgrounds. But one thing is to show the realities of inequalities in an intersectional perspective, the other is to analyse the success of such discourses and how they perform intergenerational realities, when they are included in brands' strategies. We have also to think about what kind of experiences of life may be shared by different generations of consumers in the changing cultural and technological environment. And how adults can learn from children when the socialization process is turned upside down and what we call "adulthood" is itself at stake (Garnier, 1995).

References

Aries, P. (1962). *Centuries of childhood.* Vintage Book.

Banet-Weiser, S. (2011). Branding the post-feminist self: Girls' video production and YouTube. In M. C. Kearney (Ed.), *Mediated girlhoods: New explorations of girls' media culture* (pp. 277–295). Peter Lang.

Boltanski, L., & Esquerre, A. (2020). *Enrichment: A critique of commodities.* Polity Press.

Bourdieu, P. (1993). 'Youth' is just a word. In P. Bourdieu (Ed.), *Sociology in question* (pp. 94–102). Sage.

Buckingham, D. (2011). *The material child.* Polity Press.

Burroughs, B. (2017). YouTube kids: The app economy and mobile parenting mobile. *Social Media + Society,* April–June, 1–8. Retrieved from: https://journals.sagepub.com/doi/pdf/10.1177/2056305117707189. (accessed 9 May 2020).

Cook, D. (2004). *The commodification of childhood. The children's clothing industry and the rise of the child consumer*. Duke University Press.

Craig, D., & Cunningham, D. (2017). Toy unboxing: Living in a(n unregulated) material world. *Media International Australia*, *163*(1), 77–86.

Danby, S. J., Fleer, M., Davidson, C., & Hatzigianni, M. (Eds.) (2018). *Digital childhoods. Technologies and children's everyday lives*. Springer.

Douglas, M., & Isherwood, B. (1979). *The world of goods. Towards an anthropology of consumption*. Basic Book.

Foucault, M. (2008). *The birth of biopolitics. Lectures at the Collège de France, 1978–1979*. Palgrave Macmillan.

Garnier, P. (1995). *Ce dont les enfants sont capables : marcher, travailler, nager, XVIII*[e]*, XIX*[e]*, XX*[e] *siècles*. Métailié.

Garnier, P. (2013). Objects for a 'healthy lifestyle'. Children's material culture and physical activities. *Young Consumers, 14*(4), 331–341.

Garnier, P. (2014). Childhood as a question of critiques and justifications: Insight into Boltanski's sociology. *Childhood*, 21(4), 447–460.

Holloway, D. J., Green, L., & Stevenson, K. (2015). Digitods: Toddlers, touch screens and Australian family life. *Media/Culture Journal, 18*(5). Retrieved from http://journal.media-culture.org.au/index.php/mcjournal/article/view/1024 (accessed 9 May 2020).

Hoschild, A. (1983). *The managed heart: The commercialization of human feeling*. University of California Press.

Lardellier, P. (2006). Le Pouce et la Souris. Enquête sur la culture numérique des ados. Fayard.

Lardellier, P. (2016). Génération 3.0. Enfants et ados à l'ère des cultures numérisées. EMS.

Larreau, A. (2003). *Unequal childhood. Class, race and family Life*. The University of California Press.

Martínez, C., & Olsson, T. (2019). Making sense of YouTubers: How Swedish children construct and negotiate the YouTuber Misslisibell as a girl celebrity. *Journal of Children and Media, 13*(1), 36–52.

Passuth, P. (1987). Age Hierarchies within children's groups. *Sociological Studies of Child Development, 2*, 185–203.

Pinto da Cunha Brandão, A. M., & Gadekar, M. (2020). The counterfeit market and the luxury goods. In R. Beltramo (Ed.), *Fashion industry an itinerary between feelings and technology*. IntechOpen. Retrieved from: https://www.intechopen.com/books/fashion-industry-an-itinerary-between-feelings-and-technology/the-counterfeit-market-and-the-luxury-goods (accessed 15 May 2020).

Sacks, H. (1974). On the analyzability of stories by children. In R. Turner (Ed.), *Ethnomethodology* (pp. 216–232). Penguin.

Smith, K. L., & Shade, L. R. (2018). Children's digital playgrounds as data assemblages: Problematics of privacy, personalization, and promotional culture. *Big Data and Society*, *5*(2), 1–12.

Valentine, G. (1996). Angels and devils: Moral landscapes of childhood. *Society and Space*, *14*(5), 581–599.

Van Gennep, A. (2019 [1909]). *The rites of passage*. University of Chicago Press.

Veblen, T. (1994, [1899]). *The theory of the leisure class*. Thrift Edition.

Zelizer, V. (1985). *Pricing the priceless child*. Princeton University Press.

5

Enacting global digital parenting... Alleged joint benefits for the "child-parents" consumer cluster

Valérie-Inés de La Ville

Several innovations aimed at young children such as new educational Apps available on mobile phones or tablets, as well as a wide array of connected objects, are continuously emerging in the marketplace. This profusion of innovative ideas in the digital field to improve both parents' and children's well-being has led some crowdfunding companies to launch a dedicated service such as "Start Up for kids" by Ulule[1]. Thus, digital technologies constantly increase the availability of innovative services to parents and their children, transforming parental mediation practices into "digital parenting", a polysemic term that encompasses not only the attempts by parents to regulate their children's engagement with digital media, but also, the way in which parents use digital media in their everyday parenting practices (Mascheroni et al., 2018, p. 9).

Emerging parental mediation strategies in a digital environment oscillate between contradictory principles: either restrictive (trying to control children's media time and exposure to online risks) or enabling (trying to support children's trials, errors, and increasing agency in media use (Livingstone et al., 2017). Indeed, digital parenting practices express parents' own learning path to achieve a sufficiently satisfactory balance between, on the one hand, creating opportunities for the child to develop socially valued digital literacy skills, and, on the other hand, protecting the child against constantly emerging new online risks. Moral panics about how

---

1 https://fr.ulule.com/startup-for-kids/ (accessed 9 April 2020).

to educate children in a social and cultural world transformed by pervasive digital technologies remain quite strong, as parents are confronted with contradictory guidelines or advice given by journalists, professional bodies, public policies, social researchers, and… brands.

The chapter draws on an exploration of marketing messages seeking to promote the value of 83 connected products or digital services aimed at children under 6 years. It seeks to examine how commercial messages enact the value of innovative digital services targeting parents and their young children through a subtle intertwining of, on the one hand, parental responsibilities and, on the other hand, children's developmental needs and their agency (Mayall, 2002), to offer implicit or explicit guidance about digital parenting practices.

1. Difficulties in rearing young children in an ever-expanding digital environment

1.1. Equivocal digital parenting and global brands perspective

A large array of research has demonstrated that digital technologies operate as a transformative lever for children and young people, entailing the emergence of new forms of media literacy and modes of communication and socialization that are crucial underpinnings to their future roles as productive adults and participative citizens. However, as far as young children are concerned, "there is still a paucity of research on parental mediation (…) regarding their digital media uses" (Mascheroni et al., 2018, p. 10). Indeed, the omnipresence of digital devices such as tablets or connected toys in the lives of babies, toddlers and young children raises questions about the skills actually developed by these targets when using innovative digital tools promoted by the market.

Contradictory discourses clash on the risks incurred by children due to an early exposure to various types of activities on different screens (Spitzer, 2012; Bach et al., 2013; Tisseron, 2013; American Academy of Pediatrics, 2016) and equivocal messages arise about the dangers as well as the benefits of digital activities aimed at young children. Even though the awareness of simplistic time or exposure-based guidelines is high among parents, this issue does not fit with the observed messy realities of family life (Blum-Ross and Livingstone, 2018). It seems particularly difficult for parents to make sensible choices, based on clear criteria, to support their young child's development in a digital environment. Thus, rearing a child in a constantly innovating digital environment confronts parents with unusual and uneasy issues which they have to tackle. In such a context, parental needs and concerns about why and how to develop digital parenting practices are still largely unmet. Parents are constantly in search of guidance in order to make responsible choices for the well-being of their child and an early enhancement of the child's intellectual and physical capacities.

The media environment in which young children are immersed is a complex interplay between technological advances and societal norms, in which technology-mediated interactions and ubiquitous modes of communication, as well as explicit or implicit market moralities, shape the normative requirements of digital parenting. Situations where parents make consumption choices for their baby, toddler or young child are archetypal of care-giving consumption and imply that "with these motives, consumers typically make safer, more responsible choices that account for the recipient's welfare" (Liu et al., 2019, p. 419). The rapidly expanding child-centered digital environment brings to the forefront new social and moral obligations that parents of a young child have to conform, which market discourses accompany and intensify through the promotion of digital innovations for young children. Since the seminal work by Baudrillard (1998), the study of commercial signs has emerged as a major area of investigation in consumer research. By exploiting scientific knowledge about child development or by involving child specialists in product or service design, brands offer mental and social constructions able to trigger deep emotions and evoke a large array of meanings (Mick, 1986; Floch, 1990). Brands act as cultural intermediaries to address consumers' concerns, to disseminate consumption norms and to shape the motivational structures of parental consumption (Pugh, 2005; Fenstermacher et al., 2010; Martens, 2010; Pellandini-Simányi, 2014).

Even though the underpinnings of new parenting practices are deeply anchored in diversified cultural values and moralities, the child-centered technologies apprehend the figures of the child and his/her parents as global. Indeed, the social construction operated by the market of the wired young child and his/her parents conceives them as a global target or audience. Within the realms of managerial practice, firms targeting young children under 6 years consider that their commercial offers seek to meet the basic developmental needs of every child on the planet: security, custody, emotional support, potty training, learning skills, speaking, reading, counting, fine motor skills for writing or drawing, etc. Child-centered digital technologies are expensive to develop and therefore it is necessary to make them profitable on an international market. From a managerial standpoint, marketing design will focus on the basic cognitive and social skills that every child needs to acquire before entering school. Multinational corporations conceive global offers likely to enable significant economies of scale in production and global supply chains, as well as to reduce the costs of cultural localization of marketing persuasive messages[2].

As useful windows into the marketing of "good parenting", commercial discourses and sales pitches are worth examining because they "ground their appeal in naming problems in a particular way and then offering solutions" (Pugh, 2005, p. 733). By proposing a series of cultural deals that make compromises of educational ideals, brands help parents to enjoy their parenthood, and to cope with the burden and the social pressure entailed by their parental responsibilities. "A number of companies have rushed in to address our felt need for apps that will help with parenting" (Clark, 2013, p. ix). Parenting moralities – becoming and being "good" parents – display normative requirements that underpin commercial discourses enjoining new parents to change their behavior to assume their new social role (Martens, 2010). By taking a Vygotskian perspective about consumption activities involving children (de La Ville, 2010 and 2020), we analyze marketing techniques as commercial cultural mediators providing parents and young children with semiotic tools to make sense of their engagement with digital media. This framework suggests considering mediation as a reciprocal process through which the "child-parents" consumer cluster, as both a cultural and consumption unit, is transformed. The parental mediation is not univocal as parents have no choice but to adapt to children's increasing digital skills, and to accept that, in some circumstances, their child takes the lead and guides them (Van den Bulck et al., 2016).

---

2 Opening Keynote Speech at the 1st International Child and Teen Conference – University of Poitiers, 2004, by Michael Wood, founder and former CEO of LEAPFROG – Emeryville, California, United States of America. The same managerial rationale is used by other major actors in the market: VTech, Hasbro, Mattel, Lego, etc.

In that perspective, our study aims to identify the ways in which brand discourse legitimizes certain digital innovations aimed at young children by alleging a joint benefit for the "child-parents" consumer cluster. What are the arguments put forward to encourage parents to buy digital products or services for their young children? What is the benefit claimed by these digital innovations for the development of the child and for the well-being of the hybrid "child-parents" consumer? Do they promote specific norms about the assigned meaning of good parenting in a digital environment?

1.2. Constitution of an empirical corpus and study methodology

In order to investigate the way in which digital innovations intended for young children under the age of 6 are presented, our project takes into account the semantization of market goods: "By semantization, we must understand the mechanism which consists of projecting an imaginary and social meaning onto material goods. Consumption thus induces the transformation of a material substance into a signifying substance, so that, in order to become an object of consumption, the object must necessarily transmute itself into a system of meanings" (Heilbrunn, 2018, p. 7)[3]. Building an interpretive semiological approach, Holbrook and Hirschman shed light on the semiotic rules used to create social meaning in different contexts with the purpose of reaching intermediate levels of generality: "we use the (…) term 'semiology' to designate interpretive analysis in general and the interpretation of consumption symbolism and marketing imagery in particular" (Holbrook and Hirschman, 1993, p. 232).

We conducted our study in three steps. First, we identified the circulation of knowledge about young children's skills in an environment increasingly marked by the presence of screens or connected objects from birth. This circulation involves various actors and professional networks – teachers, academic researchers, consultants, doctors, childcare professionals, journalists, bloggers, etc. – who contribute towards influencing parents' consumption choices. Next, we identified and selected a series of 83 innovations aimed at young children under 6 years of age. We went

---

[3] Our translation.

to various sites specializing in innovations (objetconnecte.net, novachild.eu) or participatory financing (kickstarter.com, Indiegogo.com, fr.ulule.com) in order, on the one hand, to select objects and services already on the market or with a good chance of obtaining the necessary financing and, on the other hand, to reject innovations recommended from the age of 6 years up. Finally, once the selection of products had been made, we carried out a content analysis of the discourse deployed on various communication media (official website, sales site presenting the brand's discourse and sometimes even the packaging). Our study enlarges and updates previous scarce research on toy catalogs (Pugh, 2005; Zegaï, 2010) by focusing on digital innovations in the baby care industries as well as web applications or connected objects and toys aiming to support parents in their practice of parental responsibility[4]…

To analyze in detail the communication strategies used by brands to prefigure the meaning of the innovations they address to the hybrid "child 0–6 – parents" consumer, we created the following grid including the following criteria:

- *The category of the product* advertised by the brand or, failing that, by its distributors.
- *The recipient*: Is it the child under 6 years of age or the parent?
- *Presentation*: Description of the product and its main features.
- *Waves*: What is the connectivity of the product? Is there any justification for it?
- *Personal data*: How does the brand handle the personal data of minors? (data collection, data security…)
- *Promise*: Characterization of the joint benefits advertised by the brand? Do the benefits relate to health issues or developmental aims of the child (cognitive, language, motor…)?
- *References*: How does the brand build trustworthiness about the solution it offers? Who are the guarantors? Do brands claim to

4 The corpus was gathered by Tatiana Picq over 4 months in 2017. Since then, some innovations have been recalled from the market due to financial shortages or security issues, whereas others have been launched on the market. Valérie-Inés de La Ville and Tatiana Picq, *Analyse de l'offre numérique destinée aux jeunes enfants de 0 à 6 ans* [Rapport de recherche pour la Fondation pour l'Enfance], Univ. Poitiers, 2020 ⟨hal-02901437⟩: https://hal.archives-ouvertes.fr/hal-02901437.

involve child development experts? Is there some factual evidence behind the stated joint benefits?

- *Publications*: What is the brand's discourse on digital technology for children, beyond its own digital offer?
- *Message*: Characterization of the tone used by the brand in its communication. Does the way in which it presents its offer leverage parental anxieties?
- *Additional information*: Does the parent play a role in the service offered (parental control, accompanying the child in the proposed activity, product customization, etc.)?

Our analysis of the convenience sample considers each website as a self-sufficient unit of analysis, a closed utterance whose meaning it is possible to interpret *per se.* By using visual social semiotics (Barthes, 1964), the first step required an understanding of how images tie diverse textual or iconic resources or several signs together to convey social meanings about the specificities of its joint beneficiary: the child and the child's parents. Claire Harrison recalls that "an image is not the result of a singular, isolated, creative activity, but it is itself a social process" (Harrison, 2003, p. 47). This analysis intends to consider the semiotic frame that interweaves functional, aesthetic, and economic dimensions to convey the meaning that a connected product or a digital service will improve the well-being of both parents and children.

The rationale of "semantic saturation" led us to group the commercial offers according to the type of benefit they claim to bring to the "child-parents" consumer cluster. By conducting a systematic comparison of the claims made by brands, we reduced the corpus of 83 digital offers into four main categories. The systematic comparative analysis allowed by the grid led us to typify four main differential narratives that seek to influence the perception of parents about the innovative value of the new digital offer. Such a reduction of the initial variety embedded in the corpus leads us to differentiate four persuasive discourses that are "ideal types" of the joint benefits provided for the "child-parents" consumer cluster. We briefly review critically the arguments used by each type of narrative to persuade the parent to purchase the proposed digital product or service, and highlight the issues raised by the portrayal of vulnerabilities and risks about the child and parental responsibility.

2. Giving meaning to the digital offer for the "child-parents" consumer cluster

The first breakdown into the four categories highlights that the commercial discourses are characterized by huge differences, not only in the depiction of the figures of the parents and the child, but also in the manner in which the relationship between children and parents is enacted… Our interpretive analysis led us to characterize four realms of value creation in digital services aimed at the "child-parents" cluster.

2.1. Baby monitoring (19 products)

This group equips the baby with objects (pacifier, diaper, body, cap, socks, patch-thermometers, etc.) that are connected to parents' mobile or tablets through service applications that allow parents to exercise control or monitor remotely their young child. This offer covers different aspects of the child's security, health and well-being with the aim of measuring and transmitting in real time the development of the baby's biological constants or his/her reactions: heart rate, breathing, movements, temperature, crying intensity, etc.

An analysis of the 19 fact sheets reveals a message that aims to reassure the parents about the child's safety and health. Some narratives leverage anxiety-provoking messages reinforcing parental responsibility in improving their baby well-being. For instance, The Owlet Smart Sock[5] claims that it "tracks heart rate and oxygen levels while your baby sleeps and notifies you if levels fall outside of a preset range" and adds "Proven to reduce anxiety and improve [parents'] sleep". The home page of the website also asserts that the company works closely with foundations and researchers, citing on the associated blog some guidelines issued by the American Academy of Pediatrics[6]. For young children, brand discourse puts forward other key stakes about child development. Gululu[7] offers to teach kids "healthy habits through play" by using an interactive bottle that not only encourages "your child to drink more water through a built-in virtual pet and an adventure game that develops as your child

5 https://owletbabycare.co.uk/ (accessed 9 April 2020).

6 https://owletbabycare.co.uk/blogs/stories/a-mothers-story-with-safe-sleep-small-items-can-create-big-problems (accessed 9 April 2020).

7 https://www.mygululu.com/.

drinks", but also includes a tracker app that informs parents about the water intake of their child. Moreover, the brand warns the parents on the blog "One in five US kids don't drink water but they do drink a lot of sugar"[8].

This cluster of products addresses the first-time parents who are worried about the possibility of misinterpreting tears and reactions of the baby who does not speak yet. Remote monitoring services warn the parents on their smartphone as soon as a key indicator is no longer complying with the standards established to appreciate the child's well-being. The joint benefit of these services is twofold. For the child, the explicit aim is to contribute to his or her well-being by reducing moments of discomfort (dirty diaper, hunger, temperature of the bottle, quality of sleep, etc.). For the parents, this type of service offers the possibility of a permanent bond with their baby, to alleviate the difficulty of not being permanently present beside the child. "Peace of Mind" is a parental benefit that appears frequently to express the relief that these services bring to parents who are concerned about their responsibility to ensure the safety of their child and to reduce the guilt associated with the unpredictable risk of cot death.

The fundamental thrust of these persuasive messages highlights the baby's extreme fragility, overall vulnerability, complete dependence on those around him and his need for security. Douglas and Michaels emphasize the underlying structure of this persuasive discourse: "The risks and problems faced by a minority – often a small minority – of infants and children become universalized, to the point of becoming potential risks for every infant and child" (Douglas and Michaels, 2004, p. 300–301). For parents, the benefit of monitoring is the possibility of being in permanent interaction with their baby or child in order to continue to protect it even from a distance. In an ethnographic study conducted during the Baby Show in Great Britain, Lydia Martens (2014) analyzed to what extent the topicality of baby safety has become a central issue between industrialists and primiparous parents. This over-emphasized focus on baby safety has enabled the childcare industry to launch a large array of connected products, while educating parents to live their new responsibility according to a medico-sanitary rationality, i.e. by conforming them to their role as active partners of the medical

8 https://www.mygululu.com/blogs/stories (accessed 9 April 2020).

world, including pediatricians, pharmaceutical laboratories and actors in the paramedical industries.

However, the very principle of "monitoring" poses delicate problems when it comes to the very young child. The interpretation of the data collected according to scientifically established standards leads a warning to be issued to the parents if a certain measure no longer conforms to the standards established to assess the child's well-being. This prevalence of universal standards established by medical science, leads parents to implement an "orthonormal" perspective over their child's development. Sometimes, the normative benchmarks intended to help parents have the opposite effect, leading parents to become deeply anxious if their baby does not begin to walk, diversify his/her diet, or begin to talk according to universal standards. Furthermore, putting at the forefront this rhetoric of parental responsibility as prevention of medical and health risks causes other types of risks to be obscured which are common to this category of products, such as the exposure of the child's body and brain to radio-frequency radiations or electromagnetic waves, and the collection and processing of personal data of minors.

2.2. Child's everyday activities (22 products)

This realm of digital innovations considers the everyday activities of the child, such as going to school, visiting friends, phoning relatives and friends, attending extra-curricular activities, shopping, wandering around in his/her neighborhood, etc. These innovations relate to the child's usual activities and to the dramas that may mark the first years, for instance the loss of personal objects such as cuddly toys or plush toys, and the need for cuddling and an adult presence. It is not surprising that the connected watch is the flagship product in this category. Indeed, the wristwatch is one of the few objects that young children are proud to wear even though they cannot tell the time, and is a personal object that they do not lose, unlike cuddly toys or other personal objects (Krupicka and De La Ville, 2005). As these innovative objects accompany children in their daily activities and their first socialization experiences outside home, they offer the possibility of customization to take into account the organization of each child's daily life.

Often focused on outdoor child safety, the products and services seek to empower children and support them in their leisure activities: "The GPS tracker for kids makes for relaxed family outings, in the knowledge that it allows you to find your child anywhere in the crowd"[9]. The commercial discourses enhance the joint benefit for parents and kids through an emphasis put on potential parental anxieties. These behavioral wearables for children help parents to tackle the need to establish healthy routines that structure children's everyday life such as walking and sleeping, meals, times for nap, playtime, and house chores. Octopus' mission states: "We help parents provide structure and routines in their children's lives. We help children develop self-discipline, self-esteem and provides [*sic*] them with the organizational skills necessary for a successful and happy life"[10]. The brand discourse emphasizes that its products are clinically tested, and introduces the members of its advisory board, who are mainly academics working in neuroscience labs. The commercial claim of a connected plush toy, which emits real cuddles at a predefined distance, highlights a bonding dimension: "Your huggable friend designed to help you stay connected", "Paris can bridge the distance between loved ones anywhere by delivering the closest thing to a real hug"[11].

The value of the service is to avoid the dramas which can affect the child's first years (loss of personal objects, getting lost, need for grown-up presence, need for cuddles, etc.) whilst reassuring the parents about the security and the context in which their child is developing. The child, who makes his/her own plans to explore the environment and extend his/her social network, is likely to confront unknown risks outside of any parental mediation. The continuity of the service ensuring the child's safety and real-time communication with the parent in case of problems is at the very heart of the joint benefit offered to the "child-parents" co-users. These applications allow the young child to smoothly acquire forms of autonomy whilst remaining permanently connected with his/her parents. The benefit provided by these digital services for children is to give them spatial and temporal reference points enabling them to increase their autonomy in their daily lives. For the parent, the claimed

---

9 https://www.weenect.com/en/gps-tracker-for-children-weenect-kids.html (accessed 9 April 2020).

10 https://www.heyjoy.io/pages/about-us.

11 https://www.kickstarter.com/projects/parihug/parihug-hug-loved-ones-from-anywhere-in-the-world/description (accessed 9 April 2020) – This Kickstarter campaign did not meet its objectives and the project was cancelled due to recent toy hacks and security breaches of toys connected to the internet.

benefit is to provide a gift of ubiquity by allowing him/her to remain close to his/her child at any time despite physical distance.

Commercial claims seek to reassure parents by offering the joint benefit of increasing child empowerment and progressive autonomy, while in the meantime, extending the sphere of parental control. Nevertheless, exercising permanent parental control over the child's activities through connected objects might reinforce parental risk-aversion in developing their child's independence, and result in a form of parental "overprotection" and "overinvestment" that characterizes "hyper-parenting" practices (Rosenfeld and Wise, 2010; Humbeeck, 2017) which comes close to the logic of permanent supervision of the child.

2.3. Training for school (13 products)

This class includes the set of digital services (games and educational toys...) claiming a significant contribution to the early development of intellectual and social skills of the child. The website homepage of the brand Alilo recalls the four "developmental benefits" for the child: "touch, hear, fun and learn"[12]. The promise of Honey Bunny, a companion for learning to speak and sing, is: "Through its amiable design, Alilo becomes doll, story teller, entertainer or simply buddy" (...) "Bunnies can be used as teaching aids in learning foreign languages and during other classes that are performed with the use of CD players or computers"[13]. Other products' positioning expresses their educational qualities by presenting the child's learning abilities and cognitive development as a vulnerable process: "The magic of human development occurs most rapidly between birth and 8 years of age, when brain cells and the connections between them form. (...) It is during this critical window that the developing brain must receive enough stimulation, and if it does not, it is very difficult to rewire later"[14]. The commercial discourses lay special emphasis on early cognitive acquisitions, as for Cubetto, a robot for kids aged 3 to 9: "The friendly wooden robot that will teach your child basics of computer programming through adventure and hands-on play"[15].

12 http://alilo-europe.com/ (accessed 9 April 2020).

13 http://alilo-europe.com/honey-bunny/ (accessed 9 April 2020).

14 https://www.heyjoy.io/pages/research (accessed 9 April 2020).

15 https://www.primotoys.com/ (accessed 9 April 2020).

The issues common to this category of digital products and services mainly include the classical "pedagogical trick" of getting the child interested in the educational activity through play (Brougère, 2005). These digital services, which are characterized by the absence of advertising integrated into the content, seek to enhance early cognitive acquisitions, and persuade parents about the effectiveness of the learning path offered, drawing on teachers' involvement in the design of the educational service, and the realization of scientific tests with researchers in educational sciences. The dashboard is the key feature of this category, as it allows parents to follow in real-time the performance of their child on several activities. The claimed benefit for the young child is that he/her will enjoy the activities and for the parents that their child will be ready for school by the age of 6. Sometimes, the joint benefit for the "child-parents" consumer cluster is stated overtly: "Don't Delay! Start giving YOUR child an Educational Advantage Today. Join hundreds of families who, as you're reading this, are giving their children a lifelong developmental head-start"[16].

The anxiety-provoking eventuality of their child getting left behind in educational terms reminds parents of their educational responsibility for the future success of their child at school (Dodson, 1970). As David Buckingham (2003) has shown, educational brands have gradually targeted parents and children as "consumers of education". This phenomenon is rooted in two concomitant cultural trends. On the one hand, the perception of a growing gap between public school education and the continuous emergence of new technologies, with which children should be acquainted at an early age, has entailed a reclassification of the home domestic space as a potential space for informal learning. On the other hand, as women have heavily entered the labor market, households with children have experienced a significant reduction of time shared between parents and children. Thus, the parents, who often feel guilty about being unavailable for their children, are in search of different types of market services for extracurricular activities and schoolwork. These educational applications transpose online the hybrid character of the extracurricular notebooks, analyzed by Pascale Garnier, which allow parents and children to "play at school" at home, and more specifically help parents to

16 https://getstarling.versame.com/starling/ (accessed 9 April 2020).

flexibly exercise a regular vigilance in order to detect whether their child is experiencing difficulties at preschool (Garnier, 2013).

Thus, commercial rhetoric by publishers of educational services aims at inculcating in parents that, in order not to jeopardize their child's chances of future success, they are required to purchase products or services that promise to bring educational benefits to their child, and to make the child's leisure time productive. Frequently, the persuasive discourses on these types of innovations refer implicitly to testing with teachers, parents and children as an extension of the datafication of education already implemented in schools in several countries (Jarke and Breiter, 2019). Moreover, the storytelling about these products often invokes the moralities of preparing the young child for the social race, hyper-competition linked to the norms ruling the schooling system and more broadly, society.

2.4. Enhancers of creativity and imagination (22 products)

This category includes digital services whose major claimed benefit is to entertain the child and enhance its creativity and imagination. This category includes innovations whose main goal is to enrich the relationship between parent and child through entertaining activities such as drawing, coloring, inventing stories, and playing roles. Thus, applications of augmented drawing, coloring, creative activities such as storytelling, puppet making, cooking, etc., seek to strengthen family bonds and memorable moments of sharing and having fun together.

An in-depth analysis of the products sheets highlights the way brands claim the cognitive benefit brought to the child by these playful activities. Oliba, a cute owl-shaped tracker tied to the child's cuddly toy communicates with an application to "share riveting stories that foster creativity"[17]. The joint benefit of Wakatoon, an App that augments the child's drawing by animating it, is for the child: "You are the artist!", and for the parents: "A fun family activity"[18]. The claim made by these commercial discourses can be classified as performative, as the shared activity between parents and children reinforces family bonds and "makes" the family. Tigouidou, the connected apron that introduces children to

---

17 https://www.indiegogo.com/projects/oliba-the-cuddly-toy-tracker-great-story-teller#/ (accessed 9 April 2020).

18 https://www.wakatoon.com/en/ (accessed 9 April 2020).

cooking by giving access to 25 recipes for pastries, emphasizes family leisure: "Sharing a pure moment of bonding with your child"[19]. The interactive wallpaper gives access to 55 stories and makes a promise of both social and emotional joint benefits: "The evening story is a special moment between parents and children"[20].

The bases of such commercial discourses that use the evolving notion of "fun" as a lever to appeal to children's subjectivities and desires have already been highlighted (Guber and Berry, 2003; NcNeal, 2007; Cook, 2012). The persuasive discourse about these commercial offers privileges a joyful pleasure between the child and the parents or grandparents through various shared activities. Analysis of the corpus reveals that the play dimension is, depending on the case, a means of helping and reassuring parents in their educational task by enriching the parent-child relationship and supporting the child's feeling of self-confidence. For the parent, the benefit provided by these types of digital products and services is their integration and involvement in the activity proposed to the child, which includes a system of immediate feedback and rewards for the child. The activity has no other purpose than its own pursuit and provides the "parent-child" dyad with a sense of immediate shared pleasure, dynamic well-being, and mastery of the activity. Interestingly, in the case of digital services aimed at very young children, "fun" is not exclusively conceived according to an individualistic stance as "an immediate psychological self-reward" (Holbrook and Hirschman, 1982), but more through the lenses of an interactive joint activity shared between the child and the child's parents. This rhetoric re-enacts the educational ideal of the creative child – spontaneous, active, hands-on learner, curious, intuitive, imaginative – that emerged in post-war America (Ogata, 2013), while offering to parents several frameworks to orientate their child's creative efforts.

The inclusion of a timer function or messages that invite the child to play off-screen activities reveals a key promise made to the parent: to help him or her reduce the attraction that screens might exert on his or

---

19 https://www.lamoretaine.com/cabinet-de-conseil-en-communication-numerique/tablier-pyjama-interactif/recettes-tablier-cuisine-interactif/ (Author's translation; accessed 9 April 2020).

20 https://www.parents.fr/bien-s-equiper/maman/parents-connectes/applications-et-site-internet/castorama-invente-le-premier-papier-peint-qui-raconte-des-histoires-aux-enfants-168229 (Author's translation; accessed 9 April 2020).

her child. Pierrick Chabi, Wakatoon founder, recalls his will to limit children's screen time by encouraging manual activities: "When I went to visit my nephew, he spent a lot of time on the screens… doing too few creative things in my opinion, and his parents weren't technophiles enough to guide him into the digital world"[21]. Indeed, while the apparent discourse of brands aims to support the child's creative efforts, there are many indications that an additional benefit offered to the "child-parents" consumer cluster lies in the dual character of the proposal. The use of the screen is limited, as it serves only to motivate the child to perform an "off-screen" leisure activity such as drawing, singing, cooking, etc. As educational controversies about the importance of screens in the lives of young children grow stronger, these innovations suggest a limited use of digital objects like tablets or smartphones to entice children to practice traditional activities that develop their creativity, storytelling capacities and sensory motor skills.

3. From "intensive mothering" to "global digital parenting"?

The objective of our explorative and qualitative analysis based on the analysis of 83 websites of digital innovations aimed at children under 6 years, was to identify recurrent rhetorical and narrative resources that brands use to promote their digital offer to both parents and children. How does the alleged benefit of innovative digital products or services become meaningful to the "child-parents" consumer cluster? Indeed, we seek to understand the creative ways through which brand content and storytelling directly contribute towards permanently reshaping family bonds and parent-child relationships in the contexts of technological novelty and new educational challenges.

Brands appear to be experts at drawing on contemporary conceptualizations of children as "beings" and "becomings" to claim the value of the digital innovations they deliver to the market that target the "child-parents" consumer cluster (Uprichard, 2008; Fenstermacher et al., 2010). The commercial discourses untangle some complex issues that modernize, within a digital realm, pre-existing interconnections

---

21 https://www.amazon.fr/l/B01KM08X10?_encoding=UTF8 &redirected From-KindleDbs= true&rfkd=1&shopping PortalEnabled=true (Author's translation; accessed 9 April 2020).

between the concepts of parental anxieties, good digital parenting and young children's developmental needs and well-being. Thus, the analysis of commercial offers appears to be a strong conceptual perspective for understanding how brand messages reshape permanently the meaning of the process of "growing up" and transform the dynamics of parenting and child care in the multi-layered temporalities of everyday life (Neale and Flowerdew, 2003). Our analysis highlights the moral dimensions put forward to promote a new good-enough parenting[22] practice that rests on digital devices. The ideology of "intensive mothering," "a logic that incorporates beliefs about how mothers should be the ones to mother children who need sacrifices of considerable time, money, attention, emotion and intellect" (Plugh, 2005, p. 731), is still present in the commercial claims aimed at persuading parents that digital innovations are meant to alleviate their burden. As mothers' work is no longer as much of a source of guilt today as it was in the 1970s or 1980s, the rhetoric of "intensive mothering" and its associated moralities are being transformed into a new rhetoric about "global digital parenting". This new parenting ideal, co-produced at the cross roads of public normative discourses[23] and private interests on the marketplace[24], opens an unexplored space for understanding the increasing ideological importance of fathering practices in relation with advances in technology targeting young children (Aitken, 2016; Croeser and Eckersley, 2019).

Our empirical corpus reveals the subtle art of paradoxical injunction that brands mobilize to remind parents of their responsibilities: "Secure your baby!" – a strong protection duty that arises all through the long-lasting period of extreme physical vulnerability and dependence of the baby and young child; "Take time to share creative activities with your child!" – the only alternative to avoid the potentially deleterious effects of screen overconsumption on child development; "Train your child for school!" within the narrow window of brain development from birth to 8 years, parental responsibility consists of transforming

---

[22] We expand on Winnicott's concept of a "good-enough mother": Winnicott, D. W. (1953). Transitional objects and transitional phenomena. A study of the first not-me possession. *International Journal of Psychoanalysis*, *34*(2), 89–97.

[23] Digital Parenting norms promoted by the EUkidsOnLine research project: http://blogs.lse.ac.uk/parenting4digitalfuture/2016/11/02/how-do-children-use-the-internet/ (accessed 9 April 2020).

[24] For instance: https://www.vtechkids.com/parent_resource or https://www.fisher-price.com/en_US/future-of-parenting/index.html.

useless leisure time in ongoing opportunities to learn; and, "Protect your child in all circumstances!" – you must maintain control over your child's autonomous activities. This persuasive communication technique that make parents feel uneasy and offers an acceptable compromise to make sense of digital innovations aimed at children under the age of 6 is what Patrick Hetzel has called "tensive rhetoric" (Hetzel, 2002, p. 267–268). It is also a perfect illustration of the historian Roland Marchand's (1985) analysis of the "therapeutic aim" of marketing, which proposes to relieve the tensions and anxieties felt by the consumer… as it strives to stage them.

The persuasive messages promote the social construction of "global digital parenting" – whose objective is to provide parents with models of educational practices and standards for exercising their parental responsibility in a digital environment which is constantly transforming. The imagery used in these commercial discourses enact a Western middle-class family, which is digitally well-equipped and confident that digital technologies make an actual contribution to strengthening the parent-child relationship and supporting the exercise of parental responsibility. This idealized global and wired middle-class family is a commercial fiction, an example of *simulacra* according to Baudrillard (1998), which enacts the parental aspirations to economic affluence and good parenting in a digital context. However, commercial messages draw on an underlying logic of muting what is implied by the permanent connection between objects belonging to the material culture of childhood and applications for the organization of activity supervision and organization of the child's activities administered by the parents. From a managerial standpoint, digital innovations that redesign children's possessions allow a hybridization of business models, which, beyond the one-off sale of a product or a toy, encourage subscriptions to services offering real-time monitoring of the baby's vitals, tracking young children's activities, and evaluation of the child's performance. Thus, key features about the child's activity are collected and processed in real time to compare them with the activity of other similar kids worldwide, and sent back to parents as meaningful data presented through different types of dashboards, parental controls, and timers to control the child and assess the child's performances. "Such practices inscribe children within an ever-intensifying network of visibility, surveillance and normalization, in which their behaviors and bodies are continually judged and compared with others" (Lupton and Williamson, 2017, p. 9). By subscribing to the digital services aimed at their young child, the parents purchase the illusion of achieving "good parenting" as a permanent practice of protecting and controlling their child, an illusion of loving care that places the child in a situation of continuously producing data that the media industries monetize to various audiences. Thus, digital innovations aimed at the "child-parents" consumer cluster rest on a logic of intimate surveillance and are effectively part of the surveillance capitalism that seeks to monetize data (Zuboff, 2015).

4. The double bind of digital parenting

Brands deploy a complex array of digital media aimed at the "child-parents" cluster that intertwines connected toys, educational and recreational apps, as well as permanent real-time apps to assist parents' efforts in monitoring their child's vitals, organizing and tracing their child's mundane activities. This technologically driven and personalized material culture aimed at children, which brands enact as innovative and problem-solving for parents, raises unprecedented issues about data production and collection from young children's activities with a commercial and promotional perspective that are likely to endanger the privacy rights of the young child and the parents (Smith and Shade, 2018). This rapidly growing field of commercial practice "(...) embodies a number of technological and sociocultural developments – the robotification of childhood, datafication and datasurveillance, and the emergence of connected and hybrid play practices – that render it an excellent point of departure for those interested in understanding, more broadly, how children's lives, and their futures are transforming" (Mascheroni and Holloway, 2019, p. v).

By developing storytelling strategies aimed at valuing digital innovations that reshape the relationships between the young child and the parents, brands expose themselves to a variety of scientific or socio-political controversies that the notion of child well-being raises in the context of increasing the digital risks to which children are exposed (Lupton and Williamson 2017). It also highlights the social, temporal, conceptual, and even political tensions underlying the notion of child well-being (Amerijckx and Humbelt, 2014).

To deepen the results of this initial research, it would be worth investigating the reception of such commercial discourses to understand the different types of compromise that parents accept in order to achieve "good-enough"[25] digital parenting. Will parents accept or resist the pervasive presence of intermediaries such as digital applications, connected toys, robot companions, etc. in the everyday life of their children? What do commercial moralities tell us about modern dilemmas of parenting by enacting the anxieties and hopes of parental responsibilities in an ever-expanding digital era (Chaolan et al., 2020)? Do parents actually feel trapped into the "double bind" of digital parenting culture, where they are criticized both for accepting the datafication and surveillance imperatives of global digital parenting and for rejecting the potential risks that these services create for the future of the child's life and his or her rights as a citizen? (Bristow, 2014).

Note: La Fondation pour l'Enfance, a French non-profit organization dedicated to the empowerment of educators and parents with regard to child wellbeing, funded this research.

References

Aitken, S. C. (2016). *The Awkward Spaces of Fathering.* Routledge.

American Academy of Pediatrics. (2016). Digital Media and Your Young Children: TV, Computers, Smartphones, and Other Screens. https://www.healthychildren.org/English/family-life/Media/Pages/Healthy-Digital-Media-Use-Habits-for-Babies-Toddlers-Preschoolers.aspx.

Amerijckx, G., & Humblet, P. C. (2014). Child Well-Being: What Does It Mean? *Children & Society, 28*(5), 404–415. https://doi.org/10.1111/chso.12003

Bach, J.-F., Houdé, O., Léna, P., Tisseron, S., Postaire, É., Bernard-Delorme, A., Descamps-Latscha, B., Macchi, O., Mouren, M.-C., & Pasquinelli, E. (2013). *L'enfant et les écrans : Un avis de l'Académie des sciences.* Le Pommier. https://www.academie-sciences.fr/pdf/rapport/avis0113.pdf.

Barthes, R. (1964). Rhétorique de l'image. *Communications, 4*(1), 40–51. https://doi.org/10.3406/comm.1964.1027

Baudrillard, J. (1998). *The Consumer Society: Myths and Structures* (C. Turner, Transl). Sage Publications.

[25] A reference to the concept of "good enough mother" by Winnicott, D. W. (1953). Transitional objects and transitional phenomena. A study of the first not-me possession. *International Journal of Psychoanalysis*, 34 (2), 89–97.

Blum-Ross, A., & Livingstone, S. M. (2018). The Trouble with "Screen Time" Rules. In G. Mascheroni, C. Ponte, & A. Jorge (Eds.), *Digital Parenting: The Challenges for Families in the Digital Age* (pp. 179–187). Nordicom.

Bristow, J. (2014). The Double Bind of Parenting Culture: Helicopter Parents and Cotton Wool Kids. In E. Lee & J. Bristow (Eds.), *Parenting Culture Studies* (pp. 200–2015). Palgrave Macmillan.

Brougère, G. (2005). *Jouer – Apprendre*. Economica-Anthropos.

Buckingham, D. (2003). Consuming Learning: Using and Reading Educational Media. In D. Buckingham & M. Scarlon (Eds.), *Education, Entertainment and Learning in the Home* (pp. 165–184). Open University Press.

Chaolan, L., MacDorman, K. F., Sabanovic, S., Miller, A. D., & Brady, E. (2020). Parental expectations, concerns and acceptance of storytelling robots for children. *HRI 20 Conference*, Cambridge, UK, 346–348.

Clark, L. S. (2013). *The Parent App: Understanding Families in the Digital Age*. Oxford University Press.

Cook, D. T. (2011). Commercial epistemologies of childhood: "Fun" and the leveraging of children's subjectivities and desires. In D. Zwick & J. Cayla (Eds.), *Inside Marketing: Practices, Ideologies, Devices* (pp. 257–268). Oxford University Press.

Croeser, S., & Eckersley, P. (2019). Theories of Parenting and their Application to Artificial Intelligence. *AIES 19 Conference*, Honolulu, HI, USA, 423–428.

De La Ville, V.-I. (2020). Child Consumption: A Vygotskian Perspective. In D. T. Cook (Ed.), *The Sage Encyclopedia of Children and Childhood Studies* (pp. 211–213). Sage Publications.

Desmurget, M. (2019). *La fabrique du crétin digital: les dangers des écrans pour nos enfants*. Seuil.

Dodson, F. (1970). *How to Parent*. Nash Publishing.

Douglas, M., & Wildavsky, A. B. (1983). *Risk and Culture: An Essay on the Selection of Technological and Environmental Dangers*. California University Press.

Fenstermacher, S. K., Barr, R., Salerno, K., Garcia, A., Shwery, C. E., Calvert, S. L., & Linebarger, D. (2010). Infant-directed Media: An analysis of product information and claims. *Infant and Child Development*, *19*, 557–576.

Floch, J.-M. (1990). *Sémiotique, marketing et communication: sous les signes, les stratégies*. Presses universitaires de France.

Garnier, P. (2013). Produis éducatifs et pratiques familiales à l'âge de la maternelle: l'exemple des cahiers d'activités parascolaires. *La Revue internationale d'éducation familiale*, *34*(2), 133–149.

Guber, S., & Berry, J. (2003). *Marketing to and Through Kids*. McGraw Hill.

Harrisson, C. (2003). Visual Social Semiotics: Understanding How Still Images Make Meaning, Technical. *Technical Communication*, *50*(1), 46–60.

Heilbrunn, B. (2018). *Médi(t)ations marchandes*. Le Bord de l'eau.

Hetzel, P. (2002). *Planète conso: Marketing expérientiel et nouveaux univers de consommation*. Éditions d'Organisation.

Hoghughi, M., & Speight, A. (1998). Good Enough Parenting for All Children: A Strategy for a Healthier Society. *Archives of Disease in Childhood*, *78*(4), 293–296. https://doi.org/10.1136/adc.78.4.293

Holbrook, M. B., & Hirschman, E. C. (1982). The Experiential Aspects of Consumption: Consumer Fantasies, Feelings, and Fun. *Journal of Consumer Research*, *9*(2), 132–140.

Holbrook, M. B., & Hirschman, E. C. (1993). *The Semiotics of Consumption: Interpreting Symbolic Consumer Behavior in Popular Culture and Works of Art*. Mouton de Gruyter.

Humbeeck, B. (2017). *Et si nous laissions nos enfants respirer? Comprendre l'hyper-parentalité pour mieux l'apprivoiser*. La Renaissance du Livre.

Jarke, J., & Breiter, A. (2019). The Datafication of Education. *Learning, Media and Technology*, *44*(1), 1–6. https://doi.org/10.1080/17439884.2019.1573833

Krupicka, A., & De La Ville, V.-I. (2005). Les enjeux liés aux innovations de rupture sur les marchés des produits de l'enfant. Réflexions à partir d'une étude de cas. In V.-I. de La Ville (Ed.), *L'enfant consommateur: variations interdisciplinaires sur l'enfant et le marché* (pp. 125–142). Vuibert.

Langer, B. (2004). The Business of Branded Enchantment Ambivalence and Disjuncture in the Global Children's Culture Industry. *Journal of Consumer Culture*, *4*(2), 251–277. https://doi.org/10.1177/1469540504043685

Liu, P. J., Dallas, S. K., & Fitzsimons, G. J. (2019). A Framework for Understanding Consumer Choices for Others. *Journal of Consumer Research*, *46*(3), 407–434. https://doi.org/10.1093/jcr/ucz009

Livingstone, S., Ólafsson, K., Helsper, E. J., Lupiáñez Villanueva, F., Veltri, G. A., & Folkvord, F. (2017). Maximizing Opportunities and Minimizing Risks for Children Online: The Role of Digital Skills in Emerging Strategies of Parental Mediation. *Journal of Communication, 67*(1), 82–105. https://doi.org/10.1111/jcom.12277

Lupton, D., & Williamson, B. (2017). The Datafied Child: The Dataveillance of Children and Implications for Their Rights. *New Media & Society, 19*(5), 780–794. https://doi.org/10.1177/1461444816686328

Marchand, R. (1985). *Advertising the American Dream: Making Way for Modernity, 1920–1940*. University of California Press.

Martens, L. (2010). Creating the Ethical Parent-Consumer Subject: Commerce, Moralities and Pedagogies in Early Parenthood. In J. A. Sandlin & P. McLaren (Eds.), *Critical Pedagogies of Consumption: Living and Learning in the Shadow of the "Shopocalypse"* (pp. 180–192). Routledge.

Martens, L. (2014). Selling Infant Safety: Entanglements of Childhood Preciousness, Vulnerability and Unpredictability. *Young Consumers, 15*(3), 239–250. https://doi.org/10.1108/YC-10-2013-00409

Mascheroni, G., & Holloway, D. (Eds.). (2019). *The Internet of Toys: Practices, Affordances and the Political Economy of Children's Smart Play*. Palgrave Macmillan.

Mascheroni, G., Ponte, C., & Jorge, A. (Eds.). (2018). *Digital Parenting: The Challenges for Families in the Digital Age*. Nordicom.

Mayall, B. (2002). *Towards a Sociology for Childhood: Thinking from Children's Lives*. Open University Press.

McNeal, J. U. (2007). *On Becoming a Consumer: The Development of Consumer Behavior Patterns in Childhood*. Butterworth-Heinemann.

Mick, D. G. (1986). Consumer Research and Semiotics: Exploring the Morphology of Signs, Symbols, and Significance. *Journal of Consumer Research, 13*(2), 196–213.

Neale, B., & Flowerdew, J. (2003). Time, Texture and Childhood: The Contours of Longitudinal Qualitative Research. *International Journal of Social Research Methodology, 6*(3), 189–199. https://doi.org/10.1080/1364557032000091798

Ogata, A. F. (2013). *Designing the Creative Child: Playthings and Places in Midcentury America*. University of Minnesota Press.

Pellandini-Simánya, L., & Pellandini-Simányi, L. (2014). *Consumption Norms and Everyday Ethics.* Palgrave Macmillan. https://doi.org/10.1057/9781137022509

Pugh, A. J. (2005). Selling Compromise: Toys, Motherhood, and the Cultural Deal. *Gender and Society, 19*(6), 729–749.

Rosenfeld, A. A., & Wise, N. (2001). *The Over-Scheduled Child: Avoiding the Hyper-Parenting Trap.* St. Martin's Griffin.

Smith, K. L., & Shade, L. R (2018). Children's Digital Playgrounds as Data Assemblages: Problematics of Privacy, Personalization, and Promotional Culture. *Big Data and Society, 5*(2), 1–12.

Spitzer, M. (2012). *Digitale Demenz: Wie wir uns und unsere Kinder um den Verstand bringen* [Digital dementia: What we and our children are doing to our minds]. Droemer.

Tisseron, S. (2013). *3-6-9-12: apprivoiser les écrans et grandir.* Érès.

Turmel, A. (2006). De la fatalité de penser la maturation en termes de développement : Quelques réflexions. In R. Sirota (Ed.), *Éléments pour une sociologie de l'enfance* (pp. 63–73). Presses universitaires de Rennes.

Uprichard, E. (2008). Children as 'Being and Becomings': Children, Childhood and Temporality. *Children & Society, 22*(4), 303–313. https://doi.org/10.1111/j.1099-0860.2007.00110.x

Van den Bulck, J., Custers, K., & Nelissen, S. (2016). The Child-Effect in the New Media Environment: Challenges and Opportunities for Communication Research. *Journal of Children and Media, 10*(1), 30–38. https://doi.org/10.1080/17482798.2015.1121897

Walderkine, V. (1984). Developmental Psychology and Child-centered Pedagogy. In J. Henriques (Ed.), *Changing the Subject: Psychology, Social Regulation, and Subjectivity* (pp. 153–202). Methuen.

Zegaï, M. (2010). La mise en scène de la différence des sexes dans les jouets et leurs espaces de commercialisation. *Cahiers du Genre, 49*, 35–54.

Zuboff, S. (2015). Big Other: Surveillance Capitalism and the Prospects of an Information Civilization. *Journal of Information Technology, 30*(1), 75–89. https://doi.org/10.1057/jit.2015.5

6

Münster's Inc. – Children as influencers balancing celebrity status, play and paychecks

Stine Liv Johansen

YouTube is increasingly becoming children's first choice when selecting media content to support their interests, for entertainment, and not least for access to social networks, often out of reach of adult's influence and judgements. YouTube allows children to participate in a number of ways, including the actual production of video content. YouTube might be described as a "wild, wild West", which children find – simultaneously – fascinating and frightening, providing a place where children and young people themselves set the agenda, separated from the agendas set by parents, teachers, and traditional media. Also, YouTube is one of several global media platforms which – for better and for worse – have come to play a defining role in the media culture of children and adolescents. Over the last year YouTube has experienced several cases and lawsuits all pin-pointing the problematic relationship between the platform and its under-aged users. According to YouTube's (and Google's) own terms of service, users who wish to have a profile on the platform must be over (at least, depending on national rules) 13 years old. This has been a point of reference in the debate and in the concrete cases since YouTube have officially recommended that this age limit is to be taken seriously and that children under the age of 13 (or older, depending on country) should only use the YouTube Kids application to access videos. It is no secret to anyone, though, that the original YouTube platform is used by many children much younger than 13 years old, whether with a profile or not. In Sweden, for instance, a recent study shows that YouTube is the most used app among age groups 0–1 years old, 2–4 years old, and 5–8 years old (Statens Medieråd, 2019).

In this chapter, I will present and discuss a specific case illustrating the increasing popularity of YouTube among children and adolescents through an analysis of a Danish youtuber, a 10-year-old girl, Naja Münster, who is among the most popular Danish-speaking youtubers. I will analyze the content on her social media channels (YouTube, Instagram and Tik Tok) drawing on a perspective of play and playfulness, applying an understanding of play as being mediatized and commercialized. The chapter will identify three categories of content in which inspiration for play and fan engagement can be found. The three categories also represent a development in the life of a girl coming of age, while at the same time growing into celebrity status as she and her family build a transmedia franchise of content across different platforms. In the final part of the chapter, I will draw perspectives towards a broader, empirical investigation of children's use of YouTube as an everyday media practice and discuss how we might approach empirical studies of children and young people as users of YouTube.

1. Focus and method

The study of Naja Münster as a YouTube celebrity is part of a larger study on YouTube as children's favorite place to be and to go for entertainment, relaxation and fun. I have followed especially Danish youtubers over the last couple of years and have focused in particular on the content on Naja's channel and the way it is positioned in the overall landscape of Danish YouTube. As the by far most popular Danish-speaking child influencer, she stood out and was difficult to overlook. I have particularly followed Naja's social media presence since 2015, when she opened her own channel on YouTube. Since then, she and her family have developed a widespread franchise of social media content, commercials, books, TV appearances, etc. In addition to online observations, I have established a personal contact with Naja and her family, initially through her management agency (Splay Denmark), where I interviewed the family's manager, Cecilie Blaksted, and got in contact with Naja's mother, Hanne. After that, I visited Naja in her home, and interviewed her and her mother. The interview was an informal meeting in the Münster family's kitchen, where Naja told me about her experience of being on the one hand a celebrity and on the other hand being 'Just Naja', as she said. Also, her mother explained how they as a family set the boundaries around Naja's use of YouTube. The interview was recorded on a smartphone and transcribed for further analysis. I have met the Münster family (Naja, her mother, her father Finn, and her brother Max) on one other occasion, where I was asked by a children's film and culture festival to do an on-stage interview with Naja and Hanne in front of an audience. At this occasion, I had informal chats with the family members and had the opportunity to observe the following meet-and-greet session, where Naja did selfies and autographs for a long line of fans. And finally, for the purpose of this chapter, I carried out a Skype interview with Naja and Hanne in May 2020, focusing on the transitions from leisure activities to more professionalized practices. I have continuously stayed in contact with the family in order to get permission to use photos, screenshots for my publications, and have also sent to them copies of articles written in Danish and told them about articles I was working on.

Studying a specific child – and her family – like this poses a range of ethical issues, which should be dealt with as part of the methodological reflections. Obviously, anonymization is not an option. There is only one Naja Münster. On the one hand, being as open as possible about my research and publication process and keeping an open dialogue with the family seems to be a reasonable way to approach this. On the other hand, this puts me in a different ethical dilemma in relation to the way in which I treat the information which I am given by the family, in relation to my analysis of the online content and the ongoing, public debate about children as influencers. My job here is not to judge the appropriateness or otherwise of building a business on the basis of a young girl's cuteness as well as her willingness and ability to appear in front of the camera in ways that are appealing to fans and therefore for commercial branding, is appropriate. From my engagements with the family I have experienced that they are very thoughtful regarding their practices and the pressure, they experience, in many ways more than I have experienced in the families of other children whom I have interviewed about their use of YouTube.

2. YouTube as children's favorite content provider

Over the last couple of years, the everyday media use by children and teenagers has undergone significant changes. In Denmark, which is the point of departure for the analysis in this chapter, there is a strong tradition of providing high-quality, non-commercial public service content to children and youth. From 2014 to 2016, Danish children (aged

3–6 and 7–12) – despite using screens for more or less the same amount of time on a daily basis – shifted their screen viewing preferences from television to streaming services (Netflix etc.) and video sharing platforms (primarily YouTube). The study of Naja is part of a larger study based on similar interviews with other children and teenagers aged 5–14. It focuses on children's and teens' own perspectives on their everyday use of YouTube and other digital platforms, on their preferences and taste in relation to content, on their parents' more or less active engagements, and on the kids' aspirations to produce content themselves. The findings from these interviews will be used as a reflexive perspective in the end of this chapter.

In 2014 38 % of 7–12-year-olds used YouTube on a daily basis. This rose to 70 % in 2016. In comparison, just 22 % checked in on DR Ultra, a TV channel (Danish Broadcasting Cooperation (DR)) specifically aimed at this age group (DR, 2017). Also, a recent study on Danish children's use of media and literature (Gissel et al., 2017) pointed to these platforms as children's favorite place to seek entertainment and to use for relaxation and "*hygge*." Especially for children aged 7 and up, a major reason for their love of YouTube is the way the platform organizes its content on channels hosted by specific influencers – or youtubers. YouTube as a platform has undergone significant changes since its launch in 2005 (van Dijck, 2013; Bärtl, 2018). From being a giant repository for all kinds of home-video content, the channel structure has paved the way for new business models and new fan communities related to individual personas and the content which they produce.

Many aspects of YouTube content relate to and remediate genres and content known from other platforms; television obviously, but also for instance blogs and how-to manuals, which in a YouTube-setting transform into vlogs (video blogs) and different sorts of play-along videos, "GRWM" (Get Ready with Me), My Morning/Evening/Workout routine etc. These types of content are common on the channels of the most popular youtubers, sometimes in ironic, remixed versions, as I will describe later in this chapter, but youtubers have also become children and teenagers' number one source of inspiration and knowledge about make-up, styling, fashion, gaming etc. Bärtl (2018), in his statistical analysis of YouTube content worldwide, points to the interesting fact that an average of 85 % of all viewing on YouTube goes to 3 % of the channels.

In this chapter, I will – as mentioned above – focus on one of the most popular Danish-speaking youtubers. Using a very small language, only spoken by approximately 6 million people, Danish-speaking youtubers could obviously never dream of being among the most viewed on the platform in general; still, it makes sense to rank them in a Danish context. Ranking can be done in several ways; by views, by subscribers, or by (estimated) monthly earnings[1]. If ranked by subscribers, the most popular Danish-language YouTube channels are Alexander Husum (387,000 followers) and Morten Münster (Naja's older brother, 366,000 followers). Naja's channel, with its 208,000 subscribers, ranks among the most popular Danish-speaking channels. Only a few Danish-speaking female influencers have a larger follower base than her, and the more than 200 videos on her channel have altogether had more than 77 million views. On Instagram, Naja has 155,000 followers and on TikTok she has 48,000 (all numbers retrieved May 2020).

3. Children as YouTube celebrities

Literature on children and YouTube, in particular children as youtubers, is scarce. The phenomenon of children starring as the main character of ongoing video publishing is new and not very well described in scholarly literature, despite the fact that some of the most influential youtubers – as well as the ones with the highest earnings – are children under the age of 10. Children like Ryan Kaji ("Ryan's World"), Karina and Roger Kurzawa ("Sis vs Bro") and Evan ("EvanTubeHD") have set the standard over recent years for high-paced, high-earning online content focused on toys and games and aimed at children in the 4–10 year age group. In 2018 and again in 2019, Ryan Kaji was the highest-earning youtuber in the world, presenting to his fans a widespread franchise of content and merchandise. Despite this intensely growing industry, only few scholars have paid children much attention as online celebrities. Jerslev (2018) and Raun (2018) focus on specific YouTube celebrities (Jerslev on UK vlogger Zoella and Raun on Canadian transgender vlogger Julie Van Vu). Marôpo et al. (2020) analyze the relationships between two teen vloggers (Portuguese SofiaBBeauty and Brazilian Manoela Antelo) and their followers as being based on intimacy and trust and resembling

---

1 www.socialblade.com.

the intimate labor (Abidin, 2013) of grown-up vloggers and influencers. Both examples in Marôpo et al.'s article started their social media presence early (at the ages of 12 and 8, respectively) and are therefore building on several years of experience although still in their teens. The article does not, however, take their history into consideration much, and therefore does not describe their social media presence as younger children. Abidin studied children who star on blogs and YouTube channels as sidekicks to their more famous parents (so-called mommy bloggers, as described by Abidin (2017)). Naja Münster also started her engagements on YouTube through regular appearances in the videos of her brother Morten. The oldest video uploaded on his channel is a vlog from then three-year-old Naja's birthday. As such, she might initially be understood as a micromicrocelebrity (Abidin, 2015), who has, by the introduction of her own channel and recently by her increasing influence on its content and performance, created a brand on her own within the overall brand of the Münster family, as I will describe in more detail later in this chapter. A few studies have focused on YouTube as a content provider for children's content (for instance Burroughs (2017) who specifically zooms in on the YouTube Kids app targeting preschool children). A range of other studies, such as Livingstone and Sefton-Green (2016), include YouTube as one of several digital platforms used by children and youth.

Rasmussen (2017) describes YouTube as a "wild, wild West", which children aged 8 to 12 find – at the same time – fascinating and frightening, providing a place where children and young people themselves set the agenda, separated from the agendas set by parents, teachers, and traditional media such as DR (Danish Broadcasting Cooperation). As such, children express an expectation of having real influence on the content which they can access on YouTube, which is contrary to their expectations regarding public service television. Further, drawing on the concept of dark play (Sicart, 2014), Rasmussen (2017) describes YouTube as a place where inappropriate, frivolous and taboo-breaking content occurs. On YouTube, there are fewer rules and content is regulated and emerges through constant negotiations between the youtubers and their followers. The content – and impact – of a specific channel on YouTube should therefore be seen in relation to an overall understanding of the interaction with fans and the collaborative practices of ongoing commenting and sharing, just as YouTube must be taken into consideration as a platform and a network with specific affordances, genres, and styles. YouTube as a platform, a network, and a community is described by

Lange (2014) and Burgess and Green (2018), who point to some interesting and important aspects of the ambiguity of YouTube as a site for participatory culture. Especially the participation aspect seems highly relevant as a point of reference in this context.

The participation, which takes place in YouTube content as well as in commentary feeds and in children's everyday encounters with the platform can be characterized as mediatized, playful practices (Johansen, 2018). Mediatized, since digital platforms function as meeting places – playgrounds even – in which practices and performances are molded and shaped by the structures and affordances given by the platforms in themselves and its users in particular. Using play as a relevant perspective in relation to the practices taking place on YouTube allows for a deeper understanding of all the silliness, the frivolity, and the disgusting stuff, which seems to be a source of endless joy and entertainment, for the youtubers themselves as well as for those watching.

As I will describe below, the content on Naja Münster's channel can in particular be seen as playful, whether she demonstrates play activities or approaches established YouTube genres (such as "routines", Q&A's, or challenges) in a specific, childish and playful manner. YouTube allows and inspires children to participate in a number of ways, including the actual production of video content on their own channel. Until the spring of 2019, all channels were open for commenting, which many children – and child youtubers – engaged in, creating playful interactions about the content of the channel (Johansen, 2018) or inventing small game-like types of comments (such as: "First Like" or "Post a number from 1–10 and I will give you a nickname"). In the beginning of 2019, YouTube decided – overnight – to close down the opportunity to comment on most channels featuring children as the primary actors. The reason for this was allegedly incidents where pedophiles had tipped each other off about videos of children in underwear, children doing gymnastics, or children jumping on trampolines, using comments with time-codes. This was obviously unacceptable, for the children as well as for YouTube as a platform, and generally this step was accepted. Still, as Naja Münster's mother, Hanne, told me, it came as a surprise to them, and neither they, nor their managers were warned beforehand. I will later describe how the family use different work-arounds to overcome the closed commentary section.

But before exploring the content on Naja's channel, I will dwell a little on the Münster family as a whole. Both from an audience and a commercial point of view, the family function as a unit and each of the members play their specific part in the overall, transmedial story of an extraordinarily ordinary family.

4. Münster's Inc.

As mentioned in the introduction to this chapter, Naja Münster (born 2009) had her own channel on YouTube in December 2015, and at the time of writing (Dec. 2019) has more than 200,000 followers on the platform. Naja is the younger sister of Morten Münster (born 1997), who is the second-largest Danish-speaking youtuber. Also, Naja and Morten's brother Max (born 2003) has a highly popular social media presence (140,000 followers on YouTube, 126,000 on Instagram). And finally, the parents of the three siblings (who also have an older brother, Dennis, who only occasionally appears in videos and images on his family's channels) started a channel in 2018 called "Mor og Far Münster" (Eng: Mum and Dad Münster) which has app. 72,000 followers. All in all, the Münster family puts a solid mark on the social media landscape in Denmark. Besides their appearance on digital platforms, over the years they have built a strong franchise of board games, books (both Naja and Morten star in fictional books, written or co-written with established children's books authors), commercial content, and in 2019 a four-episode television documentary about their lives on a national TV channel. In 2020 a clothes collection featuring Naja's name and signature was launched by the Danish children's clothes company Mini A Ture[2]. Naja has guest starred in two feature films (family comedies "Far til fire" (Eng.: Father of Four) in 2018 and 2020), and the process of filming and promoting these have been documented in several vlogs and Instagram posts.

Naja is, in many ways, an average 10-year old. The neighbor's daughter, small town middle class, portraying the Scandinavian child at its very essence. She likes to play, to be outdoors, and to tease her brothers; she loves her parents and her dog, and she holds a suitable amount of rebellious attitude, mainly expressed through her often rather explicit language (often disguised by editorial "beeps", which may in itself be emphasizing the rebelliousness). Naja provides a perhaps extreme example of children being not only consumers of media content, but also

---

2 https://miniature.dk/collections/naja-munster.

producers and participants in online communities. She represents a relevant manifestation of the fluidity of content and practices on and around digital networked platforms like YouTube.

Especially the focus on playfulness seems relevant as a backdrop for my understanding of what Naja is doing and what kind of agency she can be said to perform. There is reason to believe that YouTube has come to play a very important role in children's mediatized play as a primary source for inspiration and – for those children who are active producers themselves – as a form of play in itself. The content on Naja's channel can be divided into two main types of video, from which more in-depth analytical themes can be deduced. The following section is based on content analysis on the videos from 2015–2019. By December 2019, the channel presented 209 videos, recorded and released over this four-year period. Obviously, this period represents a development in Naja's life from preschooler to pre-teen, which is expressed in the content of the videos as well as in her appearance on the channel and on the other social media platforms on which she is present. The early videos are characterized by the staging and performance of Naja as specifically childish, emphasizing her speech impediments and funny, and rather rebellious manners, while the later videos are increasingly focused on Naja's own agenda – for instance through the involvement of her friends – while still engaging the whole family as a backdrop.

Firstly, we find the videos in which Naja takes over well-known genres and forms from other, older youtubers. "My Morning Routine", make-up tutorials, challenges (such as bean boozled, smoothie or ice cube challenge) etc. In these videos, there is always a specific, parodic twist, which could be more or less intentional, but always with an interesting effect. Her make-up turns out rather ugly, her morning routine is a mess, and sometimes she doesn't quite understand the rules of the challenges, nor is she capable of pronouncing the (often English) titles and/or genres right. In this type of video, Naja can be understood as a child playing YouTube; that is, trying out specific formats and genres through playful, interpretive reproduction (Corsaro, 2012). This is not a practice that is specific for Naja; content on YouTube – as in social network media in general – is characterized by constant mixes and re-mixes as well as references. The specificity which Naja provides to this ongoing flow is the childishness and as such the silliness which she is able to and "allowed" to represent.

Secondly, we find the videos in which Naja invents her own narratives as a playful child. She goes monster-hunting in the forest behind her house or in a two-episode video runs away from home, as such playing out a well-known narrative from children's literature and film. These types of videos have changed significantly over time, from six-year-old Naja, who talks about what to do on a rainy day, to eight-year-old Naja getting dressed for a slumber party at her friend's, flashing the latest, sponsored clothing and accessories from a well-known Danish children's clothing brand, to ten-year-old Naja hanging out with her best friend, Frigge, or vlogging from the car on her way to another award show or meet-and-greet event. This, obviously, reflects the fact that Naja is growing older and is getting different interests and orientations along the way. But it also reflects the fact that she has become a brand with increasing commercial interest for sponsors and other collaborators. For instance, she reviews a planting kit provided by a large supermarket chain, and describes how it can be used, and what the result of planting and watering seeds might be. Or she "accidently" opens her Christmas presents too early (November 2017), presenting the likely toy hits of the upcoming season. In 2019 she was the face of a large, Danish toy store brand ("BR"), which was being re-established after severe financial problems and bankruptcy in 2018. As such, she appeared massively in the printed catalogue of the store (for many years named the most popular children's "book" in Denmark).

The print appearance is supplemented by videos on Naja's own as well as on the channel of BR. An interesting feature here is that while the commentaries are disabled on Naja's channel, they are wide open on the BR channel. The videos have reached a large number of views, 2–300,000, which is high relative to the channel's modest number of subscribers (2000), and must be a result of Naja's general appeal and a well-designed transmedial marketing strategy. The campaign is particularly interesting in a gender perspective, since the toys that Naja is testing (often with her friend Frigge) include monster trucks and robots.

From a commercial point of view, her appeal must be considered relevant for both boys and girls, while promoting a non-gender-specific understanding of what good play is – and what a good toy is. Naja's parents make the decisions regarding what deals to accept in collaboration with their manager. There is a clear tendency throughout the four years during which Naja has had her channel that an increasing amount of content is sponsored, and that the sponsors are large and well-established

Danish brands, such as the above mentioned BR (which was previously owned by Top Toys, which also owned Toys"R"Us), large supermarket chains, or Legoland. Also, the family SoMe-franchise as a whole, especially videos on the parents' channel providing "behind the scenes" views into the life of a YouTube family, and Naja's increasingly independent use of supplementary platforms like Instagram and Tik Tok, points to the need to identify a third category of content, which is content about Naja's life as a youtuber. As early videos were merely mimicking YouTube life (Naja playing YouTube) she is now increasingly living the life of a celebrity herself and in different ways reflecting on the special life circumstances she lives under. In a video from November 2019, she does a "Draw my Life" where she illustrates the period where she was working on the "Father of Four"-movie. The video follows up on events which had already been documented on her social media platforms but does it in a playful way through drawing. As such, she still applies a playful and maybe even childish perspective to her content, but the neighbor's daughter has become a celebrity in herself, living a life that in many respects is different from that of her peers.

5. YouTube as a source of inspiration for play

Children have always sought inspiration for play, whether through interaction with other children, through media, or through commercials for toys. As such, youtubers – or other social media influencers – form a specific kind of hybrid, inspirational persona. Naja may at the same time function as a virtual playmate and a channel for commercial brands, in this specific case for toys and play tools, which she illustrates the intended use of and thereby provides schemes and structures for play. The recent campaign may be the most direct example – and perhaps one that even crosses the line of the subtlety, which is often the trademark of influencer marketing. This commercial is nowhere near hidden; it is directly recommending concrete pieces of toys using a "playable" scale.

But the inspiration takes on other forms, as well. Appearing as a SoMe celebrity, both online and in physical events, Naja and her family provide the opportunity to engage in fan cultures, engaging in commentaries on Instagram or meeting Naja and having a selfie taken with her in malls and toy stores all over Denmark. Since Denmark is a small country and almost all geographical locations are accessible within a reasonable car ride, it is possible for the family to appear in the northern Jutland one weekend and in Copenhagen the next, vlogging from hotel rooms and fan events. Still, the tone of these videos is consistently down-to-earth and has an underplayed sense of humor in which there is room for internal jokes, eventual swear words, and family meet-ups at cafés and restaurants with "Bajer & pommes" (Eng.: beer and fries). As such, Naja and her family distinguish themselves from the much more polished "look" on internationally famous child youtubers like Ryan Kaji, and despite their celebrity lifestyle they still appear utterly down-to-earth.

Naja would not be a YouTube celebrity if it wasn't for her brother Morten, who paved the way into social media for her and who is – although he has moved from the family home in Southern Jutland to Copenhagen – still doing the editing and curating of her content. Morten and his mother Hanne have regular Facetime meetings, approximately once a week, in which they plan upcoming content on Naja's channel. Middle brother Max makes his own content, with guidance from Morten. Hanne Münster sees this as a highly treasured family activity. "How many mothers have this kind of contact with their 19-year old sons?", she says in the interview in 2017. Also, the connection between Naja and Morten is special, she thinks. They just play and have fun, and Naja enjoys making videos and often does so without ever uploading them. She plays youtuber even when she is not on YouTube, you could say. Back then she was – according to her mother – only allowed to make content for her channel once a week, since her parents also want her to live a life which is as normal as possible, and to have other interests and hobbies. This might have changed quite a lot since then. Today, weekends in the Münster family are often spent in malls doing meet-and-greets, and Naja herself is active on social media platforms most days of the week. Presumably, this will also be the case for her peers of the same age, and may as such primarily be age-related rather than related to her role as a YouTube celebrity.

6. From leisure and fun to professional media production

As has been described above, there has been a significant development in the content on Naja's channel over the 5-year period described. This reflects changes in the everyday practices of the Münster family as a whole, as they have developed a more and more professional approach to their social media content production. In order to understand how the family's everyday life has changed and the factors determining these changes, I carried out an interview with Hanne and Naja in May 2020. Due to the Covid-19 crisis the interview was done via Skype, as we obviously could not meet physically.

According to Hanne and Naja, producing social media content is still very much a leisure activity for Naja that she finds fun and joyful. The whole family is engaged in the production of YouTube videos, and particularly during the lockdown in March-April 2020 they produced a lot of videos, since big brother Morten was home in Jutland for a longer period of time. Naja started using the video sharing platform TikTok in 2019, but did so because her friends used it, and she thought it was fun to participate in their videos. Soon after she got her own account, the number of followers rose and she now has 48,000 followers on this platform. This example shows, though, that her leisure-based social media activities cannot be distinguished from her professional social media presence, although they were not based on strategic or commercial choices to begin with.

When Naja appears in books or clothes ranges, her active participation is limited. The books are written by an author who has done an interview with the family, and Naja has not contributed to them further. She was slightly more involved in the collaboration with Mini A Ture, since she – and her mother – both found the process of choosing designs and styles interesting. These parts of the professionalization of her social media presence have therefore only required small efforts on her behalf. When she participated in the two films, though, the family had to make significant changes in their everyday life. The first film was shot on the Canary Islands, and Naja had to leave school and stay there for 5–6 weeks, while her parents had to spend their holidays to go with her. The second film was shot in Denmark, but again she had to stay in a holiday home with her mum, dad and brother Morten, who took turns in staying with her.

Being a parent of children who are engaged in such activities requires a substantial involvement, both in the creative and the commercial aspects. In early 2020, Naja's mother Hanne made the decision to quit her regular job and to work full-time to focus on the family's extensive social media presence and – as she says – to ensure coherence and structure in their family life. This means that she now will be able to accompany Naja to different events and to prepare for the videos for Naja's channel that they make on a weekly basis. Naja explains that she likes that a lot, since their afternoons can be less stressful. But at the same time this means that Hanne now relies on making a living through their social media channels, which she says has made her more conscious regarding the frequency of uploads and the quality of the content, just as she now pays more attention to the number of followers and views on her (and her husband's) own channel.

7. Perspectives – YouTube kids

The analysis of content on YouTube, as it is specifically found on Naja Münster's channel, provides insights into a specific media practice carried out by an increasing number of children and adolescents these days. The analysis of the content and the production practices is only one side to the coin, though. Children's reception and daily practices of watching and engaging with YouTube as a platform is in itself a subject worth of studying. Among other things, it holds significant explanatory power within an overall understanding of contemporary play culture and the mediatization of play and everyday life of children. There is reason to believe that YouTube has come to play a very important role in children's mediatized play as a primary source for inspiration and – for those children who are active producers themselves – as a form of play in itself. Further, the commercial aspects of the engagements with YouTube content is a relevant parameter to examine. For Naja and her family these aspects are upfront and part of the business model behind their work. For the viewers, commercial aspects relate to the concrete commercials which they have to watch in order to access content as well as the subtle relations between youtubers and brands. There is still a need for further scholarly exploration of the relationship between influencers and their followers, especially when these are young(er) children. As mentioned above, I have carried out a number of interviews with different children aged 5–14. The interviews focus on everyday practices, when and how YouTube is being used, what kind of content the interviewed children prefer – and why – and not least children's own production of content and their thoughts on their own role as both consumers and producers. Also, during the interviews, I have come to put more and more emphasis on the role of adults in relation to children's and teenagers use of YouTube, with a preliminary hypothesis pointing to a gap between children and adults (be it parents or teachers) in their experience with and attitudes towards YouTube.

The interview sessions in themselves point to relevant perspectives in relation to how children's use of YouTube is integrated into their everyday life. Although all of the interviewed children spent a significant amount of time on YouTube, all of them only rarely engage in discussions with adults about their use. They don't experience a high level of interest from adults, neither parents nor teachers, while they enjoy talking to a genuinely interested and (at least to some extent) informed adult (the researcher). The interviews revealed a very broad range of different user practices and patterns, first and foremost a broad range of content used by the children. From meditation guides to drag shows, gaming and everything in between, children's uses expose a broad set of needs and interests, which can possibly be catered for on YouTube. On YouTube, they have the opportunity to geek out with very specific interests, which they may or more often may not see reflected among their friends at school.

Children are both consumers and – to a varying extent – producers of content on YouTube. Some of the children in the interview study have their own channel on YouTube, some of them used to have one, which has now been deactivated, and some of them have plans for future content that they want to produce, once they get the perfect idea and/or the necessary skills to realize it. These very common practices often leave parents and teachers puzzled and perhaps slightly worried, which points to the need to develop a broader understanding of children's own accounts of their habits and preferences. If we want to support critical media literacy in children and adolescents, a highly relevant point of reference would be the content and the practices that they use and perform in their everyday lives.

Children's use of YouTube has – regardless of its widespread prevalence – only to a limited extent been the subject of academic investigation. This study suggests that there is reason to take these uses more seriously, and to do so from perspectives encompassing both consumption and production patterns. The case of Naja Münster illustrates how even very young children may use YouTube as a platform for fun and play, but also how a serious business may be formed out of a witty child with agency and humor whom other children find amusing and inspiring.

References

Abidin, C. (2015). Micromicrocelebrity: Branding Babies on the Internet. *M/C Journal, 18*(5). http://journal.media-culture.org.au/index.php/mcjournal/article/view/1022/wishcrys.com.

Abidin, C. (2017). #familygoals: Family Influencers, Calibrated Amateurism, and Justifying Young Digital Labour. *Social Media + Society, 3*(2), 1–15.

Bärtl, M. (2018). YouTube Channels, Uploads and Views: A Statistical Analysis of the Past 10 Years. *Convergence: The International Journal of Research into New Media Technologies, 24*(1), 99–113.

Burgess, J., & Green, J. (2018). *YouTube: Online Video and Participatory Culture* (2nd ed.). Wiley.

Burroughs, B. (2017). YouTube Kids: The App Economy and Mobile Parenting. *Social Media + Society, 3*(2), 1–8.

Corsaro, A. (2012). Interpretive Reproduction in Children's Play. *American Journal of Play, 4*(4), 488–504.

Dijck, J. (2013). *The Culture of Connectivity.* Oxford University Press.

DR Audience Research. (2017). Media Development. Retrieved from: https://www.dr.dk/om-dr/about-dr/media-development-2010-2019, May 2020.

Gissel, S. T., Hansen, S. R., & Puck, M. R. (2017). *Børns læsning 2017 – en kvantitativ undersøgelse af børns læse- og medievaner i fritiden.* Tænketanken Fremtidens Biblioteker.

Jerslev, A. (2016). In the Time of the Microcelebrity: Celebrification and the YouTuber Zoella. *International Journal of Communication, 10*(2016), 5233–5251.

Johansen, S. L. (2018). Everyday Media Play. Children's Playful Media Practices. *Conjunctions. Transdisciplinary Journal of Cultural Participation, 4*(1). https://www.conjunctions-tjcp.com/article/view/103493.

Lange, Patricia G. (2014). *Kids on YouTube.* Left Coast Press.

Livingstone, S., & Sefton-Green, J. (2016). *The Class. Living and Learning in the Digital Age.* New York University Press.

Marôpo, L., Jorge, A., & Tomaz, R. (2019). "I Felt Like I Was Really Talking to You!": Intimacy and Trust among Teen Vloggers and Followers in Portugal and Brazil. *Journal of Children and Media, 14*(1), 22–37.

Rasmussen, A. S. C. (2017). *YouTube, leg og dannelse – en undersøgelse af børns brug af YouTube i relation til DR Ultras digitale fremtid*. Master Thesis, Aarhus University. Unpubl.

Raun, T. (2018). Capitalizing Intimacy: New Subcultural Forms of Micro-celebrity Strategies and Affective Labour on YouTube. *Convergence: The International Journal of Research into New Media Technologies*, *24*(1), 99–113.

Sicart, M. (2014). *Play Matters*. MIT Press.

Statens Medieråd. (2019). *Småungar och medier*. Retrieved Nov. 11, 2019 from: https://statensmedierad.se/publikationer/ungarochmedier/smaungarochmedier2019.3348.html.

7

An expanding luxury land: A journey through the magical world which TV series are offering to their teenage audience

Ève Lamendour

American television series aimed at teenagers and young adults have recently been displaying a taste for luxury. This trend, which started in the early 1990s, has considerably developed during the last two decades, in particular thanks to such series as *Gossip Girl* or *90210*.

The progress of this particular taste in a context of mass culture is paradoxical. Indeed, mass media induces the idea that culture is shared by a large number of people and is no longer the privilege of the elite. At first, the vehicles allowing the development of mass culture were elementary schooling, newspapers, railways, and post office. The expanding level of literacy was fueled by a variety of publications made available thanks to the new infrastructures. Owing to these diverse progresses, an utterly new mass media culture has been developing starting from Western countries since the middle of the 19th Century (Mollier et al., 2009). This meant a fundamental change from previous centuries. In this development, the youth were a target as well as means. What does one see at the beginning of the 21st century? Mass culture aimed at young people promoting a form of elitism made up of conspicuous luxury consumption, success, and extensive leisure. It may seem a tribute to Thorstein Veblen's *The Theory of the Leisure Class*, first published in 1899. The reinvention of elitism through mass media is at the core of this research.

One of the contributions to the analysis of the influence of mass media comes from the Frankfurt School. Leading figures of this social theory and critical philosophy movement include Theodor W. Adorno,

Max Horkheimer, and Walter Benjamin, whose main contributions were published between the 1920s and the 1940s. Their ideas continue to significantly influence how we think about the effect of mass media. These authors considered that popular culture, *via* the mass media, is merely a form of alienation that is typical of industrialized societies. The analysis these intellectuals put forward is that the people will not benefit from the culture reserved for the elite. Furthermore, crushing of the elite culture by the mass media signals the decline of any possible sense of culture. Jazz, cinema, cartoons, and radio programs symbolize the social slide into complacency and indulgence.

Here I propose to look at a typical contemporary mass culture production aiming in particular at a young target, namely TV series. To examine to what extent TV series participate in the spread of an adolescent culture leaning towards luxury, firstly the focus is put on the recent history of North American television series aimed at teenagers. Using the theoretical approaches of reception, I propose a guideline to better understand the need for fiction. Secondly, an analysis of a corpus of TV series allows me to highlight the type of attributes associated with the staged luxury. Relying on a semiotic approach, I will present a typology of the fictitious high school students who benefit from a dreamed adult-like life. Eventually, my aim is to identify the luxurious attributes and signs of a fictitious and luxurious adolescence. Thus, a typology of the teenagers as hyper-consumers as staged on the small screen is elaborated. In conclusion, I will reexamine this new trend using Benjamin's concepts of authenticity and aura (2008).

1. TV Series as a transitional object for teenagers

The choice of North American TV series is justified by their wide broadcasting on regular channels in the U.S.A. and abroad and by their accessibility through streaming websites. Mass media is an evolving landscape with the explosion of streaming (VOD or peer-to-peer websites), the ubiquitous access to TV series and films through subscriptions to distribution platforms such as Netflix, and one-upmanship in the production of television series that compete, particularly among the youngest customers, with the cinema offer.

Furthermore, media consumption by youngsters has increased tremendously. On average, recreative screen use for an American teenager is 7 hours 22 minutes daily[1]. Their choice is more and more influenced by their peer group, thanks to the autonomy afforded by the equipment they benefit from: by the age of 12, 69 % of the American teenagers have their own smartphone[2]. The most popular activity on screen remains watching TV or videos, over playing games.

The TV series favored by teenagers come in many genres. Nevertheless, the fact that a significant proportion of these series depict high school students provides an echo chamber for an adolescent culture. The latter point is particularly visible on the forums of the streaming websites and on the other social media.

1.1. The high school narrative

The plot focusing on a group of teenagers living under an arbitrary rule (school, parents, captain…) is an old television recipe. It is obviously an older recipe owing to novelists such as Mark Twain or Jules Verne. As television is concerned, it has been indulged in by the main networks, i.e., ABC, The CW (and earlier UPN and the WB), Fox, and NBC. This type of storyline is to be found in TV series as different as *Fame* (1982–1987), *Dawson's Creek* (1998–2003) or *One Tree Hill* (2003–2012). For this research, a study was made of 56 American TV series broadcasted between 1952 and 2019 whose plot dealt with teenagers (see Tab. 1). A classification by decades is a convenient way to display longitudinal data. Each decade has its specific tone. Nevertheless, some representations live on through time (the ever-happy nuclear family), sometimes in a minor form, and some representations fade away or gain in visibility.

During the 1950s and 1960s, the narratives' focus is the family. The teenagers are essentially represented as members of a family. The focus begins to shift in the 1970s owing particularly to *Happy Days*, aired on ABC from 1974 to 1984. The show focuses mainly on the everyday life of teenagers. Family appears as an anchor and a reference for them. But their concerns are diverse and mainly centered on the group of friends. The show "is the epitome of the idealization of adolescence in the United States. Its nostalgic glint (the action is set in a tight-knit

1 The recreative use of screen excludes homework and time spent for school. The survey sample covers 1677 young people aged 8 to 18. *The Common Sense census: media use by tweens and teens* 2019.

2 *Ibidem*, 2019.

Tab. 1: The High School Narrative through Time

Decades	Frequent narrative	Luxury trend	Emblematic TV series	
			Title & broadcast	Luxury theme
1950s	The plot focuses on a middle-class family; the children are depicted as part of it.	Not a subject (3 shows listed)	Father Knows Best CBC 1954–1960	None
1960s	Idem with a more diverse definition of family (blended family, lone parent)	Not a subject (5 shows listed)	Brady Bunch ABC 1969–1974	None
1970s	The plot focuses on the life of teenagers (friends, high school, going out, and family). Friends don't mix genders.	Not a subject (15 shows) Visible through a rare character, i.e., the spoiled rich girl in *The Facts of Life*	Happy Days ABC 1974–1984	None
1980s	Idem with a bigger emphasis put on the romantic aspect (dating or not). The group of friends is mixed (race, gender).	Not a subject (5 shows) Visible through an occasional main character, i.e., the millionaire adoptive father in *Rags to Riches*	Saved by the Bell NBC 1989–1993	Given by a character: a teenager from a wealthy family wearing designer clothes at school
1990s	Adolescence as a time of friction (bullying, sexual abuse, drug use, etc.) and involvement in a more diverse group (gay friend, vampire slayer, etc.).	A possible theme among others (3 shows on 8 listed)	Beverly Hills 90210 Fox 1990–2000	Main theme: the ostentatious lifestyle of a group of teenagers
2000s	The everyday life of a group of teenagers quite autonomous from their parents.	A subject for 8 shows out of 12 listed and a central theme for 4 of them.	Gossip Girl The CW 2007–2012	Main theme: the ostentatious lifestyle of a group of teenagers
2010s	The search for identity by an isolated teenager or a group of friends in difficult times (deceit, accident, suicide, murder).	The main theme for 7 out of 8 shows listed.	Pretty Little Liars ABC 2010–2017	Background theme: wealthy lifestyle, desire for luxury coming from the less well-off characters

community during the mid-1950s to the mid-1960s), the jovial tone (the well-integrated blameless boy, his friends and family) make the series an expression of the American way of life and may explain its national and international success. The series has been broadcast for 11 seasons and 255 episodes. It had given rise to several related shows and to a movie by George Lucas. If the series' plot is centered on a group of white male pupils, the following teen sitcoms have begun to display mixed casts. For instance, *Saved by the Bell*, aired by NBC for 5 seasons beginning in 1989, was more representative in terms of ethnicity and gender. A year later, the same company broadcasted *The Fresh Prince of Bel-Air*, which focuses on an aimless teenager from a proletarian background sent from Philadelphia to Los Angeles to live with his successful uncle. The protagonists are all from African American origin"(Lamendour, 2020). Furthermore, in the 1980s, the plots put a new and bigger emphasis on the romantic aspect. Dating or not dating becomes an issue. The next decade builds on new subjects which are more controversial. Examples are *Buffy, the Vampire Slayer* (1997–2003) or *My So-Called Life* (1994–1995). The latter ABC show appears to be a revival of the earlier ABC program, *Afterschool Special*, begun in 1972. This serialized version covers the same type of topics, i.e., addiction to alcohol or drugs, sexual abuse, bullying, homophobia, etc. During the 1990s, adolescence tends to be more often depicted as a time of friction within the collective of youngsters or vis-à-vis the adults in charge. It is also the decade which marks a turning point in the conception of TV shows. The growing impact of marketing is visible, specifically in the gender targeting. Before that, most shows were aiming at family viewers or at a given age group. If this is still the case with *The Fresh Prince of Bel-Air*, it is no longer the case with *Beverly Hills* (1990–2000) and later with *Gilmore Girls* (2000–2007), clearly targeting a female audience. With the 2000s, the representation shows an increase of the autonomy of the youngsters, living a life quite independent from their parents.

From the 1970s to the 2000s, adolescence is represented as a tight-knit collective entity. This image begins to flicker through the 2010s. The isolated teenager is a new protagonist (*Jane by Design*, *The Carrie Diaries*, *13 Reasons Why*). The search for identity appears as a major issue (*Switched at Birth*, *The Lying Game*, *The Vampire Diaries*). And, as a novelty, the difficulties face by teenagers are strongly emphasized.

1.2. Luxury as a new trend in teen TV

Throughout the historical digest of American TV series, one sees an expanding offer directing teen protagonists in order to touch an audience rather composed of teenagers than the whole family. The narrative tends to gain a glamorous polish based on the staging of luxury goods, brands and lifestyle. The consumption of luxury goods or brands is not a theme throughout the earlier period (Tab. 1). It gains in visibility with the inclusion of a specific character during the 1970s (secondary character) and 1980s (main character) before becoming a possible theme during the 1990s and turning into a main subject since the 2000s.

In order to pinpoint the appearance of luxury-seeking behavior in TV series aimed at teenagers, one needs to define what is luxury. The distinction between luxury brands and non-luxury brands has been operationally defined by Vigneron and Johnson (2004) as the distinction between brands exhibiting five perceived values, contingent on a particular socioeconomic framework.

1. The consumption of luxury brands is viewed as a signal of status and wealth, and whose price, which is expensive by normal standards, enhances the value of such a signal (perceived conspicuous value).
2. If virtually everyone owns a particular brand it is by definition not prestigious (perceived unique value).
3. The role-playing aspects and the social value of luxury brands can be instrumental in the decision to buy (perceived social value).
4. For a brand which satisfies an emotional desire such as a luxury brand, a product's subjective intangible benefits such as esthetic appeal clearly determines the brand selection (perceived hedonic value).
5. Prestige is derived partly from technical superiority and the extreme care that is taken during the production process. For instance, a Rolex Sea-dweller works 1,220 meters underwater and is hand-crafted (perceived quality value).

This interpretation recognizes that the definition of luxury may vary for different people, depending on their socioeconomic background. Translated into marketing terms, consumers develop luxury meanings for objects and brands based upon interactions with people (e.g., aspired and/or peer reference group), object properties (e.g., best quality), and hedonic values (e.g., sensory beauty). Such interactions occur at personal and social levels. Thus, a brand's luxury quality is created from a multitude of interactions between the consumer and elements within the environment. Luxury-seeking behavior is the result of multiple motivations, but in particular the motives of sociability and self-expression. Those are two of the characteristics of the teenagers' age group, i.e., the importance of the peers and the search for one's identity. At a time of identity building in one's life, one depends on all the help available, either the leather jacket of Fonzie, the quite innocuous bad boy of *Happy days*, or the cocktail dress worn by Serena in *Gossip Girls* – anything that makes one belong in the sense of being understood and accepted by the group of peers and still remains unique and distinctive.

Through the TV series, one finds that the luxury trend begun in the 1990s offers teenagers a numbing panoply to tame the difficulty of their age.

1.3. Theory of reception

I would like to lean here on a recent study concerning the appeal of fiction (Lamendour, 2017). The main point is to understand what fictions (TV series, films, or novels) represent for their audience or readers (Fig. 1). The model proposed is based on semiotics (Barthes, 1964; Eco, 1985; Greimas, 1987). I propose considering the model as the reference matrix to assess what is generically the use of fiction. It provides a reading grid that distinguishes five modes of reception of fiction as existential postures. The use of fiction by its audience can be described as an initiatory journey throughout these five postures.

The reading of this matrix applied to a teenage audience has to start from the majority position: fiction as an active way of being in the world, endowed with a specific and sustained sociability. It means, for instance, being involved in peer to peer streaming websites, either doing the translation for the subtitles, or commenting on and creating lists (the best 2000s teen shows, etc.), or even participating in crowd funding (in order to promote the continuation of a cut-short TV series such as *Veronica Mars*, for instance).

Then, it distinguishes two complementary postures that put the viewer in motion. In the first one, fiction is used as a transitional object to tame a time of change, or a new status. The path from childhood to adolescence and to adulthood is not easy. TV series based upon teenage characters give something to refer to, to discuss amongst peers.

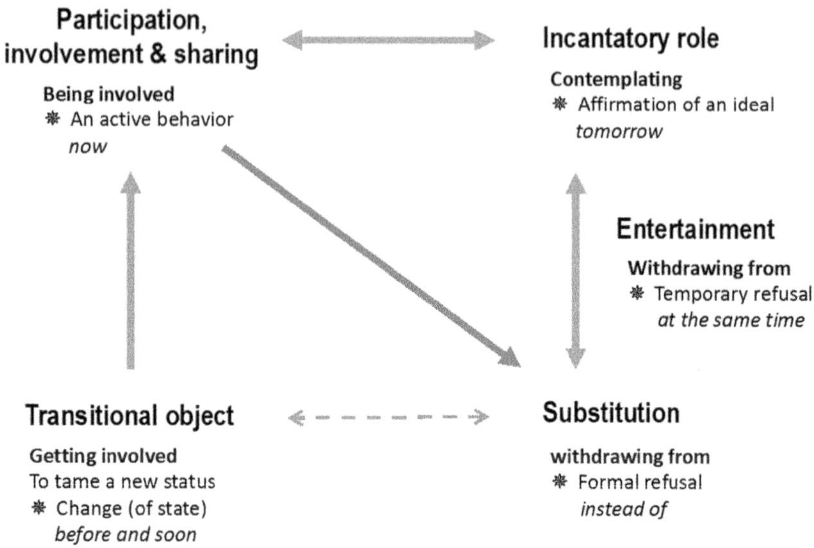

Fig. 1: The Matrix of the use of fiction

Characters in TV series or real persons in TV reality shows offer a sample of behaviors to discuss, praise or ridicule. In what could be described as a sophisticated Legoland, they provide versatile possibilities to play with before engaging in real situations.

The second posture sees fiction as an incantation to beget a new condition or state of mind. This condition that still has to happen is a promise of an enviable future – a future that would be likely to modify the relationship the teenage viewer has with her/his present situation. Characters (or real persons in TV reality shows) have a stronger hold on their viewers; they become a behavioral model for teenagers. The situations depicted in fiction become an image of an ideal future. Watching TV series, they discover what they want to be.

The model provides a fallback posture in opposition to these three positions. This latter posture marks a refusal of a current condition. It could be either a temporary refusal where the time dedicated to entertainment is preferred to actual life (dealing with parents, doing homework), or it could be a stronger rejection. It would then be marked by a bulimic dive into a fictional existence that replaces the real one. The practice of binge watching, the excessive mode of watching TV series, would be an expression of this posture.

Adapted to a teenage audience, the journey this matrix defines takes the form of a rite of passage. It begins with a time of change, when fiction provides a transitional object necessary to project oneself into adulthood and be able to eventually participate in it. The incantatory role of fiction shapes the nature of the involvement imagined by the youth. If or when the journey becomes too challenging, this youth may find solace in a protected harbor and delve into fiction. This withdrawal may help temporarily or become a shield against a demanding or disappointing reality.

Thus, through this matrix one can appreciate how a teenage audience will be susceptible to the programs it heavily consumes daily. We will then focus on one of its recent trends, the glamorous veneer.

2. The attributes of a luxury youth

The original corpus is composed of 56 TV series produced in the United States between 1950 and 2019. As described previously, the 2000s have seen a transformation in the representation of teenagers, i.e. the addition of a glamorous veneer. Although this representation existed in the 1990s, it was unusual. Beginning in the 1990s, and continuing through the following three decades, I pinpointed 13 programs (see Appendix 1) and used them to examine three aspects of adolescent life: living spaces, leisure activities and social markers. This evaluation identified how they form an overall system that values the luxury goods and accessories that are typical of conspicuous consumption.

2.1. Living spaces

The fictitious luxury youth begins with an embedded identity. Its main characteristics are a spatial affiliation and a distinctive living space. In most of the TV series examined, the action takes place in the house of the parents (mansions, XXL villas) or in a luxury hotel suite situated, preferably, in an iconic district (Orange County, when the action is located in California, or the Upper East Side when in New York). The zip code is used as a referential marker in the 1990s TV series *Beverly Hills*. Furthermore, after running for 10 seasons, this series was revived in 2008 under the title *90210*. Addressed at teenagers, the action has to involve high school students. Similarly, in *Veronica Mars*' first season, the zip code is a key factor that distinguishes well-to-do pupils from others, in a context where there is no middle class: "This is my school. If you go here, your parents are either *millionaires* or your parents *work for millionaires.* Neptune, California. A town without a middle class," as the protagonist explains in the opening scene (season 1, episode 1). 90909 is the fictitious zip code attributed to the city of Neptune, which is situated between Orange and Balboa counties, CA. Pupils used the phrase "09ers" as a synonym for the wealthy kids.

The swimming pool plays an important part in teenagers' social lives. A mirror of the mansion it is attached to, it can be monumental (as in *The Orange County*, *Pretty Little Liars* and *Veronica Mars*) and offers a stage to demonstrate one's coolness.

But, for these teenagers, the domestic space is not restricted to the house-garden-pool area. The distinctive spaces they enjoy extend beyond these ordinary limits. Meals are taken in five-star hotel's restaurants, or in country clubs. The choice of food underlines the exclusivity of the location: *croque-monsieur* in truffle oil, served on request because it is not on the menu (e.g. *Gossip Girl* season 1, episode 1) or champagne drunk by high school students (e.g. *Gossip Girl* season 1, episode 1). Before the existence of Uber Eats, wealthy pupils had their meals delivered to them at school (*Veronica Mars*).

2.2. Leisure activities

The leisure activities of teenage characters are likely to differ from their audience's. First of all, they do not watch TV. "No one does anymore" states a pupil in *Gossip Girl.* Their life is full of events. A day at school, followed by a meal shared with the family, as seen in earlier TV series, seems difficult to fit into the agenda.

Time with peers is not only spent around the swimming pool (either during the day or at late-night parties), but also at the country club, in exclusive bars or fashionable nightclubs. Serena and Blair, high school students, are shown meeting in a bar for cocktails at 7:30 pm on a school day (*Gossip Girl*, season 1, episode 1). Their outings illustrate their membership of the jet set. Numerous cameos reinforce the message: for instance, Paris Hilton appears several times in *Veronica Mars* and *The Orange County*, while both Quincy Jones and Donald Trump, among hundreds of others, made an appearance in *The Fresh Prince of Bel-Air.*

Social events include invitations to trendy events such as fashion shows, galas and gallery openings, or debutantes' balls. Holiday locations reinforce the sense of exclusivity (Martha's Vineyard, Paris).

All of these indulgent activities are made possible by the significant amount of independence these teenagers have to manage their on-screen agenda.

2.3. Luxury markers

This analysis distinguishes different types of markers (notably brands, either visible or quoted in the dialogue). The main markers are clothes and accessories, the choice of means of transportation, and high-tech props.

The extent of the wardrobe is seen in the existence of a dressing room adjacent to the teenager's bedroom. For girls, it contains an extensive collection of handbags, shoes, and jewelry. Here, there is no need for the fashion police. These teenagers are masters of using brands and their accessories. Being fashionable is desirable – even if the route to *haute couture* is a long one for characters coming from a middle-class background (*The Carrie Diaries*, *Jane by Design*, *One Tree Hill*). But it can be a way of life for other characters; one example is the evening dress designed by a renowned brand that is offered to Serena by her mother for a teenagers' party (*Gossip Girl*). Fashion awareness is emphasized by the physical attitude of teenagers. Thus, *The Lying Game* focuses on twin sisters, who have been separated at birth. Their appearance is quite revealing. The one living in a wealthy family reproduces[3] the pose commonly used since the 2010s to advertise handbags. Fig. 2 shows a comparison of two images, a snapshot presenting a face to face of the twin sisters, the other, an advertisement for Longchamp's handbag. Between 2013 and 2017, the brand relied on a socialite, Alexa Chung, to promote its products.

In this corpus, the teenager is the master of her or his appearance. Both genders have perfect hair and are expert users of cosmetics. A recent Netflix series, *Elite*, puts a new emphasis on the male wardrobe. The preference for Lacoste among male pupils has had a strong impact on discussions on social media and forums. For instance, one discussion begins with the question: "Why TF is only wearing Lacoste clothes like

---

[3] Unless it is the other way around, and advertising copies fiction.

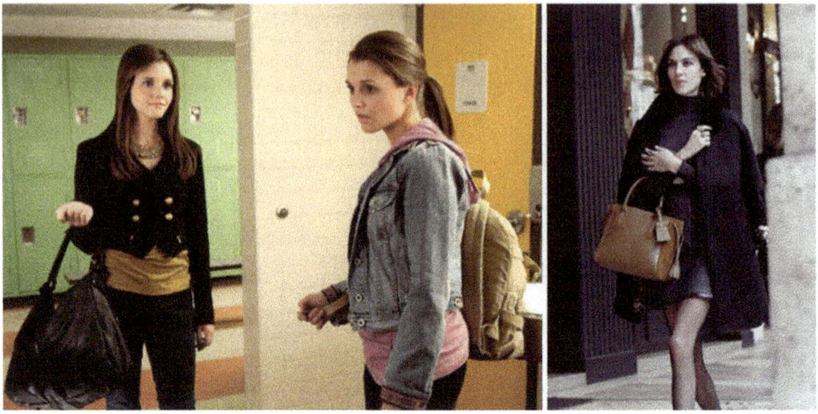

Fig. 2: The handbag pose.

literally every single item is Lacoste even his underwear?"[4]. The answer given to this web user explains the brand's positioning.

The twins separated at birth in The Lying Game vs. a Longchamp© advertisement

The second marker of luxury is the selected means of transportation. Here, a simple list will suffice to illustrate their standard of living: taxis, limousines with a driver, a distinctive personal car (a Porsche for the high school student in *The Lying Game*), extending to a private jet (*Veronica Mars*). Moreover, teenagers enjoy the newest high-tech products, notably smartphones and laptops, whose logos are highly visible onscreen.

3. Luxury land

In the corpus analyzed, high school students are depicted as emancipated hyper-consumers who are living an adult dream life that could seem quite shallow. It is possible to pinpoint a typology of characters who enjoy an easy life, which is a mix of teenage leisure and adult independence.

4 See for instance https://www.reddit.com/r/EliteNetflix/comments/d7zkmj/is_lacoste_a_luxury_brand/.

3.1. Autonomous high school students

Teenage characters enjoy VIP treatments and have a strong sense of independence that looks a lot like adulthood. In fact, they live in a time and world that is separate from the world of their parents and other adults. The attributes of a luxury youth can be summed up as an ethos of distinction (Bourdieu, 1984), combined with freedom from any constraints. This ethos is made up of consumer habits and reinforced through their ability to know how to dress, where to mix, with whom, which party to go to, and which college to attend. Each of these items are treated as equally significant. This confusion between form and substance, or rather the way in which appearances are equated with life choices, establishes some common ground with the daily life and worries of their audience.

The freedom experienced by emancipated TV teenagers comes from their absentee parents, and leads to a contemporary trope: the alcohol and sex combo. Addictive behaviors are commonplace in fiction, whoever the protagonist. It may be the wealthy heirs of absentee fathers and deceased mothers, such as Chuck in *Gossip Girl* or Logan Echolls in *Veronica Mars*. It can also be working-class children who rub shoulders with the great and the good (*The Lying Game*, *Pretty Little Liars*, *Elite*).

If heirs or heiresses are some of the main parts, they are joined by the sons or daughters of the *nouveau riche*. For instance, the Waldorf family in *Gossip Girl* represents "old money." This is shown through debutantes' balls, holidays at Martha's Vineyard, the practice of endogamy, the wedding of the heir to the throne of Monaco, etc., while Serena boasts connections to an artistic family. The showbusiness element is embodied in Echolls' father, an A-list star in *Veronica Mars*. The business world appears through the ability to make money (in *Veronica Mars* Cassidy Echolls develops a successful real estate business while still in high school).

3.2. Luxury appreciation and rejection

A full representation of the behaviors of fictitious teenagers towards luxury goods can be shown in a schema (Fig. 3). Their lifestyle can be understood not only as the sum of attributes, but also as a whole system. The first axis describes the protagonist's proximity to the realm of luxury (social class, consumption habits, way of life, etc.). Extremes are located

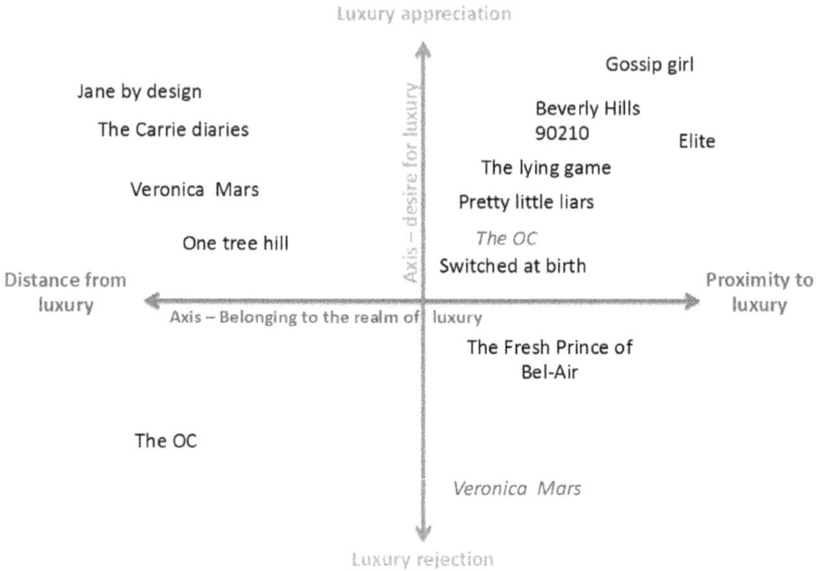

Fig. 3: The representation of luxury in teens' fiction

at both ends: on the one hand, in *Jane by Design*, the heroine is an aspiring high school student from a working-class background who wants to become a couture designer; on the other hand, the heiress in *Gossip Girl* is certain to attend the best college on the east coast.

The second axis distinguishes degrees of desire for luxury. For instance, a working-class protagonist may be drawn towards it (*Jane by Design*) or may maintain a certain detachment (*The Fresh Prince of Bel-Air*).

There are few examples of the rejection of luxury: the main cases are found in *Veronica Mars* and *The Orange County*. In the former series, the protagonist, Veronica, initially embodies a desire for a luxury world, which is illustrated through her choice of friends and boyfriend. The plot then leads her to express a more critical view of luxury, and of a discriminatory culture that endorses values based on appearances, abuse of power, and money. In *The Orange County*, one of its protagonists, Ryan Atwood, is presented as a character immune to luxury. As a young, underprivileged offender, he is taken under the wing of his lawyer and discovers a way of life he had never imagined. In the series, he finds it difficult to come to terms with his new status.

3.3. Connivance and efficiency

Quotes and references from one series to another, and from TV series to social media, convey a strong sense of connivance between a specific series and its audience. This helps to maintain a distinction *vis-à-vis* the world of adults who do not understand and cannot see what is obvious to teenagers. A good example of this is the fact that the voice of the eponymous gossip girl, a manipulative character who is heard but never seen, is that of Kristen Bell. This actress played the part of Veronica in *Veronica Mars*. Crowdfunding permitted the production and release of a movie version of the TV series, which is a powerful testament to the attachment of viewers to their series.

Certain characters act as intercessors between fiction and reality. One example is the figure of the rock star in *Gossip Girl* or *Veronica Mars*. In the latter, the singer of the rock band *The Dandy Warhols* was invited to appear in an episode, while one of the band's songs (*We used to be friends*) is used in the credits for an entire season.

The transmedia visibility of series, their characters, and their interpreters are attractive factors for brands. Cross-references encompass numerous, diverse practices ranging from brand placement (or products, or individuals such as Paris Hilton or Andie MacDowell) to the placement of characters in advertisements. A prime example is Leighton Meester, who plays Blair Waldorf in *Gossip Girl*, and who has appeared in numerous advertisements (for Nikon Coolpix, for the Reebok "Fly Generation" line in 2009, Bulgari, for the haircare product Herbal Essences in 2010, the perfume Lovestruck by Vera Wang and Missoni in 2011, and the French brand NafNaf in 2013). These practices[5] go as far as creating a brand ambassador – namely, Blake Lively for Gucci, who was discovered when she played Serena, the second protagonist in *Gossip Girl*. Onscreen characters benefit from their actresses or actors' use of Instagram or Snapchat, and *vice versa*.

---

5 To know more about the creative communication and image policies displayed by luxury brands, see Fonrouge and Lipovetsky (2013).

The luxury tone of a significant part of contemporary TV series is not innocuous. It drives a taste for specific types of goods that are more-or-less affordable for young viewers and their families. It exposes them to a range of values on a scale that promotes, above all, conspicuous consumption, social distinction, and hedonism.

4. The new aura

The evocative universe that is developed in these TV series makes them an effective marketing tool for any brand wishing to orient itself towards a younger target. The social media visibility of series, their characters and their interpreters is an attractive factor. The question of the use of such leverage is one of ethics. The capacity to absorb and appropriate criticism (which is the mark of the new spirit of capitalism, according to Boltanski and Chiapello, 2007) is clearly seen in quotations and multiple references from one series to another. In one of the rare critical TV series, *Veronica Mars*, the eponymous character is the narrator. From the very beginning, the story is told through her voice. In *Gossip Girl*, the same voice is heard through the whole TV series. It is the voice of the same actress and it is the voice of the eponymous character who, never seen, hides behind social media under the anonymous name Gossip Girl. The tone, which is critical of social discrimination in the former TV series, is turned into a socially harmless and personally hurtful one. By deflecting criticism, the narrative merely gives a description of a way of life that appears desirable because it is pervasive and uncontested. My point of view is not that of a moral censor but of an observer who witnesses the transformation of the aura. The concept of aura, developed by Walter Benjamin (2008), refers to the time that preceded the age of mechanical reproduction through reprography, photography, postcards, sound and films recordings, etc. Then, works of art benefited from an aura made of authenticity and of physical uniqueness. They were received for their cult value (religious sculptures or paintings) and, to a lesser degree, on rare occasions, for an exhibition value (during processions, for instance, and later on in the sanctity of museums). In this line of thought, a copy would be deprived of the quality of aura. How could a manufactured product, a brand, or a TV series reclaim the strength of an aura?

The brand culture among teenagers has been amply studied (Strasburger et al., 2008; Delannoy, 2016). They are consumers and, as such, they become a marketing target: 39 % of their income is spent on clothes, accessories and footwear[6]. The desire to belong to their peer group explains the knowledge teenagers develop for specific brands as well as the shared knowledge of TV series. The latter knowledge also testifies of an aspirational desire to tame the grown-up world and make it into a playful and enchanted scene (Lamendour, 2017), as described earlier. The teenagers' relationship with luxury brands may be described as a powerful vector capable of maintaining the magic. Their search for identity revolves around the notion of possession enhanced by peer review. In an age of social media and expression through selfies, exhibition tends to become a core value. In this context and for this population, aura is not defined by a substance, i.e. authenticity and uniqueness (existing at a specific time in a specific place as one original), but rather by an insubstantial quality resting on repeated exhibitions and ubiquity.

The increasing development of counterfeit luxury goods fits in with this change in the nature of aura. Thus, luxury brand enthusiasts tend to view a continuum between counterfeit products and genuine luxury goods (Turunen et al., 2011). The latter occupy the ultimate position of the desired objects, while the former are considered a lesser version. In their evaluation, these consumers tend to reject no-brand products even more. Both genuine and counterfeit luxury goods realize a social function (prestige, peer acceptance) as well as a personal value (through experiences or memories attached to the product). Here, genuineness is defined by the high price, the rarity (among the general population, not among the peers) and the perceived quality, i.e. the fact that the manufacturer whose brand is visible on the product is the one that benefits from its sales. The fact that the authentic product is often manufactured in the same country where its counterfeit is produced is not irrelevant to understanding the continuum between genuine and counterfeit goods. The perceived conspicuous value may be found in the exhibition of the brand and its ubiquity among peers, through social media and TV series.

The TV series promoting a luxury lifestyle bring about numerous blogs, personal and commercial websites whose purpose is to help TV viewers, male or female, to find the clothes or accessories staged in the TV series. Some of these websites offer links to the real things while

6 Piper Jaffray 27th semi-annual taking stock with teens survey, Spring 2014. Survey conducted on 7,500 teenagers in the U.S.A.

others propose a mix of genuine items and others "to help transform you into a fashion icon, without the heavy price tag"[7].

This new trend of promoting a luxurious lifestyle in TV series can be described as a biased understanding of elitism. It would, however, be an elitism deprived of any ambition, with a core that simply revolves around the idea of ownership. Any conspicuous brand is a sign for an audience. The new aura is thus to be found in appearances, through repeated exhibitions thanks to its ubiquitous quality.

References

Adorno, T. W. & Horkheimer, M. (2012 [1947]). *Kulturindustrie. Raison et mystification des masses*. Allia.

Barthes, R. (1964). Rhétorique de l'image. *Communications*, *4*, 41–51.

Benjamin, W. (2008 [1936]). The Work of Art in the Age of Its Technological Reproducibility: Second Version. In M. W. Jennings, B. Doherty, & T. Y. Levin (Eds), *The Work of Art in the Age of Its Technological Reproducibility, and Other Writings on Media* (pp. 19–55). Harvard University Press.

Boltanski, L., & Chiapello È. (2007 [2006]). *The New Spirit of Capitalism*. Verso.

Bourdieu, P. (1984 [1979]). *Distinction. A Social Critique of the Judgement of Taste*. Harvard University Press.

Cook, D. T. (Ed.). (2020). *The Sage Encyclopedia of Children and Childhood Studies*. Sage Publications Ltd.

Eco, U. (1985 [1979]). *Lector in Fabula*. Grasset.

Fonrouge, C., & Lipovetsky, G. (2013). Les entrepreneurs du luxe: une analyse historico-sociale. *International Management*, *17*(3), 31–35.

Greimas, A. J. (1987 [1970]). *On Meaning*. University of Minnesota Press.

Lamendour, E. (2017). *Éloge de la fiction*, Qualification to supervise PhDs in management sciences, Poitiers University.

7 Pinterest, https://www.pinterest.fr/louc_45/blair-waldorf-style/. See also https://www.justwomenfashion.com/ (accessed 21 June 2020).

Lamendour, E. (2020). Teenager television series. In D. T. Cook (Ed.), *The Sage Encyclopedia of Children and Childhood Studies* (Vol. 4), Sage Publications Ltd.

Mollier, J.-Y., Sirinelli, J.-F., & Vallotton, F. (Eds.). (2009). *Culture de masse et culture médiatique en Europe et dans les Amériques, 1860–1940*. Presses universitaires de France.

Turunen, L. L. M., & Laaksonen, P. (2011). Diffusing the Boundaries between Luxury and Counterfeits. *Journal of Product and Brand Management, 20*(6), 468–474.

Veblen, T. (1973 [1899]). *The Theory of the Leisure Class: An Economic Study of Institutions*. Houghton Mifflin.

Vigneron, F., & Johnson, L. W. (2004). Measuring Perceptions of Brand Luxury. *Brand Management, 11*(6), 484–506.

Appendix 1

Tab. 2: Selective Filmography

Title	First season	Number of seasons	Places	Pitch	Role of luxury
Beverly Hills, 90210	1990	10	California: Beverly Hills	Teenagers' everyday life in a well-off area of Los Angeles	Bling-bling as a way of living
The Fresh Prince of Bel-Air	1990	6	California: Bel Air	A lost teenager from a proletarian background in Philadelphia is sent to live with his successful uncle in L.A.: frictions and friendship with his 3 cousins.	Everyday life and contrastive effect
The Orange County	2003	4	California: Orange County	A lawyer takes a lost teenager from a proletarian background home. Frictions and friendship with the lawyer's daughter and son.	Everyday life and contrastive effect. Desire for luxury by some characters.
One Tree Hill	2003	9	North Carolina: Tree Hill, fictitious city	Two half-brothers compete in order to join the basket team of their high school.	On the margins: one of the female characters wants to work in fashion.
Veronica Mars	2004	3	California: 90909 Neptune, fictitious city resembling Orange or Balboa county	In a high school where the rich and the poor go, Veronica, the teenage daughter of the sheriff rejects the race for popularity and has developed an activity as a private investigator.	Everyday life and contrastive effect. Rejection of luxury by Veronica Mars.
Gossip Girl	2007	6	New York: Upper East Side + The Village	The life of two extremely wealthy girls made of love, sex, alcohol, best universities application files, and two middle class teenagers whose father wants to send them to a good school.	Everyday life and contrastive effect. Desire for luxury by some characters.

Title	First season	Number of seasons	Places	Pitch	Role of luxury
90210 Beverly Hills	2008	5	California: Beverly Hills	A former student of Beverly hills comes back to live there with his wife and children: a daughter and an adoptive black son.	Everyday life and contrastive effect.
Pretty Little Liars	2010	3	Pennsylvania: Rosewood, fictitious city	A murdered teenager and 4 of her BFFs from middle class to upper class background involved in the inquiry while being blackmailed.	Everyday life and contrastive effect Desire for luxury by some characters.
The Lying Game	2011	2	Arizona: Phoenix, Arroyo High school	Twins separated at birth meet eventually. The one living in a wealthy household goes looking for their mother while the other plays her part.	Everyday life and contrastive effect.
Switched at Birth	2011	2	Kansas: Kansas City and its wealthy suburbs, Mission Hills	A wealthy couple and a Latino single mother discover that their respective daughters were switched at birth.	Everyday life and contrastive effect.
The Carrie Diaries	2012	2	New York and Connecticut: Castlebury	Carrie Bradshaw as a teenager: the discovery of New York.	Curiosity for luxury.
Jane by design	2012	1	New York + suburbs	A teenager gets an internship in the fashion industry by lying about her age.	Desire for luxury.
Elite	2018	2	Spain: an elite high school	3 working-class friends are given scholarships to an exclusive private school.	Desire for luxury & frustration.

Part 3

Circulating and enriching content aimed at children: Transmedia/Media mix...

Gilles Brougère

This part, which has four chapters devoted to very different productions, while dealing with the question of the transmedia(1) and the circulation of contents on different media, shows us a diversity of mechanisms and strategies. Although in all four cases displayed there is transmedia, albeit in varying forms and degrees, the transmedia fulfils different objectives in each case.

Transmedia refers to the distribution of the story on different media (Jenkins, 2006), which may be more or less close to an adaptation, while *media mix*, beyond this distribution, takes into account marketing and commercial considerations, in particular the profitability of a television series through its tie-ins (Steinberg, 2012). Behind these different forms, we discover a plurality of ways of addressing a children's audience and of conceiving the interaction between different media. The four texts in this section reflect these differences, and one could argue that there is nothing in common between *Pokémon* on the one hand and *Secret Path* on the other – they are two worlds that seem to be at odds with each other. However, the presence of two other productions, *Petit Poilu* and *The Long Long Holiday*, allows us to overcome this opposition between a mass market product on the one hand and a critical, militant and esthetically innovative product on the other, by providing a less clear-cut diversity.

These products can be arranged along a line, always in the same order, that will be our guiding thread in this presentation: *Pokémon* (*Po*), *Petit Poilu* (*Little Hairy, PP*), *The Long Long Holiday (LLH*), and *Secret Path*

(SP). We can thus consider that we are going from the most mass-produced and most widely distributed to the most marginal, cultural, educational, even artistic. Thus *Po* is a historical example of mass distribution (Tobin, 2004), which although it is no longer at the level it was, remains important and continues to increase the number of products available, through games but also a new film that is no longer a cartoon, *Detective Pikachu*. At the other end of this same line, *SP* does not seem to have anything in common with it. However, this linear distribution is also present on other dimensions that we will analyze one after the other.

1. Transmedia(l), product enrichment and meeting the public

Hence this line makes it possible to arrange products according to the importance and mechanism of transmediality. *Pokémon* is an extreme case of a Japanese-style media mix (Steinberg, 2012), very quickly combining a video game (the origin of the franchise), a cartoon and trading cards, then developing on all possible media, including the interior and exterior decoration of the plane of a Japanese airline. There seems to be no other limit to the extension of the franchise than its acceptance by the public. The strategy is one of maximum expansion. *Petit Poilu* shows the next stage down – a limited expansion, from a comic book to a cartoon that uses the stories from the albums but adds more to reach a sufficient number of episodes, and has seen some development of a few tie-ins (various products including a plush toy, with a distribution that is not comparable to that of *Pokémon*). While the starting point is an adaptation, for the cartoon the situations produced by different screenwriters increase in number, and extend the universe according to a transmedial mechanism. *The Long Long Holiday* is a cartoon which is not the adaptation of a pre-existing work – a rather rare phenomenon. Moreover, it is not a set of episodes that can be broadcast in any order like *Pokémon* (at least within one season) or *Petit Poilu*, and which will only end when the audience become tired of it. This latter format makes it easier to increase the number not only of episodes, but of seasons and tie-ins, following a mechanism of repetition with a few variations. On the contrary, *The Long Long Holiday*, like *Secret Path*, tells a story with a beginning and an end, which does not favor transmedial proliferation. In the case of *LLH*, apart from the novelization as a return to inspiration from children's literature, the offer is only supplemented by two products – an activity book and a free educational game, offered for reasons of promotion and valorization more than for directly economic reasons. *Secret Path* is a work that combines poems and music (the starting point), drawing and then animation. The transmediality relies on different media to convey a message and offer a coherent set of three products: an album of 10 songs, a book drawn without text but explicitly associated with the album, and a cartoon that, in a way, sets the first two products in motion and makes them more accessible.

This graduation of greater or lesser transmediality covers other distinctions between the first two products (*Po*, *PP*) and the last two (*LLH*, *SP*) which are not the work of chance. In the first two products, it is imagination which prevails, with characters who, in the case of the pocket monsters (the *pokémons*) as much as in the case of *Petit Poilu*, are imaginary beings that relate to the place given in children's productions to animals or to characters which resemble animals. In the latter two products, it is history and its realistic dimension which are presented. For LLH, there is a literary invention and the freedom to imagine, but it is within a precise historical background that frames the fiction. This fiction must be historically credible, which is not the case in imaginary worlds, even if *Pokémon* takes place in the everyday contemporary world. *SP* proposes a work that is both realistic in relation to a real event that is being considered – a 1967 article being the primary source – and dream-like, which gives great graphic freedom. On the one hand (*Po* and *PP*), this difference translates into the proliferation of characters and more or less fantastical universes that allow for the multiplication of narratives and facilitate transmedia. On the other hand (*LLH* and *SP*) it translates into two punctual narratives in a world that is ours (past, certainly, but present in memories and narratives) and closed, unlike the potentially unlimited expansion of the other two.

The transmedia and the richness of the media mix invite exploration, a notion central to Quentin Gervasoni's text (in this volume): "the *Pokémon* experience can be understood as a "designed exploration" produced by the intersection of game design, marketing strategies, fan engagement and collective fandom production, which leads fans to navigate in the *Pokémon* universe, especially on the internet." Transmedia, the abundance of tie-ins and the incessant renewal of basic products (games, cartoons or films, cards) leads to exploration and discovery. The consumer is invited not only to consume a specific product but to discover the diversity of associated products. Even when more limited, transmedia invites the consumer to explore the different products and go beyond the reference universe, whether it is fantasy, dreamlike or realistic: to go from cartoons to comic albums for *PP*, to read the novel adaptation or play the game for *LLH*, to discover songs, book and animation for *SP*.

However, and perhaps this is the main thing, all products try in one way or another to use this transmedia or adaptive mechanism to cater for their audience. This mechanism of extension is obvious for *Pokémon*, which is in the tradition of the Japanese media mix. With *Petit Poilu*, the cartoon makes it possible to increase the audience, compared to a comic strip that addresses the parents/child cluster (Valérie-Inés de La Ville in this volume) and needs to have gained the interest of the parents (or other adult mediators such as librarians or teachers) before being able to address the children. This argument convinced the authors to move on to cartoons despite the risks of having less control. The aim is to guarantee the durability of their comic strip, which could benefit from spillovers from the cartoon's audience. This has a paradoxical effect: what was at the origin of the adaptation becomes a by-product, in a media mix that reverses the chronology in a new commercial mechanism making the cartoon the dominant medium, insofar as its audience is potentially the largest.

In *LLH* the serious game relates to promotion and educational enhancement of the cartoons. For *SP* it is rather a creative variation, in a combination of music and narrative without words except for the lyrics of the songs. However, this also allows the audience to be extended by allowing different audiences, depending on the medium, to hear the political message underlying this production.

2. Which child?

The transmedia or media mix can thus refer to a mechanism of audience extension, so as to address new audiences, for example in terms of age and gender, but also in terms of interest in a particular type of medium. As François and Garnier (in this volume) point out, one cannot dissociate the addressing of children from their representation in the various products, which all have the characteristic of featuring children, realistically in three, and more unrealistically in *PP*, which proposes a mix of child and animal.

Pokémon, originally formatted through video games and card games aimed at pre-adolescent males, has broadened its audience through cartoons and certain licensed products (such as stuffed animals) towards younger children and girls, for example by focusing on the Pikachu character and his cuteness (Brougère, 2004). In addition, its longevity and the appearance of new games, including in 2016 the "augmented reality smartphone video game *Pokémon GO*," have made it possible to develop an older audience of teenagers and young adults, without forgetting the effect of nostalgia for those who knew Pokémon when they were children and who maintain their interest in the franchise (Gervasoni in this volume).

The authors of *Petit Poilu* do not conceive the child as an audience to be conquered, but as an addressee to be respected, "taking children seriously," to use the expression of François and Garnier (in this volume) which defines *LLH* as following the same path. Thus a dimension of responsibility and transmission of values appears, even if these values are far from taking up the mainstream conception of a child to be protected and supervised, referring rather to the vision of an autonomous child, capable of making contact with strangers, of exploring the world in a mode close to truancy. It is interesting to note that other narrative means are very close to the vision of childhood that emerges from *LLH*. This cartoon is a realistic presentation of the children's point of view at an important moment in history. The addressing of the child is reinforced by the emphasis on child characters who are confronted with difficult situations that make them a mix between adults and children, as can be found in literature aimed at pre-teens and teenagers, such as Enid Blyton's *Famous Five*. This mechanism is the one that Chombart de Lauwe and Bellan (1979) had emphasized in works for children, with their child heroes having adult characteristics, particularly with regard to their autonomy from the adult world, which can undoubtedly be found in all the child characters in the four examples.

One can also note how the four productions try to overcome gender stereotypes. We mentioned this for *Po* even though it remains a product marked by a masculine dimension. The other products each try in their own way to avoid being part of a narrowly gendered logic, regardless of whether their heroes are male or a combination of girls and boys; for instance, in *LLH* the effort is made to highlight the role of girls.

It is therefore necessary to understand the relationship between addressing children and their representation. It can be considered that these works avoid being enclosed in an aseptic vision of the child, aiming to preserve him or her from any risk linked to imitation in the real world of what is seen in cartoons. For *LLH* "the rural context of the 40s also gave the opportunity to show children with greater freedom than those in today's cartoons: some children in *LLH* use knives, three of them go on a bicycle without any helmet, etc." (François and Garnier in this volume).

This issue can also be found in *Petit Poilu*, which distanced itself from the sanitized vision expected by the first Canadian producer and, after the break-up, maintained the atypical vision that emerged from the comic strip. We can also mention the debates around *Pokémon* and the criticism of supposed violence that was claimed to make it unsuitable for children. As for *SP*, it is far from mainstream products, particularly because of its dramatic ending and the desire to convey a message capable of transforming Canadian society in its relationship with indigenous populations.

Multimedia products not only address children, they also invite them to participate (Steinberg, 2012). Transmedia thus allows them to explore and deal with a variety of products. It is the products that are most oriented towards mass production that develop participation the most, insofar as participation contributes to the commercial development and multiplication of products. In the case of *Pokémon*, we can also highlight the commitment of the fans, who, more often than not, are no longer children: they contribute to the enrichment of the universe by offering "walkthroughs, encyclopedias, news about the franchise, as well as online communities to participate in, constituting resources for exploration and participation" (Gervasoni in this volume). The more children participate, the more they become involved in the consumption of products. Play is one of the ways to make this participation possible, hence the importance of recreational products for a franchise that allows children not only to receive a story but to (re)produce it. This is an issue that Ito (2010) raises by taking the example of Pokémon to underline the centrality of consumers' creative activity, a participation that has a learning dimension and the production of new meanings.

While *Pokémon* is the most participation-oriented product, if only because of its origin in a game and its radical media mix dimension, *Petit Poilu* and *LLH* offer limited by-products (games, various media) to involve their audience, and *SP*, in a different mode, invites the spectator to be also reader and listener, to move from one media to another.

3. Value, authorship and legitimation

The line we have evoked seems to be that of greater cultural legitimacy – as explained by François and Garnier (in this volume) – linked to more asserted artistic intentions. But behind this question we can grasp that of the place of the author and the control of the process. With *Pokémon* there are no authors, at most a creator of the game and of the original idea (Satoshi Tajiri); subsequently the author becomes pluralized and relates to the commercial control of copyright and franchising. However, the role of the fans who also wish to exercise control complicates this and creates a tension between the company holding the rights and the fans who contribute to enriching the universe, helping consumers to find their way around, commenting on new releases but sometimes criticizing and hijacking official proposals. Moving towards greater cultural legitimacy means moving towards a more assertive presence of authors. Beyond a collective work to produce a cartoon, *PP* and *LLH* are characterized by the presence of an author (a couple in the first case), the creators of the comic strip or the designer of the idea who try to maintain their conception and authorship through the intervention of many collaborators. Finally, *SP* is a testament to the control of the songwriter, accompanied by the author of the drawings, in the context of a product which is controlled by its authors.

Behind the author, the issue is that of intentions, as Brougère says about *PP* (in this volume). *Pokémon* is a collective product, as Condry (2013) was able to document. While there is copyright control, there are multiple authors, and the intentions do not have a single source. It is a flow that associates a multitude of authors, without any question of one author, even if the original idea, which he does not own, can be attributed to Satoshi Tajiri. In the production of the cartoon *Petit Poilu* the authors of the comic try to maintain the intentions even if they have to do so with the intentions of contributors, in particular the scriptwriters, the storyboarders or the director. They enjoy a status that gives them this power, but time and technical constraints make maintaining intentions a challenge that increases with the expansion of the field through the multiplication of episodes and tie-ins. The logic of *LLH*, a story and not multiple autonomous narratives, makes it possible to justify the necessary coherence and respect for intentions that guarantee it even if this means working with a team of professionals. The initial author undoubtedly succeeded here in ensuring that her intentions were taken up (but also enriched or clarified) by the various participants. What is important is not then total control but ensuring that the initial intentions are taken into account even if the original author does not intervene at all stages. With *SP*, where the number of participants is limited, it is a configuration where intentions are easier to maintain throughout the process with the presence of two authors, each with specific skills, lyrics and music for one, drawing for the other.

Legitimacy and control of authors are partly reflected in the place of education in these different universes. The importance of education follows the same progression along the same line. *Po* stimulates learning within the world and invites the public to learn *Pokémon* in a scholarly and encyclopedic setting. The authors of *PP* have a vision of education through truancy, which relates to the learning achieved by the character in his multiple encounters, allowing children to learn from the character's adventures. *LLH* combines entertainment and historical knowledge, which is underlined by the derivative game which aims to highlight the educational dimension of the series even though it was designed with entertainment in mind: "LLH was not designed just as an entertaining program, but also as an educational tool contributing to the culture of its audience, i.e. working for the memory of younger generations" (François and Garnier in this volume). *SP* seems to be moving away from pure entertainment to offer an expression that raises awareness of the situation experienced by indigenous children. It is about proposing an education with a transformative and militant purpose.

If there is education in the four universes it is in relation to the logic of entertainment, it is at most edutainment, none of the products mentioned being strictly an educational product, let alone a school product. And this is all the more so because in these four universes there is a distance from formal places of learning, or even a criticism of them (at least implied through their absence) and an openness towards other learning spaces, whether it be hunting and relationships with *pokémons*, the discovery of a fantasy world, the autonomy left by a war or traditional indigenous education.

Beyond their differences and the transmedia means used, these four products offer the vision of a child capable of learning by himself/herself, even if the more dramatic *SP* shows an individual failure that must serve the cause of social transformation. The underlying idea is then that one could just as easily learn with entertainment products that make use of transmedia richness.

Perhaps it is necessary to end this confrontation of four universes and their analysis by rejecting to some extent this line of growing cultural legitimization, and by highlighting the potential wealth, increased by the transmedial mechanism, that can be found in each of these products, including the one most oriented towards mass consumption. All four products are thought-provoking and invite consumers to explore their world as a means of access to a wide variety of forms of knowledge.

References

Brougère, G. (2004). How Much Is a Pokémon Worth? Pokémon in France. In J. Tobin (Ed.), *Pikachu's Global Adventure: The Rise and Fall of Pokémon* (pp. 187–208). Duke University Press.

Chombart de Lauwe, M.-J., & Bellan, C. (1979). Enfants de l'image: enfants personnages des médias, enfants réels. Payot.

Condry, I. (2013). *The Soul of Anime. Collaborative Creativity and Japan's Media Success Story*. Duke University Press.

Ito, M. (2010). *Mobilizing the Imagination in Everyday Play: The Case of Japanese Media Mixes*. Mashup Cultures, 79–97.

Jenkins, H. (2006). *Convergence Culture: When Old and New Media Collide*. New York University Press.

Steinberg, M. (2012). *Anime's Media Mix: Franchising Toys and Characters in Japan*. University of Minnesota Press.

Tobin, J. (Ed.). (2004). *Pikachu's Global Adventure: The Rise and Fall of Pokémon*. Duke University Press.

8

Is *Pokémon* for children?
How fan participation and transmedia practices transform age boundaries of audiences

Quentin Gervasoni

Although video games initially appeared as an adult hobby (Triclot, 2011), they then became associated with children and teenagers. Later on, video game audiences grew older again, with some young adults even playing the same games as children and adolescents to some extent (Cross, 2010). This porosity of age boundaries is part of a wider trend observable mainly in the leisure world that has been associated with transformations related to media, although Cross argues that "the cult of cool" is a core factor. *Pokémon* is usually known as a children's game, and even though its audience has grown older as old-time fans keep buying their products and actively engaging with the franchise, the video games are still mainly designed for children. Yet, the internet of *Pokémon* seems to be mainly populated by adolescents past the age of 15 and young adults, even up to 30 years old, according to my observations as well as my casual experience as a fan. Younger children are there, but are less visible. I argue in this chapter that this is a consequence of the fact that the online spaces I study, which are mainly the ones with the highest visibility[1], are built by adults and older adolescents, for adults and older adolescents. While the younger part of the *Pokémon* audience is likely to have less access to the internet, this does not suffice to explain the relative

---

1 I study some "niche" communities such as one based on a role-playing forum, however, the one I chose is the most populated and most visible one among the French role-playing forums, with several dozen to a hundred active members.

invisibility of younger adolescents[2]. As such, fans' online practices of circulation and enrichment of the *Pokémon* franchise are part of what makes it broaden its audience.

According to Jenkins, "a participatory culture is one which embraces the values of diversity and democracy through every aspect of our interactions with each other – one which assumes that we are capable of making decisions, collectively and individually, and that we should have the capacity to express ourselves through a broad range of different forms and practices" (Jenkins et al., 2015, p. 2). This idea of participatory culture as a movement toward a democratization of participation tends to minimize the fact that participation is primarily about power (Kelty, 2013). Indeed, adult-children relationships are grounded in power, as age constitutes a "principle of justification of action between adults and children" (Garnier, 2014, p. 453) which contributes towards the legitimizing of adult domination. This means that the study of the online participation of children, adolescent and adults of the same fandom must take adult domination into consideration. Thus, although it is undeniable that the internet has raised some opportunities for participation, it is important to keep in mind that the skills and resources required for such participation are not evenly distributed across social categories such as social class (Helsper and Eynon, 2013; North et al., 2008) and age (Meneses and Mominó, 2010), as, unsurprisingly, children need to develop their digital literacy, contrary to what the criticized concept of "digital natives" would suggest (Bennett et al., 2008; Lardellier, 2016)

Gary Alan Fine argues that the success of leisure organizations mainly depends on their ability to provide resources to participants (Fine, 1989). Resources can be material, such as infrastructures or physical tools, but also immaterial, such as knowledge. Explaining the success of *Pokémon* is beyond the scope of this chapter. Rather, Fine's Provisioning Theory incites people to consider the role played by resources produced online by The Pokémon Company (TPC) and by the *Pokémon* fans with respect to fans' participation and the age dynamics among the online fandom.

---

2 It is impossible for me to make a rigorous quantitative claim about the age stratifications of the French *Pokémon* audience, in general or online, since such data is unavailable and would require a complex and expensive methodology. France also lacks rigorous data on the use of internet by children and younger adolescents. The surveys conducted by the Ministry of Culture on the matter only concern people aged 15 or more (Donnat, 2009).

How do the resources provided by TPC and the online fan communities influence fan trajectories in the *Pokémon* world? How do those resources participate in framing the intergenerational online fan participation with *Pokémon*?

First, I present the *Pokémon* franchise and the data and methodology which this chapter draws on. In the second part, I argue that the *Pokémon* experience can be understood as a "designed exploration" produced by the intersection of game design, marketing strategies, fan engagement and collective fandom production, which leads fans to navigate in the *Pokémon* universe, especially on the internet. The third part emphasizes the role of fans in the construction of the internet of *Pokémon*, and the fourth part investigates what various barriers this induces for children's participation. The fifth part furthers this point by highlighting adult-targeted online communication by TPC.

1. Investigating the internet of *Pokémon*

Pokémon was launched in Japan in 1996[3] as a video game before it quickly became a media mix (Steinberg, 2012) with the production of an *anime* as well as a trading cards game. Satoshi Tajiri, the man behind the original games, was a fan of beetle collection and hoped to foster a taste for the exploration of nature in children of the new generation (Tobin, 2004, p. 57). After a period of "Pokémania" around the 2000s, the franchise was prophesied to fall out of trend (Tobin, 2004). Despite the apparent end of "Pokémania", the video games of the main *Pokémon* series[4] still usually hit 10 million sales each year[5]. *Pokémon* came back into the spotlight with the 2016 augmented reality smartphone video game *Pokémon GO*, which was the object of much academic focus, as it raised issues related to public health (Althoff et al., 2016; Ayers et al., 2016; Oidtman et al., 2016; Zach and Tussyadiah, 2017) and economic impact (Frith, 2017), and academics investigated the potential reasons

---

3 *Pokémon* official website: https://www.pokemon.com/us/about-pokemon/.

4 Fans refer to the series of *Pokémon* video games which are iterations of the first ones as the "main" series. They consist of a young adolescent (around eleven years old) setting out on a quest to become a *Pokémon* master by challenging trainers in *Pokémon* battles, while beating an evil team in the process.

5 See for instance the ranking for the best Nintendo 3DS sales (official website): https://www.nintendo.co.jp/ir/en/finance/software/3ds.html.

for its success (Keogh, 2017; Vella et al., 2019; Yang and Liu, 2017). Thus, while it is unlikely that *Pokémon* has managed to revive Japanese kids' taste for nature and beetle collection, it succeeded in encouraging many people to explore cities. However, the world that *Pokémon* fans usually wander through is rather the virtual, intertextual world of the franchise itself, and one of its widest spaces may be found online.

This chapter draws on a study of the francophone online fandom of *Pokémon*, focused mostly around the video games, which are at the center of the *Pokémon* media mix (Gervasoni, 2018; Ito, 2010), though the broader context of the franchise is taken into account[6]. Rather than mapping *a priori* the space of our fieldwork and its boundaries, I started with participant observation of a few online *Pokémon* fan spaces, and drew on the "orientations" (Boutet, 2008) of the users themselves who participate in constructing the internet of *Pokémon*[7]. This means our fieldwork is dynamic and the limits are drawn based on practical criteria but not taken for granted. In this chapter, I mostly focus on observational data gathered on four kinds of online spaces: Facebook fan groups, YouTube videos and comment sections, Twitter, and fan websites. This leaves out several major online spaces, such as Discord[8], and forums. According to my observations, which have been confirmed by several testimonies, forums have been largely emptied of their active users, who left to Discord. Discord is a very scattered space, with a very complex and messy organization. At this point of my research, my understanding of the Discord *Pokémon* fan ecosystem is too shallow for me to exploit the data rigorously.

This chapter also draws on 19 semi-directive interviews, most of which were conducted online with fans contacted in online fan communities and other online spaces not dedicated to Pokémon. Online, written interviews were done through Discord for most part, although a few of them were carried out on Messenger.

6 This chapter draws on an ongoing PhD thesis about the role of the internet in the attachment to the *Pokémon* franchise, under the supervision of Pascale Garnier and Vincent Berry of EXPERICE research center, Université Sorbonne Paris Nord 13. This PhD thesis benefits from a grant from LabEx ICCA.

7 I use the term "internet of *Pokémon*" to refer to the complex set of online spaces dedicated to *Pokémon*.

8 Discord is an application which allow users to easily create servers with direct message channels for written conversation, and vocal channels. Discord also allows private direct messages and calls.

Some face to face interviews were also conducted with pupils of the high school I used to work at (as a supervisor) in late 2017 and early 2018. The choice to use mostly online, written interviews is driven by several factors. It is easier to get fans to agree to an online interview than a face-to-face one, and it allows me to do away with geographical barriers. Although interviewees are less likely to be focused on the interview due to the multitasking habits of internet users (Béliard and Brossard, 2012), online interviews also allow them to opt for spontaneity rather than well-considered responses, and make it possible for the researcher to come back to the interviewee in later days in order to ask for clarifications, precisions, or finish aborted interviews. In this chapter, all quotes from interviews are translated from French. I try to respect the tone and style of the interviewee to a certain extent. Interviewees are also given a pseudonym.

2. The "designed exploration" of the *Pokémon* world

> I love the culture they created in the games, with a mythology, a history, events, as well as self-references between games. But most of all the exploration/discovery of new regions with each new game[9].

Kurt Squire argues that video games are to be considered as "*designed experiences*, in which participants learn through a grammar *doing* and *being*"[10] (Squire, 2006, p. 19), by which he means that any ideology or intent is injected during the development of a game, and gamers are active producers of a gaming experience that is framed by the design. *Pokémon*'s experience appears to be mainly focused around exploration and adventure. I use the term *designed exploration* here to examine the ways in which the *Pokémon* game design, and even *Pokémon* as a whole, incite and frames diverse exploration practices.

Indeed, one of the main pleasures of *Pokémon* stems from the possibility to explore a complex living world. As was noted earlier in the chapter, Satoshi Tajiri's goal when developing *Pokémon* was to give kids the will and the pleasure to explore nature. In this respect, *Pokémon GO* may look like the achievement of that original goal, although the game design favors the most urban areas over "nature" (Colley et al., 2017).

---

[9] Nicolas, 20, M.

[10] Italics in the original text.

Still, *Pokémon* video games from the main series are about setting on a quest to help a scientist learn everything about *pokémons*[11] by exploring the region. The *Pokémon anime*, another core part of the *Pokémon* media mix, also tells the story of a young adolescent who explores the world of *Pokémon*. The French and English versions of the emblematic opening of the first season both mention this fact[12]. Indeed, *Pokémon* was designed "not as something you consume, but as something you do" (Sefton-Green, 2004). *Pokémon* fans are incited to navigate through the fictional world of *Pokémon*, engaging with products of the *Pokémon* media mix (Steinberg, 2012). Becoming a fan of *Pokémon* involves learning about hundreds of creatures, gaining and sharing information within the community of fans. Such a quest for information may lead fans online (Vasquez, 2003). When she was younger, Marjorie[13] "loved to visit *Pokébip* to read articles about the *anime*". All the fans I interviewed converged in their discourses of how they started searching for online *Pokémon* content. At some point, they needed information about how to get past an obstacle, or about where to find a *pokémon*. They figured that the internet might be the place to find a solution.

For instance, Morgane[14] started checking *Pokémon*-related materials "at the end of primary school, to find walkthroughs on forums". The *designed exploration* of *Pokémon* is not only a product of media mix strategies which foster active engagement with cultural products, but also of game design itself. *Pokémon* contains several hidden and semi-hidden in-game features. For instance, *pokémons* have Individual Values (IVs), hidden values which influence the *pokémon*'s combat characteristics. Such hidden values can be evaluated thanks to online calculators[15]. In the recent games, some Non-Playable Characters

---

11 Although TPC prescribes the use of *Pokémon* both for referring to the brand and to the creatures, we consider it less ambiguous to write "*Pokémon*" when referring to the brand, and "*pokémons*" when referring to the creatures which inhabit the world of *Pokémon*.

12 The English and French lyrics of the *Pokémon* first season *anime* opening on the largest *Pokémon* fan-made wiki. https://bulbapedia.bulbagarden.net/wiki/Pok%C3%A9mon_Theme; https://www.pokepedia.fr/Th%C3%A8me_Pok%C3%A9mon.

13 20, F.

14 19, F.

15 For instance, using Serebii (a famous fan website) IV calculator. https://www.serebii.net/games/iv-calcsm.shtml.

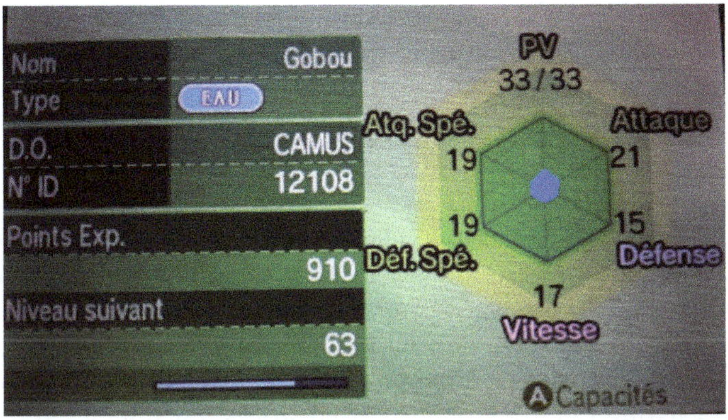

Fig. 1: Author's picture of a stats screen of a pokémon, Mudkip (Gobou in French), in *Pokémon Ultra Sun*. His nature is "Hasty," which lowers his Defense by 10 % and boosts its Speed (Vitesse) by 10 %, as suggests the colors in which they are written

(NPC) give hints about IVs, although one needs to know such values exist in order to understand what the NPC is talking about. Some other features are not completely hidden but not explicit either, such as "nature". Pokémons can be of one of 24 natures, 4 of which are "neutral". The 20 other natures give a 10 % boost to one battle characteristic[16] and reduces another one by the same amount (Hit Points are not affected by nature). This feature is not explicitly explained in the video games and players usually learn this in the fan websites and communities. The recent games give hints about the effects of natures in the User Interface. The boosted stat is written in red and the lowered one in blue (Fig. 1). However, the interviews revealed, not surprisingly, that only those who already know about the mechanics behind the "nature", realize what the colored stats mean, and some do not even realize they are differently colored. *Pokémon* is already too vast for a player to know everything about it by simply playing and passively consuming products. Such game design features make it even more important for players to engage more intensively, and

16 *Pokémons* have 6 battle characteristics: Hit Points, Attack, Defense, Special Attack, Special Defense, and Speed.

online participation is the most common way to further one's knowledge about the games thanks to the resources provided by fans.

Through the media mix strategies embraced by TPC and a variety of game design features, *Pokémon* incites a form of involvement which guides people toward "curious exploration" (Auray, 2017) of online spaces, which can be seen as a potential gateway to participation, or even a form of participation in itself (Jenkins et al., 2015), although it does not leave obvious traces. The fact that the content fans engage in once online are, in part, produced by other fans, suggests that the "designed exploration" is framed not only by TPC, but also by the collective action of fans. Although the exploration of online content appears to be of a different nature than that of the virtual spaces in-game, we argue that there is a continuity between both.

3. Fan digital labor

While *Pokémon* is a *copyrighted subculture* (Fine, 1989), and Nintendo is known for its conservative approach to copyright and authorship (Newman, 2018), much of the internet of *Pokémon* is the result of fans' *digital labor* (Scholz, 2013) through which they provide walkthroughs, encyclopedias, news about the franchise, as well as online communities to participate in, constituting resources for exploration and participation. Although TPC has now seriously entered the internet, putting effort into an official YouTube channel, advertising on Twitter with a Community Manager, fans have been pioneers in building the internet of *Pokémon*. Since 2013, *Pokémon* now has official channels in several languages including English and French, which boast millions of subscribers each. Yet, some *Pokémon* fan channels sometimes attract even more viewers than the official channel. The official French language *Pokémon* channel has 205,000 subscribers, and most of its videos about the video games get between 50,000 and 200,000 views. One of the most popular recent videos, the first *Pokémon Sword/Shield* trailer, got 203,915 views on November the 6th in 2019. At the same time, the Pokémon Trash YouTube channel has 800,000 subscribers, and most of its videos about the video games get over 100,000 views. A telling example is that of the video "Que cache le trailer de POKÉMON ÉPÉE BOUCLIER?" [What's behind the *Pokémon Sword/Shield* trailer?], published on July 8, 2019, 3 days after the trailer it refers to, which got more than 270,000 views. In comparison, the official trailer got slightly over

104,000 views[17]. Fan participation also results in a large body of fan production, such as artwork or even fan-made video games. In other words, fans are the active builders of the internet of *Pokémon*, and as such, they are the core providers of transmedia resources which enable and foster participation. In his study of 1980s role-playing games, Fine (1989) already observed this process: the players participated in providing resources in *copyrighted cultures*, however, he still insisted that it was highly framed by the game creators. While TPC plays a central role in shaping fans' activity and the way resources are organized, nonetheless the way the resources circulate, especially on the internet, is now determined in a more complex way by both the company and the fans. I avoid talking about a "coproduction" of the franchise and its online spaces, because such a term tends to hide the fact that the relations between fans and companies are ones of uneven power. For instance, when fans produce video games which gain too much attention, TPC does not hesitate to make legal threats and force the amateur to shut his game down[18].

Nonetheless, the internet has given the opportunity for fan communities to be active producers and to play an important role in the production and circulation of *Pokémon* content online. Fan websites are run by fans who recruit other fans to gather information about the franchise as fast as possible in order to share news, and as such become important sources of information for fans. Two of the main *Pokémon* French fan websites, Pokébip and Pokémon Trash, boast around 1–2 million visits a day, while the official website can be estimated to usually get about 1.5 million French visits a day[19]. Much like mainstream news outlets, fan websites draw on each other's work, as well as a network of information sources. For instance, in February 2019, a Twitter account which had leaked a conference a few weeks earlier tweeted the message "Pokémon

17 Every trailer on the official French-speaking channel is published in two versions, with one presented as the Belgian version, although I have not found any difference between those versions. Links to the Pokémon Trash video and the official trailer: https://www.youtube.com/watch?v=FVhgglVg7TQ; https://www.youtube.com/watch?v=qHLJXe8PUYs.

18 Pokémon Uranium, which boasted over a million downloads, may be the most famous recent example. https://www.polygon.com/2016/9/21/13007798/pokemon-uranium-shutdown-downloads-development-canceled.

19 According to SimilarWeb (https://www.similarweb.com). The 1.5 million number for the official website was obtained by applying the percentage of visits from France to the total.

soon". Pokékalos, a French fan website, shared that news through their own Twitter account, and other websites such as Pokémon Trash wrote articles in anticipation[20] of a supposed "Pokémon Direct"[21] coming soon. As a result, although TPC own *Pokémon* and are the first-hand producer of the franchise, the circulation of the information is largely done for free by fan websites which act as mediators. They are essential actors of the affective economics (Jenkins, 2006) of *Pokémon* in that they provide information about the franchise not only as fans, but also as fan communities. For instance, Pokémon Trash is known for its humorous editorial line which heavily draws on subcultural elements of internet and gaming communities, such as internet memes[22], which act as important shared references for online groups (Miltner, 2014) and constitute repertoires of practices (Gutiérrez and Rogoff, 2003), in that they become important aspects of participation in fan communities.

Indeed, not only are memes used in Pokémon Trash articles, but sharing memes is also one of the main activities in some Facebook fan groups and Discord servers. Pokémon Trash runs a Facebook Fan Page which advertises some of the website's content and shares some funny posts. A private group called Pokémon Trash Talk is associated to this Fan Page. While Discord servers are scattered online spaces, which are subject to very complex patterns of use, maybe in part because Discord written communication is done only through instant messages, Facebook group patterns of use are a little easier to characterize. Usually, people post and comment on "*Pokémon* memes." For a meme to qualify as a *Pokémon* meme and thus be relevant in a *Pokémon* fan group, it must at least feature a *Pokémon* in the image or be about *Pokémon*. Some memes

---

20 The article about the rumors on the Pokémon Trash website names and thanks Pokékalos for finding and sharing the information. https://www.pokemontrash.com/news/rumeurs-annonce-plus-coquiperl-go.

21 Nintendo broadcasts live streams called "Nintendo Direct" on streaming platforms such as YouTube and Twitch to reveal and discuss trailers, expose their marketing strategies, or simply communicate with their fanbase. *Pokémon* now has its own live streams called "Pokémon Direct."

22 Internet memes can be defined as "groups of digital items sharing common characteristics of content, form, and/or stance, which were created with awareness of each other and were circulated, imitated, and/or transformed via the Internet by many users" (Shifman, 2014, p. 41). The most common examples of memes rely on images called "templates," usually viral pictures, often took from popular culture media products, which are either posted in a fitting context or captioned in a slightly different way from the original.

use images from *Pokémon*, such as the "surprised Pikachu" meme which got famous online even outside of the *Pokémon* fandom[23]. "Surprised Pikachu" was originally a zoomed image of Pikachu from the *anime*, in which he had his mouth wide open and looked shocked. A lot of "surprised Pikachu" memes posted in *Pokémon* fan groups were not really about *Pokémon*, such as one which was painted on a car hood, with the caption "*Engine blows up*", surprised Pikachu thus representing the reaction of the car owner. Relevant *Pokémon* memes can also be more standard memes which do not draw on *Pokémon* content if the meaning of the meme has something to do with *Pokémon*. In such a context, fan groups largely function under an emotional regime (Reddy, 2001) of *fun*, that is, the activity of the group is largely driven by the production and the circulation of content with the purpose of producing a playful atmosphere.

As such, fans do not just circulate *Pokémon* content with some minor added value; they are, at a collective level, very active producers of *Pokémon* content. This fact is most obvious during periods in which new *Pokémon* content is revealed or commercialized, which triggers an emotional regime of *collective effervescence*, marked by an expression of *hype*[24], but also disappointment and even anger[25]. This emotional regime, alongside the regime of *fun*, is dominant in the live chats of live stream announcements on platforms such as YouTube and Twitch.tv, as well as in the comment section of YouTube trailers, for instance. Fan Discord servers and Facebook groups are also affected. In Facebook groups, the daily activity rises in the days subsequent to announcements and leaks[26]. Fan artists are also very active right after trailers and announcements. For instance, as soon as a new *pokémon* is revealed, many works of fan art are produced and circulated, and such fan art even seems to participate

23 Knowyourmeme page of "surprised Pikachu": https://knowyourmeme.com/memes/surprised-pikachu.

24 I use the term *hype* in the way fans do, to refer to the strong, collective feeling of anticipation and impatience. French fans also use the English word *hype*.

25 See the #Dexit and #BringBackNationalDex on Twitter for examples of strong, collective fan "voice" mobilization. These hashtags followed the announcement that not all former pokémons would be included in the next games.

26 Sometimes, information which TPC does not want to give away is leaked. The most recent, massive leak happened in November 2019. The entirety of the pokémons to be available in *Pokémon Sun & Moon*, including the new ones which had not yet been revealed in official trailers, were leaked.

in feeding the *hype*. Wooloo, a basic and cute sheep-like *pokémon*, which is the equivalent of usually bland, early-game *pokémons*, received an enthusiastic response and inspired fan artists a lot. The female playable character, with its Scottish look, also inspired fan artists, who drew on clichés about the Scottish such as their accent and their alleged love of alcohol, which guides much of the production of fan art of this character.

While *Pokémon* is a copyrighted culture and The Pokémon Company sometimes has a conservative stance concerning copyrights, nonetheless fans and fan communities participate actively in the production and circulation of *Pokémon* content online. Not only they do engage with resources provided by The Pokémon Company, but the fan communities have also built social infrastructures which in turn provide relevant resources for participation, such as repertoires of practices and online spaces for learning and mobilizing those repertoires, among other resources. In that sense, fans play an important part in the construction of an online ecosystem which favors the development of a participatory culture.

4. Barriers to children's participation

> So, everyone's 30 years old, you follow *Pokémon* like kids, the group's called trash talk, but we can't trash talk? It seems like we've got the elite over here[27].
>
> A game for crybabies who are going to have great fun grooming their pokémons, giving them hugs, and throwing a plastic pokéball at the TV screen, because It'S So CoOl[28].
>
> And on the other hand, we take away battles with wild pokémons from the game, and to make things worse we add some of this *Pokémon GO* shit.
>
> Can't wait for the next RPGs, hoping they'll think about their very first players[29].

These two instances of online posts by fans capture the tensions that pervade the *Pokémon* audience and fandom in relation to age. As the first

27 Facebook publication done by a member of the Pokémon Trash Talk group. He was banned or left the game thereafter.

28 I write in such a way to highlight the fact that the original French comment writes this phrase with a very bad spelling in order to make it look stupid and signify sarcasm. Another way people do so in the internet, which is much easier to translate, is by alternating upper and lower cases, usually in reference to the Mocking SpongeBob meme: https://knowyourmeme.com/photos/1267323-mocking-spongebob.

29 Comment on the first trailer for Pokémon Let's GO Pikachu/Eevee on the official French-speaking Pokémon YouTube channel. Link to the video: https://www.

one suggests, albeit exaggeratedly, the majority of the active members of the group are adult. On November 15, 2019, a member of the fan group Pokémon Trash Talk posted a survey asking for the age of other members. People voted in categories including 10–14, 14–18, 18–20, 20–25, 20–30 and 30+, alongside many less serious choices added by other members such as "age is just a number". While this is obviously not a rigorous survey, it can be used to determine broad tendencies. The highest age category was 20–25, with 232 answers, followed by 18–20 with 124 answers, 25–30 with 87 answers and 14–18 with 45 answers, while 10–14 only had one, although an earlier survey in September 2017 had 10 self-declared members aged 13 or less, all of whom did not seem to be lying according to their Facebook profile. These surveys suggest that the majority of the active members of the Facebook group are over 18 years old. Although this may not be the case of the *Pokémon* online audience in its entirety, Pokémon Trash Talk is arguably the biggest French *Pokémon* fan community, and the most visible. The second quote is a YouTube comment which aggressively exposes a stance which is held and expressed in hundreds of other comments on the official French-speaking YouTube channel. Online debates and discussing in *Pokémon* spaces can be perceived as so toxic that some interviewees have reported that they avoid participating openly due to this. Hamza[30] reports that "sometimes [he] refused to ask questions or share stuff on the website because [he] was afraid too many people would be mean to [him] or make fun of [him]". He later sent me a screenshot of a segment of the comment section of a post on the Pokémon Trash Talk group, in which someone asked what the use of a particular *Pokémon* move was. The first person who answered assumed he was asking about the effect of the move, and answered, in what was interpreted as an aggressive way, that one can use Google to find answers to such questions, before explaining the effect[31]. Hamza highlighted that "he's the kind of person because of whom [he doesn't] want to post stuff". If adults are deterred from participating due to a "toxic atmosphere," it is likely that some children would be too,

youtube.com/watch?v=8b-FZT9O6C4&list=PLVXmcWvDTic9Rq6I1oSu3PX-2lLwiE4sb_.

30 26, M.

31 In the main series of *Pokémon* video games, pokémons learn moves (4 at a time at most) which they can use in turn-based battles. Some of these moves are not very useful during usual solo play but can be strategically useful in player-versus-player, and their usefulness isn't always obvious.

especially when many fans claim that children are responsible for what they consider a decline in quality of *Pokémon* video games, which feeds mechanisms of exclusion analogous to some of the mechanisms which exclude women from online gaming spaces (Fox and Tang, 2017; Gray, 2012; Gray et al., 2017). Still, one must be wary of immediately drawing a parallel between these two forms of domination, as these claims require further inquiry.

The potential exclusion of children from online fan spaces and communities does not only arise from explicit exclusionary mechanisms such as an open hostility toward childhood. After all, the publication present in the first quote in this section was followed by several opposing comments. Members of Pokémon Trash Talk reminded the person who posted it that this was not a group for "trash talking", a discussion group of the Pokémon Trash community, hence the name. At the time, a member also noted that "there are also children in this group (some comments are made by 12 years old)". All the more, participation requires the acquisition of *repertoires of practices* (Gutiérrez and Rogoff, 2003) which are associated with specific subcultures. It is unlikely that younger adolescents and children understand most of the pop culture references which internet memes draw on or more subtle forms of humor which memes can convey, which require specific, new literacies (Procházka, 2014) to be fully grasped. Indeed, a lot of memes are references to typically adult worlds, such as workplace culture, drug, sex, and politics.

Not only do children and younger adolescents lack specific kinds of literacy, they also do not necessarily share the same interests and the same culture as older adolescents and adults. Even though the "cult of cool" has weakened age barriers in the domain of leisure (Cross, 2010), differences still subsist between the leisure worlds of children and adults, starting with some shared popular culture references which may be largely restricted to a generation or the other. Alban[32] had "acquired a writing 'style' (nothing exceptional but, as a result, nobody knew about my exact age until the first IRL gathering)". He had therefore developed skills which allowed him to be a news writer for the Pokémon Trash website when he was in junior high school, which means he had a status, and was recognized by the community. Yet, even though he did not always get talked down due to his age, "[he] felt little connection with their

[32] 26, M.

humor, their interests". Being an important member of the community was important for him as he was in a "violent school" and a difficult overall social context, he wrote during the interview. His status in the community allowed him to feel cool and important. In another context, the lack of connection with his older peers' culture would likely have been a barrier to his participation.

5. *Pokémon* is adult business

In the recent years, The Pokémon Company has put more efforts into their online presence. While their games still seem to be targeted at children, their online activity, paradoxically, seems to be turned towards their older fans. This results in tensions with regards to the reception of the online communication surrounding *Pokémon* video games.

One of the core reasons for lasting attachment of fans to the franchise is believed to be nostalgia (Carter, 2014; Keogh, 2017; Yang and Liu, 2017), as suggested by the success of *Pokémon GO* among adults. Nostalgia acts as a sort of disposition ready to be re-ignited on certain conditions. It is an emotion that has long been strongly commodified (Cross, 2017), and *Pokémon* plays heavily on it. A year after the creation of the official *Pokémon* YouTube channel, before announcing the *Pokémon Sun & Moon* games, the official channel posted a series of short videos called *Pokémon Generations* which acted as a tribute to the history of *Pokémon* generations. Among the trailers for *Pokémon Let's GO Pikachu & Eevee*, several videos were clearly made to appeal to nostalgia. One of the trailers shows Lavender Town, an iconic town of the first games famous for its creepy atmosphere, which inspired a famous creepypasta (creepy urban legend) about Japanese kids who allegedly committed suicide because of the music[33]. Pikachu is present in most games, and every generation has its "Pikachu-like" (Fig. 2) new *pokémon*, except for the second generation which brought Pikachu's baby counterpart, Pichu, which evolves into Pikachu. This can be understood not only as a tribute to the franchise mascot, but also as a tribute to the first generation. To a lesser extent, Charizard, another first-generation *pokémon* and one of the most iconic of the franchise, also had special treatment. It had several

33 "Lavender Town", Know Your Meme. 2011. http://knowyourmeme.com/memes/lavender-town-syndrome-creepypasta.

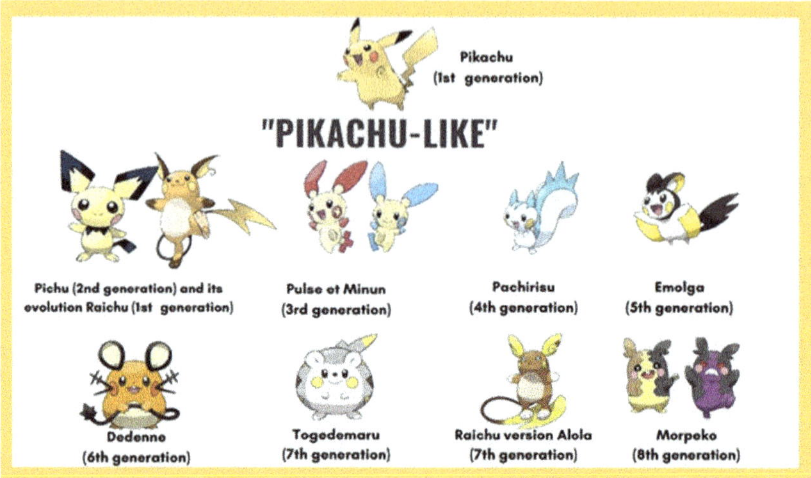

Fig. 2: Fan art presenting Pikachu and the "Pikachu-likes," as well as his two evolution forms and his baby form

special forms, such as two Mega-Evolutions, when not every *pokémon* had one and none other than it had two, and it also got a Gigamax form (Fig. 3). In the trailer which revealed its Gigamax form, four others are revealed, and they are also from first-generation, iconic *pokémons*. Not surprisingly, Pikachu is one of them, and its Gigamax form is made fat, which is understood by fans as a reference to the fat design of Pikachu in the first-generation games. Eevee, which was featured as one of the two main *pokémons* of the *Pokémon Let's GO* games, Meowth, which is famous for being a main antagonist of the animated series, and Butterfree, an important *pokémon* of the main protagonist in the first season of the *anime*, were also revealed to have a Gigamax form. Butterfree is famous for the emotional scene where he was released by Ash, the main protagonist, so that he could live with his romantic partner. This scene has become a meme which made fans cry, and still does.

More subtly, fans also noted that the fifth generation of games, *Pokémon Black/White*, was largely inspired by the first generation[34].

TPC communication also strongly draws on aspects of online culture which are unlikely to appeal to younger fans. Junichi Masuda, composer,

34 An article from Smogon, a fan website which mainly focuses on competitive play. The article argues based on the many similarities between 1st and 5th generation

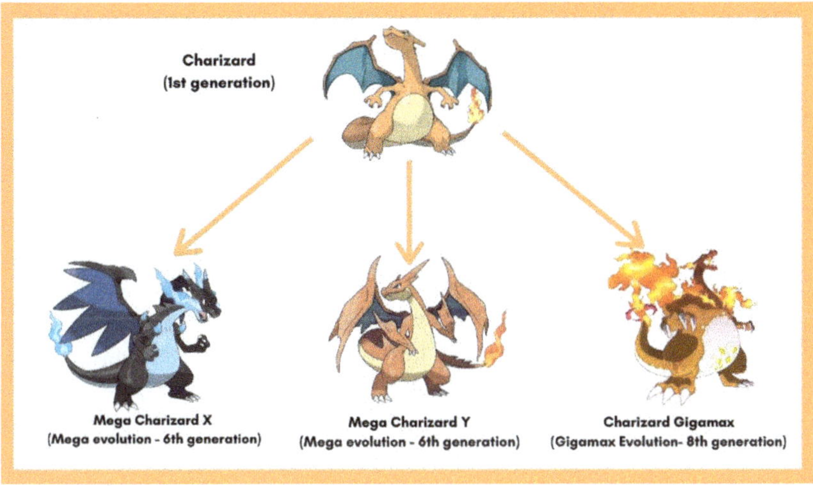

Fig. 3: Fan art presenting Charizard and his Mega-Evolutions and Gigamax form

director and producer of *Pokémon*, has the habit of sharing subtle clues about upcoming content. While exploration and riddles are not specifically adult leisure activities, he shares those on Twitter, which is mainly a network for adults and, to a lesser extent, older adolescents[35]. For instance, in February 2019, Masuda shared a screenshot from *Pokémon GO* which showed a *pokémon* which had 226 candies[36], without any context. Fans deduced that an announcement would happen on February 26, 2019 (2/26)[37], and were right. Another most telling case of online communication directed towards adult fans may be the 24-hour live stream which took place on the October 4, 2019. For most part, it was just a still view of a mysterious forest where nothing happened

games. https://www.smogon.com/smog/issue14/firstvsfifth.

35 According to the Pew Research Center, only 32 % of U.S. teens say they use Twitter, while the numbers are 85 % for YouTube and 51 % for Facebook, for instance. All the more, only 3 % say they use Twitter most often. https://www.pewresearch.org/internet/2018/05/31/teens-social-media-technology-2018/.

36 In *Pokémon GO*, the player amasses candies as he captures *pokémons*. Candies are used to evolve and boost *pokémons*.

37 An article from Pokémon Trash which relays the information: https://www.pokemontrash.com/news/rumeurs-et-tumeurs.

on screen. In 24 hours, only a handful of previous-generation *pokémons* and one from the current one, which had already been revealed in a previous trailer, appeared. The only novelty was the revealing of Galar Ponyta, the Galar form of a first-generation *pokémon*[38]. Hence only one new *pokémon* was revealed in a 24-hour stream. Fans, and especially fan websites which had to gather and share the information, followed the entire stream. This sort of commitment is unlikely to happen with children and younger adolescents, due to them not being able to do this, but it is also highly unlikely that they find enjoyment in doing so, not that adults seemed to enjoy it all that much.

Many adult fans believe that TPC does not really care about them when designing its video games, and still targets children. An employee of Asmodée, the French company in charge of the distribution of *Pokémon* cards, informally confirmed that TPC does not focus all that much on satisfying its adult fanbase. This may however be partly untrue, in that, although they do not seem to design their video games mainly for that part of their fanbase, they still provide resources which seem to be specifically targeted at them. In-game "Easter eggs" are common. For instance, in *Pokémon Sun* and *Pokémon Moon*, which were released in 2016, a feature allows players to take in-game pictures of wild *pokémons* and receive comments from fictional social network commenters. Sometimes one can get the comment "7.8/10 Too much water ¯_('-- ')_/¯", which is a reference to a popular IGN Entertainment Inc. review which became a famous internet meme[39]. More generally, the media mix strategy has long allowed *Pokémon* to broaden its audience's age range. For instance, the *Pokémon Adventure* manga is considered to target an audience older than that of the *anime*, for instance. It tackles more serious and political subjects, has humans targeted and hurt near death in *pokémon* battles, and some *pokémons* die gruesome deaths, such as an Arbok, a snake *pokémon*, which gets cut in pieces and lies in its blood. Another one, the last one before the release of the games, revealed that the game featured famous human characters from the first generation of games and manga.

38 An article from Pokémon Trash was written live by members of the writing team: https://www.pokemontrash.com/news/les-24h-du-pokmans.

39 An IGN article which lists *Pokémon Sun & Moon* Easter eggs, including the one about the IGN review: https://www.ign.com/wikis/pokemon-sun-pokemon-moon/Easter_Eggs_and_References#Other_References.

6. Children's participation in the adult fandom of *Pokémon*

Throughout this chapter, I have made the case that, by circulating and transforming resources provided by TPC, *Pokémon* fans and fan communities are essential actors of the enrichment of the "Poke-world" (Sefton-Green, 2004), by taking part in cooperation networks similar to those observed in "art worlds" (Becker, 1982). In this "Poke-world", fans engage in a "designed exploration", induced by *Pokémon* game design and its media mix nature, and framed by the online ecosystem of resources for participation which results from the combination of industrial production and fans' "digital labor" (Scholz, 2013). Among such resources are the vast and varied information fans have collectively gathered and shared in online databases and websites, as well as the many fan productions such as fan art and fan-made video games. These resources act as a support both for the initial gaming experience, with walkthroughs and guides, and for the enrichment of gaming possibilities.

Alongside informational resources are social resources, such as fan communities, which allow fans to build their identity as a fan by participating in communities of practice (Lave and Wenger, 1991) in varying degrees, by writing news, sharing information, or simply publishing internet memes and participating in debates. This makes *Pokémon*, an initially single-player game for the most part, into a collective experience. Active, public participation, however, is limited by dynamics of exclusion. The perceived toxicity of some internet spaces can be a deterrent for some fans, and the hostile discourse toward children makes the internet of *Pokémon* a space which paradoxically may not be completely fit for children's participation.

Since this chapter draws mostly on qualitative data, and quantitative data in online participation is very difficult to grasp, especially regarding children, as well as being scarce and of limited quality, I cannot say with certainty that children are deterred from participating online due to all of this. Indeed, they are likely to be in lower numbers in the first place in the online spaces I observe. They may also participate in online *Pokémon* spaces which I have not explored yet. Still, since I investigated the spaces with highest visibility, their absence there is important to note. Furthermore, however great or small the effect is which the exclusionary dimension of the resources has on children's participation, the internet of *Pokémon* still appears to be an age-segregated space built largely by adults, for adults.

References

Althoff, T., White, R. W. & Horvitz, E. (2016). Influence of Pokémon Go on Physical Activity: Study and Implications. *Journal of Medical Internet Research, 18*(12). https://doi.org/10.2196/jmir.6759

Auray, N. (2017). *L'Alerte ou l'enquête: une sociologie pragmatique du numérique*. Presses des Mines via OpenEdition.

Ayers, J. W., Leas, E. C., Dredze, M., Allem, J.-P., Grabowski, J. G. & Hill, L. (2016). Pokémon GO: A New Distraction for Drivers and Pedestrians. *JAMA Internal Medicine, 176*(12), 1865–1866.

Becker, H. S. (1982). *Art Worlds*. University of California Press.

Béliard, A.-S. & Brossard, B. (2012). Internet et la méthode ethnographique: l'utilisation des messageries instantanées dans le cadre d'une enquête de terrain. *Genèses, 88*(3), 114. https://doi.org/10.3917/gen.088.0114

Bennett, S., Maton, K., & Kervin, L. (2008). The 'Digital Natives' Debate: A Critical Review of the Evidence. *British Journal of Educational Technology, 39*(5), 775–786.

Boutet, M. (2008). S'orienter dans les espaces sociaux en ligne. L'exemple d'un jeu. *Sociologie du travail, 50*(4), 447–470.

Carter, L. (2014). Pokémon and a Fandom of Nostalgia. *Reflexive Horizons: Film Philosophy and the Moving Image*. http://www.reflexivehorizons.com/2014/03/24/pokemon-and-a-fandom-of-nostalgia/

Colley, A., Wenig, N., Wenig, D., Hecht, B., Schöning, J., Thebault-Spieker, J., Lin, A. Y., Degraen, D., Fischman, B., Häkkilä, J., Kuehl, K., Nisi, V., & Nunes, N. J. (2017). The Geography of Pokémon GO: Beneficial and Problematic Effects on Places and Movement. *Proceedings of the 2017 CHI Conference on Human Factors in Computing Systems – CHI '17*, 1179–1192. https://doi.org/10.1145/3025453.3025495

Cross, G. (2010). Valves of Adult Desire: The Regulation and Incitement of Children's Consumption. In D. Buckingham & V. Tingstad (Eds.), *Childhood and Consumer Culture* (pp. 17–30). Springer.

Cross, G. (2017). Nostalgic Collections. *Consumption Markets & Culture, 20*(2), 101–106.

Donnat, O. (2009). Les pratiques culturelles des Français à l'ère numérique. *Culture Études, 5*, 1–12.

Fine, G. A. (1989). Mobilizing Fun: Provisioning Resources in Leisure Worlds. *Sociology of Sport Journal, 6*(4), 319–334. https://doi.org/10.1123/ssj.6.4.319

Fox, J. & Tang, W. Y. (2017). Women's Experiences with General and Sexual Harassment in Online Video Games: Rumination, Organizational Responsiveness, Withdrawal, and Coping Strategies. *New Media & Society, 19*(8), 1290–1307. https://doi.org/10.1177/1461444816635778

Frith, J. (2017). The Digital "Lure": Small Businesses and *Pokémon Go. Mobile Media & Communication, 5*(1), 51–54. https://doi.org/10.1177/2050157916677861

Garnier, P. (2014). Childhood as a Question of Critiques and Justifications: Insights into Boltanski's Sociology. *Childhood, 21*(4), 447–460. https://doi.org/10.1177/0907568213491770

Gervasoni, Q. (2018). Pokémon as Hybrid, Virtual Toys: Friends, Foes or Tools? In G. Brougère & M. Allen (Eds.), *8th International Toy Research Association World Conference*. https://hal-univ-paris13.archives-ouvertes.fr/hal-02170789

Gray, K. L. (2012). Intersecting Oppressions and online Communities: Examining the Experiences of Women of Color in Xbox Live. *Information, Communication & Society, 15*(3), 411–428. https://doi.org/10.1080/1369118X.2011.642401

Gray, K. L., Buyukozturk, B., & Hill, Z. G. (2017). Blurring the Boundaries: Using Gamergate to Examine "Real" and Symbolic Violence against Women in Contemporary Gaming Culture. *Sociology Compass, 11*(3). https://doi.org/10.1111/soc4.12458

Gutiérrez, K. D., & Rogoff, B. (2003). Cultural Ways of Learning: Individual Traits or Repertoires of Practice. *Educational Researcher, 32*(5), 19–25.

Helsper, E. J. & Eynon, R. (2013). Distinct Skill Pathways to Digital Engagement. *European Journal of Communication, 28*(6), 696–713. https://doi.org/10.1177/0267323113499113

Ito, M. (2010). Mobilizing the Imagination in Everyday Play: The Case of Japanese Media Mixes. *Mashup Cultures*, 79–97.

Jenkins, H. (2006). *Convergence Culture: Where Old and New Media Collide.* NYU Press.

Jenkins, H., Ito, M., & Boyd, D. (2015). *Participatory Culture in a Networked Era: A Conversation on Youth, Learning, Commerce, and Politics.* John Wiley & Sons.

Kelty, C. M. (2013). From Participation to Power. In A. Delwiche & J. Jacobs Henderson (Eds.), *The Participatory Cultures Handbook* (pp. 22–32). Routledge.

Keogh, B. (2017). Pokémon Go, the Novelty of Nostalgia, and the Ubiquity of the Smartphone. *Mobile Media & Communication*, *5*(1), 38–41.

Lardellier, P. (2016). *Génération 3.0. Enfants et ados à l'ère des cultures numérisées.* EMS éditions.

Lave, J. & Wenger, E. (1991). *Situated Learning: Legitimate Peripheral Participation.* Cambridge University Press.

Meneses, J. & Mominó, J. M. (2010). Putting Digital Literacy in Practice: How Schools Contribute to Digital Inclusion in the Network Society. *The Information Society*, *26*(3), 197–208. https://doi.org/10.1080/01972241003712231

Miltner, K. M. (2014). "There's No Place for Lulz on LOLCats": The Role of Genre, Gender, and Group Identity in the Interpretation and Enjoyment of an Internet Meme. *First Monday*, *19*(8). https://doi.org/10.5210/fm.v19i8.5391

Newman, J. (2018). Kaizo Mario Maker: ROM Hacking, Abusive Game Design and Nintendo's *Super Mario Maker*. *Convergence: The International Journal of Research into New Media Technologies*, *24*(4), 339–356. https://doi.org/10.1177/1354856516677540

North, S., Snyder, I., & Bulfin, S. (2008). Digital Tastes: Social Class and Young People's Technology Use. *Information, Communication & Society*, *11*(7), 895–911. https://doi.org/10.1080/13691180802109006

Oidtman, R. J., Christofferson, R. C., Quirine, A., Espana, G., Kraemer, M. U., Tatem, A., Barker, C. M., & Perkins, T. A. (2016). Pokémon Go and Exposure to Mosquito-Borne Diseases: How Not to Catch 'Em All. *PLoS Currents, 8.*

Procházka, O. (2014). Internet Memes – A New Literacy? *Ostrava Journal of English Philology*, *6*(1), 53–74.

Reddy, W. M. (2001). *The Navigation of Feeling: A Framework for the History of Emotions*. Cambridge University Press.

Scholz, T. (Ed.). (2013). *Digital Labor: The Internet as Playground and Factory*. Routledge.

Sefton-Green, J. (2004). Initiation Rites: A Small Boy in a Poke-world. In J. Tobin (Ed.), *Pikachu's Global Adventure: The Rise and Fall of Pokémon* (pp. 141–164). Duke University Press.

Squire, K. (2006). From Content to Context: Videogames as Designed Experience. *Educational Researcher, 35*(8), 19–29.

Steinberg, M. (2012). *Anime's Media Mix: Franchising Toys and Characters in Japan*. University of Minnesota Press.

Tobin, J. (Ed.). (2004). *Pikachu's Global Adventure: The Rise and Fall of Pokémon*. Duke University Press.

Triclot, M. (2011). *Philosophie des jeux vidéo*. Zones.

Vasquez, V. (2003). What Pokémon Can Teach Us about Learning and Literacy. *Language Arts, 81*(2), 118–125.

Vella, K., Johnson, D., Cheng, V. W. S., Davenport, T., Mitchell, J., Klarkowski, M., & Phillips, C. (2019). A Sense of Belonging: Pokémon GO and Social Connectedness. *Games and Culture, 14*(6), 583–603. https://doi.org/10.1177/1555412017719973

Yang, C. & Liu, D. (2017). Motives Matter: Motives for Playing Pokémon Go and Implications for Well-Being. *Cyberpsychology, Behavior, and Social Networking, 20*(1), 52–57.

Zach, F. J. & Tussyadiah, I. P. (2017). To Catch Them All – The (un) Intended Consequences of Pokémon GO on Mobility, Consumption, and Wellbeing. In R. Schegg & B. Stangl (Eds.), *Information and Communication Technologies in Tourism* (pp. 217–227). Springer.

9

Maintaining an author's position during media circulation: The case of an animated cartoon created from a comic strip[1]

Gilles Brougère

"European-style authors don't just let go of their baby like that." (A scriptwriter)

"We put ourselves in the children's shoes in a very empathetic way, like that, in a very natural way." (PB)

"Authorship is therefore about control, power, and management of meaning and of people as much as it is about creativity and innovation" (Johnson and Gray, 2013, p. 4)

1. Presentation of *Petit Poilu* and research framework

Petit Poilu (Little Furry) is a comic strip by Pierre Bailly (PB, cartoonist) and Céline Fraipont (CF, scriptwriter) published by Dupuis and aimed at children who cannot read yet (it is a silent comic strip, i.e. one without text), from 3 to 6 years old, even if the authors do not want to lock themselves into what they consider to be a straitjacket, and also see a wider potential audience. Addressing young children (preschoolers) is a characteristic of the product that not only fortifies but also shifts the traditional addressee of the comic strip. As part of research on product

---

1 The topics of this text were the subject of a communications under the title "*Petit Poilu s'anime: d'une bande dessinée d'auteur(s) à la production collective d'un dessin animé*" during the International Conference "*La fabrique de l'Animation. Une industrie culturelle saisie par les sciences sociales*" Université Sorbonne Nouvelle, June 6, 2017, published in Brougère, 2019.

design for children (CoCirPE)[2] a study on this aspect was the subject of a first publication (Brougère, 2018).

It highlighted a very strong collaboration between the scriptwriter and the cartoonist, who do not work in a separate manner, distinguishing between two phases (the script and the drawing), but instead through various interactions back and forth, until the feeling is gained, seemingly based on intuition, that it works. If the story and the universe in which it takes place are different each time, there is a template that is at the very origin of the concept and to which the authors are very attached, insofar as it characterizes the singularity of their work. Thus in each album (and then in each episode of the cartoon) the following moments are presented: rituals of getting up, going out of the family home, a transfer to another world, a meeting and a challenge, crying and leaving the picture with his mother, solving the problem, building a friendship translated by a gift that *Petit Poilu* brings home, a quick return, eating and sleeping with the gift. This matrix and more generally the work are conceived in relation to the child recipient.

This addressing relates first of all to the couple's child, to whom they wished to pass on their passion for comics. But this transmission only works insofar as the authors feel like children: it is a matter of putting themselves in the children's shoes, of finding the child within them. The author's dimension and the addressing of the child are articulated by being a little childlike oneself. But what makes such a comic book specific, which is not the case with the television series, is that the child, in order to access it in most cases, is dependent on the adult, which implies addressing adults, parents or prescribing teachers, which results in the presence of an educational dimension with which the authors are ambivalent. On the one hand, they wish to transmit values and accept the idea of a comic book which, due to the absence of text and esthetic choices, allows the child reader autonomy. On the other hand, the educational conception that is reflected in the albums is that of truancy, a school of life far removed from publisher's strategies of finding a place for these albums within the nursery school with very formal educational proposals (cards for example). The educational dimension can be set aside in the cartoon or at least remain in a mechanism of informal learning.

---

2 *Conception et circulation des produits pour enfants*, a study financed by Labex ICCA (Laboratoire d'excellence Industries culturelles et création artistique).

Finally, the analysis of the production of comic strips, due to the development of merchandising within the framework of a mail order system available to the publisher, has shown authors who are not hostile to the circulation of their creation on various media but who at the same time are careful to ensure that this process takes place within the framework of maintaining the values and meaning of their creation. They assert themselves as the authors of a work that must set the tone for what circulates and not of a character that could circulate without reference to the comic. Authors want to keep their hand on meaning and not see the production of new meanings emerge according to the diversity of media and supports: "They are authors who are extremely interventionist, who have a very precise idea of what they want to do with their character, their brand, and they do it very well." (Marketing Manager, *Petit Poilu*)

In this chapter we will focus on the second phase of the study, which allowed us to follow the realization of the cartoon. Indeed, after an unsuccessful attempt with a Canadian channel, *Petit Poilu* became a cartoon financed by the Canal+ group and RTBF, producers and broadcasters of the series. It is a 2D cartoon of 78 7-minute episodes (including credits).

In this case study we will analyze the relations or articulation between, on the one hand, the collective nature of the production of the cartoon, which contrasts with the more solitary work of creating a comic strip studied in the first phase mentioned above, and the affirmation or rather the management of a position of author(s), a dual author, scriptwriter and cartoonist, marked by the question of addressing the child as we have analyzed for the comic strip itself. In the context of the transition of the latter to a cartoon, a collective work, the authors risk disappearing in a new creative process that could produce a distancing from their original work. How do the authors try, with varying degrees of success, to maintain their status as "European" authors in this media circulation, to maintain the values and meaning of the comic and to ensure that their intentions presented in the comic are still present in the cartoon?

After having discussed the methodology of the study, we will present some of its results, starting with the question of the passage from comics to cartoons, we will next, pursuing this relation with the original and legitimate source, investigate the author's position combined with the addressing of children, which will lead us to track down the question of intentions and their clarification. We will illustrate this based on the question of sound, which has the particular feature that it is an original element in relation to the albums (which, moreover, are silent and therefore not only without sound but also without speech), before discussing the limited control of authors in the framework of a collaboration rather than a real cooperation.

2. Research methodology

We were able to follow the production of the animated cartoon in real time over two years. We combined interviews and observations, and also carried out what we called interview-observations, i.e. interviews that took place during parts of the work and when certain tasks were being carried out whilst the interviewer was present. Almost everyone involved was interviewed, including the two authors of the comic books who were also involved in the creation of the animated cartoon, the script manager, three scriptwriters, the production manager, the director, the animation managers, the multi-media manager, contacts in the two co-producing TV channels and the royalties manager. We carried out interview-observations with a storyboarder, the design manager of the cartoon animation, the musicians and the sound designer. The observations involved several meetings between the authors and the animators, between the director and the authors, plus the recording of the voice tests, the animation studio in Belgium, the recording of the final voices, the mixing, the celebratory party at the end of the pre-production phase – all were accompanied by informal interviews. This chapter will use only a small part of the data collected to analyze them in relation to the issue mentioned above. As a starting point we based our research on certain theoretical elements concerning addressing children (Brougère and François, 2018). Our approach was that of the "adaptive theory" of Derek Layder (1998), which consists of enriching the theory of new references as well as transforming or producing concepts from data.

Indeed, in this chapter the approach is strongly empirical, the theoretical references being called upon only to interpret, if necessary, the data without a specific theoretical framework having preceded their collection. As a starting point, we will simply adhere to Caldwell's remark (2008, p. 2) "that industrial reflexivity needs to be understood as forms of local cultural negotiation and expression as well, for the lived production communities that create films, programs, 'making-ofs', behind-the-scenes, docs, DVD bonus tracks, show-biz reports, and cross media film/TV franchises." We will try, despite the difficulty in the context of a reduced format of one chapter, to report on the ethnographic dimension of the approach, to rely as much as possible on the actors' point of view.

3. From the comic books to the animated cartoon

We can highlight as a starting point the continuity between the comic books and the animated cartoon, which put the authors in a position of strength. Each book corresponded to a single episode and they were able to adapt 17 out of 18 books published at this time with few changes and use the scenarios from two further books. This silent strip limits the elliptical closures in order to ensure that the story is understood; thus it was quite easy to transpose into an animated cartoon. This continuity gives an important place to authors by limiting translation work. The comic books (not just the character and the underlying values but also the sequence of each episode and their matrix, which we mentioned) served as a model: particularly as this production was taken on following the initial failure of a Canadian team who modified certain aspects of the comic books enormously and excluded the authors; this led them to be more attentive, realizing that by accepting one change after another, before vetoing it, they risked totally transforming their comic strip into something else, in this case, according to the scriptwriter, a "male Hello Kitty who spends his time saying that he loves everyone."

However, this continuity cannot obscure the difference between two ways of telling a story. As a storyboarder pointed out, in comics where there is total freedom, there is no limit to creativity, whereas the animated cartoon will have limits, particularly relating to cost, which are constraints (limitation of characters, the sets, certain movements, etc.). Thus, using the example given by a scriptwriter, in a comic a character can change clothes as many times as one likes, whereas this might prove to be too expensive in the case of an animated cartoon. However, despite these differences, which for the most part reflect the limits of a budget for this type of production intended for television, a scriptwriter emphasized the fundamental continuity between the two:

> They made us a 'bible' but in reality, their comic is very close to the animation. In effect the adaptation is minimal. There was no need to do anything very different with it because they had kept to the system of a puppet theatre. There is not much scenery, no depth of field, it remains as little boxes and it's as if the camera moved from one to the next. I think it remains pretty close to their comic books.

According to the director this continuity relates to the expectations of the child audience:

> I put myself in the place of the child who reads *Petit Poilu*. He is told "there's going to be an animated cartoon". That happened to me when I was little; I had comic book heroes who I loved and suddenly I heard that there was going to be an animated cartoon. It was great! I said to myself "I'm going to see the same stories on the screen, with music". I remember how often I was disappointed; it was nothing like the comic because they had changed so many things, it was a new project. The idea for *Petit Poilu* was to say "I want the child, who knows the books by heart, to find them again in the images".

4. An authorial position

The similarity to the comic books and the fact that the adaptation was minimal established the comic books as direct models and empowered the authors, who were ensuring this continuity, to start with the adaptation of their 17 books.

However the position of authorship created by the authors was complex. On the one hand, concerning their work with their comic books, they criticize the image of the all-powerful author and illustrated the recycling aspect of their work and their use of prior ideas from the comics of other authors: "For me, all those who tell stories, it's just a mix of how they feel and a recycling of ideas" (PB).

On the other hand, they endeavored to control the production of the animated cartoon, assuming authorship: they checked and modified the 59 original scenarios created by the scriptwriters, and asked for and obtained the status of co-director of the animated cartoon for the cartoonist of the comic books.

Their position as authors was tested in the animated cartoon project led by a Canadian chain which requested multiple changes. The authors proposed numerous adjustments until a split became inevitable, especially when the Canadian producer actually questioned what the authors had to do with the matter!

As soon as the comic books contract was signed, the authors asked to be involved in the animated cartoon project where appropriate; this desire was expressed well in advance to ensure the animated cartoon would not be made without them and to assert their position as authors.

In fact, in the authors' opinion all adaptations of comics into animated cartoons had been failures, hence their request to be co-directors.

According to them it was less a question of claiming their position as authors but more of defending the quality and integrity of their comic books, which nevertheless amounted to them exercising their moral right with regard to authorship and copyright:

> I do not think it's a question of being the author or not, I think it's more a question of wanting the project to achieve a certain standard. The comic strip was loved so much that we want the animated cartoon to be just as good. Therefore our requirements are evident, based more on a demand for quality rather than of being the authors. (PB)

The authors also made it clear that they were not "artists" whose intention was to complain, but that they were there to serve the public and ensure that the technical and artistic solutions chosen were made based on a sense of communication. This is the case of the choice made of the type of drawing on the first album after many different styles had been tried. It is a desire to choose the technique at the service of the message and the public, which brings the question of the author back to that of addressing the public, here to children. The author is not an artist but the one who guarantees that the message will be well understood by the target audience, which is related to the authors' integration in the popular comic strip symbolized by their publisher (Dupuis) as opposed to an artistic comic strip defined as far away from the public. It is in this context that they are authors without really wanting to be.

- I don't feel like an author, from the very beginning, so that already answers your question. (PB)
- I can't really define myself with that label either, I feel like I'm carrying a project that's us, but I'm not looking over my shoulder. (CF)
- We're demanding with ourselves in our work and we ask people to be almost as demanding as we are, because it's not easy, but it's in terms of requirements, on concrete things, that it's played out, it's not at all on the… (PB)

Consequently, it is a question of preventing others from setting themselves up as authors in the context of illegitimate appropriation. If they question the notion of authorship, it is not to give others the opportunity to take this position. However, this position refers to the role they give themselves with regard to taking the public into account. No one but them would bring up the issue of addressing children by constantly putting themselves in children's shoes in a very empathetic way:

- They don't talk about it; nobody talks about it. They're on the technical side. (CF)
- In my comments I often talk about the young spectator, the kid, the thing… careful because the young spectator won't have enough eyes to understand that… the kid will never understand that… careful you mustn't take him for an idiot… (PB)
- All the time, me too, in the scenarios… (CF)
- … the children won't understand, and I think that's a… we put ourselves in the children's shoes in a very empathetic way, like that, in a very natural way… (PB)

They are therefore, within the framework of the collective, the guarantors of a certain way of considering children, which sets them up as authors who are responsible for taking the final addressee into account. The author is not there to enhance himself but to enhance the recipient, which constitutes the whole paradox of the position:

> So I think you really have to trust them and that's what really annoys me is to be faced with adults who make a product for children and don't consider the children to be up to the same level as what we put in their… and so that's where it's tricky because we're the guarantors of that, but chances are it's still a bit of a miss, you know. I'm still not sure that the show will be successful in terms of what we want to transmit. We remain watchful, it's an everyday job and that's what's tiring. (CF)

5. The necessary explanation of intentions

Unlike the case of the comic books in which the two authors controlled the essentials of the process, and outside interventions were marginal and had no influence on the actual theme of the books, for the animated cartoon they had to work within a complex system of production in which numerous people were involved. Whilst in the comic there is no gap between the intention and the results of the work (rather that the intentions are only those that can be deduced from the work[3]), when producing an animated cartoon the authors were obliged to make their

---

3 This should be qualified by mentioning the collaboration between the scriptwriter, who produces an illustrated storyboard, and the cartoonist. There are therefore

intentions explicit, and in writing (e.g. e-mails, briefs, literary "bible", corrections, sketches of drawings) and intervene in person (e.g. telephone or video conferences, appointments and meetings).

The question of intentions being understood via material supports and not through the author's thought process, making the intentions objective, is borrowed from the analyses of Burnett (2013). Although the intentions of the authors were already present in the strip cartoon (they emphasized the need for all the contributors to read the comic books which were present in every workplace and a scanned version was available online for those who worked from home), they were not necessarily understandable to everyone. Hence the need for constant explanation requiring the producer to circulate very long emails received from the authors. The analysis of the data highlights the omnipresence of the issue of, and even the term, "intentions".

Thus, during a meeting with the animators in the studio in Belgium, the authors' presentation of the series' features immediately mentions the main intentions: "*Petit Poilu* is a 2D digital animated television series for preschool children. However, the stories, which are without mushiness and are as eccentric as one could wish, are aimed at everyone." From the outset, the definition of the series is accompanied by intentions that strongly refer to addressing children: not being locked into an infantilism rejected by the authors. A certain way of addressing children without doing so as criticized products do. And the rest of the speech emphasizes intentions rather than technical details: "It is by plunging into the depths of himself, listening to his creativity, and above all, by developing his empathy towards the other characters, that *Petit Poilu* will find the way to overcome the obstacles and thus… will grow up by a hair's breadth!" The animators are therefore asked to respect and translate the intentions of the authors who came for this.

According to the authors it was a case of avoiding, among other things, a schmaltzy vision of a product intended for children, and of conveying a certain view of this public for whom the authors considered themselves to be the guarantors. This refers back to the interviews that effectively made the authors the "people to turn to" with regard to how to address children. However, the wish to respect the sense of the comic

---

traces of the scriptwriter's intentions, which were moreover shown on the occasion of a travelling exhibition (intended for libraries) on the *Petit Poilu* albums.

led the scriptwriter to intervene regularly in the scenarios of the new episodes:

> The problem I had at the beginning was that I realized very quickly when the story wasn't good and continued not to be good and I felt it was getting bogged down, that I was tending to change the story myself and sometimes quite a lot of the story… It's true that at some point having done it a few times we discussed it. I said there is a problem; I am re-working the stories, sometimes by up to 70%, for people who afterwards are going to retain copyright on this animated cartoon, which will be accepted even though I have changed 70% of the story. What should we do? (CF)

When it comes to authorship the question of copyright is never far away. With regard to the images it was a question of defining the style of each episode so that it conformed with what the authors were expecting: "I define the scenery, the settings, how the characters come in, go out, how it will be staged… a kind of first draft so that it fits a little in the style of *Petit Poilu*", a means of getting across the intentions through drawing. "That was the main difficulty, it was to make everyone understand that we're not in the limelight, neither in perspective nor in volume, that we're not in a flashy esthetic, we're in a flattening of a narrative process".

The whole problem with the production is therefore enabling the transmission of intentions without the other participants being deprived of their artistic contribution. As the production manager points out: "The authors are always explaining, we have emails that are two pages long, they always have arguments…". It's a question of listening to the author (which seems to have been done by the director, who is appreciated by the authors) without encroaching on the work of the other participants, such as the storyboarders. It is indeed a question of respecting the author's intentions, but of thinking that professionals are needed to translate them into an animation series, whereas the authors would tend to control all the stages of the cartoon to make sure that their intentions are respected.

6. The flow of intentions and their technical translation

Thus, the intentions of the authors were caught up in "a flow of intentions" (Burnett, 2013) and these needed to be translated using technical devices that they did not master (contrary to the comic books where external interventions were limited):

> No intention has a simple life, after all: some intentions remain relatively stable during the inventive process, but given the complexities of production, this is something akin to a story of survival in the wild. Other intentions are less fortunate: they are rejected entirely or undergo significant transformation. Ultimately, the story of how an original intention filters through creative practice, how intentions undergo moment-by-moment adjustments on the set, is so mere curiosity for the obsessive; these shifts and refinements – how intentions *move* – more so than "visions" or "worldviews" provide reliable explanation for the finer aspects of authors' work. (Burnett, 2013, p. 112)

Although each contributor was supposed to adhere to the intentions of the authors (and the authors' stance was that their intentions should be paramount), and each contributor did refer back to them, others were able either to introduce their own ideas (the scriptwriters in particular) or carry out their own translation that could never be without interpretation. There were many interpretations that were to a greater or lesser extent appreciated by the authors.

The difficulty was that these intentions needed ultimately to be perceptible to children, but in the authors' view some of the contributors' visions of children would be an obstacle. Consequently they needed to ensure that the original intentions, those of the comic book "models" and of the "bible", were clear to children, albeit with the added difficulty of the absence of language, in particular words, to express the characters' emotions and feelings:

> In fact I realized that what is really difficult is making people understand the motivations of the characters. The fact that they do not express themselves, for example they can't say, "oh, I'm angry, I'm going to punch you", we are obliged to understand: "ah, he's angry, he's going to punch him". Therefore that… that takes time. In fact, it's like miming; the actions of the character really have to be drawn out over a long period. Before the character reacts it's necessary for the young spectator to be aware of his motivations. (CF)

However, as it was not technically possible for all of them to do everything, they all had to rely on the contributions of others to make such a necessarily collective work possible. We can define the role of the scriptwriters in this way: they were obliged both to work from the intentions of the authors and to create an original story which carried these specific intentions, thereby participating in this "flow of intentions." They can therefore claim the position of author sanctioned by authors' rights.

> Yes, we are authors because we still propose our ideas, our own imagination. It's clear that we're under a sort of constraint of orders. At the same time, it's an exercise, it's as if we had a framework, you bring your ideas, your imagination, your way of seeing things and at the same time, you mustn't go beyond. But it's not bad if you go a bit further. (A scriptwriter)

The need to create a universe for each episode[4] and the characters linked to this universe opened a creative opportunity for the scriptwriter. However, this could also be considered to be a threat to the security of the creation:

> So, all the time you have to invent something new, new characters, something very meaningful, it's not easy. It's not an easy series to write.
>
> The script is still a working tool and you're not behind the next person, who is the storyboarder, to tell him what you have in mind. So we have to get as many things across as possible with our script and in fact, we have to write quite a lot. (A scriptwriter)

Scripting is a way of telling others what to do next. It is about maximum clarification of intentions:

> Since we have so many people reading after us, at some point everyone has to agree and see the same story.
>
> If we want to be understood as well as possible, it's already a literary genre in itself, to contribute the maximum amount of our vision, even if we know, once again, we're completely aware that in cartoons, it's the boarder, afterwards, who changes things, the director... It's obvious that what we'll see in the picture won't be what we had in mind. (Scriptwriters)

There is also a need to ensure that these new intentions are understandable to the targeted children:

> The difficulty is rather to say to oneself "they are 4–6 years old, it's not the same thing as talking to 6–8 or 8–10 year olds". [...] Sometimes, I might tend to put in *intentions* that are not in fact basic enough, not visual enough. It has to be very burlesque and funny; it has to be fun and at the same time, there have to be these little moments of emotion. (Scriptwriter) (our italics)

---

4 The specificity of *Le Petit Poilu*'s stories in both albums and television series is that each episode, once it leaves the family home, takes place in a different universe with non-recurring characters.

Furthermore, these creations were reviewed, adapted and remodified so that they could be placed in the settings and images by the storyboarder and the director. Storyboarders need to transform scenarios so that the intentions are feasible and understandable. It is a matter of making all intentions clear.

> So we, the boarders, do the drawings, so all the *intentions*. Sometimes we add things because we find that the script is not clear. It must be clear, clear. So sometimes we moan at the scriptwriters because... in the script, things can happen, but in the image when it gets stuck, it gets stuck, and it has to be immediately understandable. [...] what we have always been asked and what is correct, is to give the *intentions* so that it is clear, to avoid it not being understood if it goes off to China some time, so in general we write it and put the dialogue. (A storyboarder) (our italics)

Storyboarders have to add intentions that are not in the script:

> All the *intentions*, we put them... they're not necessarily indicated in the script and I think it's great, for example, to establish a relationship of... for example a character who is going to impose his law on another character, who is going to crush him and that, it won't necessarily be indicated. But for me, I think it's absolutely essential that we feel there's pressure between the two characters, or complicity, or a relationship of tenderness between brothers and sisters. (A storyboarder) (our italics)

It implies the need for an interpretation of the intentions of both the scriptwriters and the authors, and also the production of new intentions relating to the animation that the very literary text of the scenarios could not always predict. Consequently, there were gray areas that provided room for new interpretations and creations and this also contributed to the "flow of intentions". Finally, always in the background, there was the need to ensure that all this work, having been repeatedly reviewed and modified, could be understood by children without any test ever having been carried out. Thus, according to the director:

> When I read the script I have quite a clear idea of what it should look like. Often there are many things in the scenarios that do not work because the scenarios are written by people who are very literary but do not always think in terms of visuals. Sometimes there is something that would seem to work in writing but once it is created visually, the *intentions*, the objectives do not work at all. It would not be understood. Sometimes it's a problem of comprehension, sometimes it's also a problem of complexity. Someone writes a sentence, it appears easy but actually setting it out becomes a laborious business. There are many things that I change at script time. (Our italics)

Thus the role of the director is to make the different interventions coherent, to make "it works" so that the intentions can be understood. In a way it is about maintaining those intentions as validated by the authors:

> My role is to put this script into images *and to ensure that everything is clear, comprehensible, that people can understand the intentions of the characters*, that is, the point of the story: what is going to happen, why is it important, why he is sad, etc. (The director) (our italics)

Animators, for their part, tend to be situated in a mechanism not of artistic contribution, but of interpretation of the intentions of the authors, the scriptwriters, the storyboarders, the director, within the framework of a style of animation that has been defined through discussions between the director and the authors in a spirit of fidelity to the comic book and its intentions. The whole product must allow the public to understand these various intentions. The result is a certain invisibility of the interpretation work carried out in the animation studio.

The intentions are esthetic, narrative and also educational because the authors are the guarantors of a certain ethic and moreover a representation of the child. Behind these ideas it is the question of how to address children that is pivotal, as the authors perceive it, and for which they are perhaps the only authority. Therefore they had to ensure that the ideas of the other contributors, particularly of the scriptwriters, and how they were interpreted by the different contributors, conformed with the general intentions that reflect the values that *Petit Poilu* portrays and must continue to portray, and particularly from the point of view that the animated cartoon is a new medium which, contrary to the abandoned Canadian project, should not challenge the values to which the authors are attached. It is on this question that the authors claim legitimacy when they do not have it from a technical point of view:

> And I think it's a very pragmatic vision of the work, that is to say that we realized over the development of the project over years and years that even if at the beginning we're not sure of ourselves, we realized that we had a certain know-how for this particular project, Celine as a scriptwriter, as a acting director, as a director in relation to the emotions, and all that, and me as a designer, so we affirmed a legitimacy of… when we weren't sure of that legitimacy before, we asserted it as we went along. (PB)

7. Collaboration and intention: The example of sound

We will illustrate this aspect by using the subject of sound. Although the comic is related to the animated cartoon it is silent, firstly because it proposes no dialogue that is specific to it, but also, as in the case of all comics, other than the occasional exclamation or musical note, there is no soundtrack, which is an essential element of an animated cartoon.

Therefore in the authors' "bible" the following was written:

> In this series no-one speaks but they all emit rumblings, sounds, noises that are there to support the *intentions*. The music and the sound effects will therefore play an essential role because they will transmit not only the atmosphere of the adventure but also the emotions of the characters. (Our italics)

Though the authors may have had their own ideas for the voices of the characters (who speak a language made up of onomatopoeia, devoid of meaning but yet coherent), the music and the sound effects were original creations. Thus the original voice tester created a style of speaking for the principal character that was validated and in the main used for the definitive voice. According to the authors: "She invented a kind of vocabulary almost of her own, between Japanese and gobbledygook. In fact it wasn't bad." It is evident that this actress made a real contribution to the final creation although the actress who performed the final voice of Petit Poilu felt, from her point of view that, as she was following the work of the original, she did not bring any new element to the creation. However, the final production involves not only the actors, but also a sound engineer and the director, and it is constantly necessary to check whether the voice recorded on the image (in this production, the image precedes the final voice) does indeed translate the intentions of the characters. It is a question of giving meaning especially where the image could be ambiguous.

The sound designer had extensive discussions with the authors, who live in the same Belgian town, yet he produced a sound universe that was his own interpretation of their ideas: "here, the *creative process* is more the overlaying of a certain number of sounds to obtain a new texture rather than creating a sound from nothing using a synthesizer or whatever" (our italics). The sounds translate an intention that cannot simply be understood by an image, such as the blow of a hammer, the sound of which makes it possible to capture the force with which it was used.

Apart from the theme tune of the opening sequence proposed by one of the authors, the music was a relatively minimalist and original creation. In a cartoon animation the purpose of the music, according to its creators, is to express emotions and thereby translate the *intentions*: "we just need to be clear with regard to the emotion, then it's our job to translate that emotion into music."

This was less the result of an overall plan for the sound but more a "back and forth" between the ideas of the authors and the interpretations of the different contributors. However, the translation of intentions is a creative work, especially when it takes place in this sound space that is absent from the comic book.

8. Limited control

The authors did not have total control. Although they dreamed of having total control of the project of creating the animated cartoon of *Petit Poilu* in stop motion, they recognized the difficulties, and though they were favorable to turning *Petit Poilu* into an animation, they were obliged to accept the group dimension of such a project. The necessary speed of the process for reasons of cost was one of the initial factors limiting their control. For the authors the question of time, the need to respect a tight schedule (two episodes per week for all the stages) appeared to be a race against the clock and did not give them enough time to react thoroughly. The director himself emphasized this speed of production (that related to the use of computers) which reduced the time for reflection.

According to the production manager the authors did not appreciate the organization process that required that everything be in place so that the work was available to everyone at the right time, and that they regarded it as an unbearable time pressure (racing against the clock). It was a question of cost, of course, but not solely that, it was also a question of managing the time constraints of a large number of people, many of whom were casual or freelance workers and not immediately available employees.

Perhaps what made a difficult situation more complex was that it was a joint project but without any real cooperation; it was a long way from the operation described by Coundry (2013) concerning Japanese animation. Several participants complained that there was a lack of relationships to better understand what needs to be done. For example, one scriptwriter said:

> When we meet storyboarders at drinks, there are often people who reproach us, who say we write stuff that can't be drawn. But if we don't meet them and they don't explain it to us, we can't know. The more experience we have, the more we manage to feel it, but it's obvious that we always write things that seem very good in our head but that, in the end, are not drawable.
>
> That's the whole difficulty of the animation scriptwriter and in my opinion, and we're all pretty much in agreement, it's just incredible that there's not more contact between a team of scriptwriters and the storyboarders, the people who create the image.
>
> It's absurd that we animation scriptwriters can't know more about how to make a cartoon. I miss that because I think I would go much faster, that's why there are many animation scriptwriters who themselves were storyboarders, who in my opinion understand faster.

Two aspects made this collaboration difficult and, as a consequence, also made the collective construction of ideas and their interpretation difficult: the isolation of the different contributors, which appeared not to be a constraint but just a way of management, and the aspect of authors' rights, which concerned some but not others, and which led to an individualization of the work in relation to the copyrights.

9. Intention, collaboration and recipients

There are the explicit intentions (such as briefs and oral communications) which circulated to ensure the collective aspect of the animated cartoon creation. However, these intentions were not only those of the original authors (who were constantly present and trying to control the translation of their ideas), but others also produced their own intentions (such as the scriptwriters), or produced them in the gray areas where there were no given intentions (the storyboarder), or designed a specific level of intentions (the voices, the production), or interpreted the original ideas and contributed to the "flow of intentions" which fed into the animated cartoon. All of this was to ensure that it would be comprehensible, that it would work, particularly for children, all in spite of a project with very little overall collaboration (at best one could only speak of "little islands" of collaboration).

Collaboration consists of making the intentions of the authors (and of a few others such as scriptwriters) accessible and understandable within the framework of this particular medium that is the animated film. The authors are the ones who produce intentions, and the others make them accessible to the public. Not all elements can be mastered by the authors as in a comic book, as the example of music has shown: the musicians put the question of intentions at the center, but use their creativity to do so and think that they can make certain intentions that are difficult to convey understandable (especially to children).

In a production where the authors have a strong legitimacy because of the continuity between the comic book and the animation series, one perceives the complexity of the concretization of the intentions which must be combined with other intentions and which will only be accessible through a constant work of translation (from the idea to the script, the storyboard and then to the animatic which integrates the exact temporality and the vocals, to the final animation with the post-production which integrates the final voices, the sounds and the music). In the end, are the authors' intentions understood by the children? This is of course undecidable due to the variety of receptions, characterized here by differences in the age of the audience. Nevertheless, the fact remains that being an author implies that intentions are conveyed, participating in a collaborative work out of necessity means accepting the presence of other intentions and the constant translation of one's own. But here it is in the name of the child audience, and respect for it, rather than their work, that authors justify their interventions and the need to maintain the original intentions despite the complex production process.

This configuration, distinct from the mechanisms at work in other contexts (such as Japanese anime or American cartoon) gives legitimacy to the interventions of the authors of the original work; yet they still need to be justified and explained. It is not enough to assert oneself as an author, one must succeed in making one's intentions known and effective in complex modes of communication and collaboration, moreover characterized by time pressure. But how can one be an author without wanting to drape oneself in the garment of the almighty creator? It is by being as much as an author, the spokesman for the recipient, the judge of the degree to which the child has been respected, as conceived and written in the original comic book, that authors justify their position. Thus, they make it part of the mechanism of a controlled circulation of their franchise, making their character a bundle of meanings and values that they have to maintain in a relative integrity. It is not a question of developing a transmedia mechanism in which each medium could contribute to modifying these meanings, but rather a mechanism of adaptation which must never lose the link with the original production in the light of which the new products must be appreciated.

References

Brougère, G. (2018). Adresser une bande dessinée aux jeunes enfants: le cas *Petit Poilu*. In G. Brougère & S. François (Eds.), *L'enfance en conception(s). Comment les industries culturelles s'adressent-elles aux enfants?* (pp. 47–74). Peter Lang.

Brougère, G. (2019). *Petit Poilu* s'anime: auteurs, collaborations et adressage aux enfants, *Revue française des sciences de l'information et de la communication, 18*, http://journals.openedition.org/rfsic/7956.

Brougère, G. & François, S. (Eds.). (2018). *L'enfance en conception(s). Comment les industries culturelles s'adressent-elles aux enfants?* Peter Lang.

Burnett, C. (2013). Hidden Hands at Work: Authorship, the Intentional Flux, and the Dynamics of Collaboration. In J. Gray & D. Johnson (Eds.), *A Companion to Media Authorship* (pp. 112–132), Willey-Blackwell.

Caldwell, J. T. (2008). *Production Culture. Industrial Reflexivity and Critical Practice in Film and Television*. Duke University Press.

Condry, I. (2013). *The Soul of Anime. Collaborative Creativity and Japan's Media Success Story*. Duke University Press.

Johnson, D. (2013). *Media Franchising. Creative License and Collaboration in the Culture Industries*. New York University Press

Johnson, D. & Gray, J. (2013). Introduction: The Problem of Media Authorship. In J. Gray & D. Johnson (Eds.), *A Companion to Media Authorship* (pp. 1–19). Wiley-Blackwell.

Layder, D. (1998). *Sociological Practice. Linking Theory and Social Research*. Sage.

10

The creation of cultural value in children's media:

Studying the production and circulation of a quality TV cartoon

Sébastien François and Pascale Garnier

France is not only the third-largest producer of animated contents in the world (CNC, 2019), but also occupies a unique place in the global animation industry (Furniss, 2017), through the production of movies with ambitious artistic goals (Noesser, 2016; Commin et al., 2017). For instance, since around twenty years, the works of Michel Ocelot (*Kirikou and the Sorceress*, 1998; *Azur & Asmar: The Princes' Quest*, 2006; *Tales of the Night*, 2011; etc.) or Sylvain Chomet (*The Triplets of Belleville*, 2003; *The Illusionist*, 2010; etc.) have embodied the so-called "French touch" (Neupert, 2011, p. 124–161; Valière, 2017). Their *original* creations are often opposed to the existing (and vast majority) of animated contents, be it the movies released by "big" studios (e.g. Disney, Pixar, Dreamworks, Illumination Entertainment, etc.)[1], productions adapted from comics or other original sources or, above all, cartoons designed for TV. However, the latter cannot be denied any cultural value just because they are apparently more commercial and are more explicitly intended to incorporate children's media cultures (Caronia and Caron, 2008; Buckingham, 2009; Drotner and Livingstone, 2011).

This chapter illuminates precisely this kind of cultural distinction, by documenting the creation of a specific cartoon series called *Les Grandes grandes vacances* (*The Long Long Holiday*), first broadcast on the French

---

1 For an economic and overall perspective on the animation studio as a cultural industry, see Yoon and Malecki (2009).

TV public service in 2015 and winner of different prizes in France and abroad. Thanks to empirical data coming from interviews with the various and numerous actors involved in the production process (showrunner, animators, producer, director, broadcaster, agent for animation artists, etc.), our analysis is focused on the creation of artistic and cultural "value" in the realm of children's TV. For example, how has this animated series, from the very beginning, created a positive and very unique image, in comparison to more common and standardized TV products for children, in order to rally supporters and the production teams? How has it managed to appear to be the result of a cottage industry, even though its production remained largely industrialized?

We emphasize here the role of the cartoon's theme – World War II as experienced by young children – as a key element in gathering a network of professionals to implement this project, in gaining the attention of private and public funding (especially in the French context), as well as national and international broadcasters. The historical period, narrated from children's perspective, in particular helped to transgress the norms that traditionally constrain the making of children's TV cartoons. Thanks to this case study[2], we also point out not only the role of professionals' expertise and reputation, but equally the importance of their collaboration based on a shared vision of children's skills and agency. Thus, the concrete production of *The Long Long Holiday* (*LLH*) was supplemented by a "valorization" process, i.e. the project went through various "arenas" and "trials" (Boltanski and Thévenot, 2006 [1987]), to convince stakeholders and animation professionals that it was worth making it happen. This means that here we combine production media studies and pragmatic sociology frameworks[3]: we argue, following Luc Boltanski and Arnaud Esquerre's work (2017), that the cartoon's production process was regularly "enriched" and transformed into an "exceptional good." This approach takes into account people's distinction strategies (Bourdieu, 1984[1979]) – in the case of *LLH*, the comparison with the

---

2 This study was part of a larger research project about the design and circulation of cultural goods aimed at children (CoCirPE), directed by Gilles Brougère and funded by the academic cluster ICCA (Cultural Industry and Artistic Creation) from the university consortium "Université Sorbonne Paris Cité." We also would like to thank all the professionals who agreed to participate to this study.

3 Our theoretical model, which tries to articulate different approaches of cultural creation, was the central point of a previous presentation (Garnier and François, 2017a).

common production of animated contents – but does not limit the construction of cultural value to the latter. We put into perspective the cartoon's story and content as well as its slow maturation, through multiple "modes of existence" (Souriau, 2009), the building of cooperation networks (Becker, 2009) and specific media circulation strategies (*Strenae*, 2011; Steinberg, 2012). Within the scope of this chapter, we will not develop all the dimensions of this valorization, but demonstrate that it relies on different (and intertwined) modes of justification embedded into the professionals' ordinary work.

Through a presentation of *LLH*, the article first shows how these justifications emerged and initiated the valorization process quite early during the cartoon's creation, while mobilizing professionals for an "atypical" project. Then, we explain how the value of *LLH* was constructed upon the assemblage of a congruous group of professionals, i.e. those sharing the objectives of the initial author, as well as cultural tastes about (legitimate) animation and children's culture. Finally, it appears that the cartoon's criticism both of childhood's assumed vulnerability and of the "moral panics" usually associated with children and media also structured the professionals' attitude towards the project The historical period depicted in *LLH* actually convinced numerous actors of this cartoon's ability to enhance children's agency – be they children on screen or among the presumed audience.

1. A case study: The Long Long Holidays

1.1. Studying the making of animation

Our choice to analyze the production of only one cartoon is related to the state of the art in animation studies: even though animation techniques are rather well documented and theorized (e.g. Wells, 2010; Williams, 2012) – among other things, in relation to future animators' training – social sciences have rarely considered them and, more broadly, the production process of animation, as a potential object of study.

Most academic works so far have focused on the content of animation, very often from an aesthetical perspective (Pilling, 1998; Wells, 1998). Such works sometimes point out the social and moral issues raised by animated contents explicitly addressed to children, but it is a more common topic in the studies about the reception of children's TV. The latter which frequently refer to the recurring moral panics concerning mass media and children (Critcher, 2008; Buckingham, 2009), usually discuss the effects of cartoons on children (e.g. Baton-Hervé, 1999; Pecora et al., 2006; Bermejo Berros, 2007) or highlight their potential appropriation by young audiences (Buckingham, 1993 and 2011), but have regularly ignored the production itself of animated contents. Of course, there are also a couple of publications specifically on children's TV and networks. But if some historical approaches (Poels, 2013; Perlmutter, 2014) or works more centered on educational television (Fisch and Truglio, 2000; Morrow, 2008; Duccini, 2013) provide important details about the production process, others tend to uncritically include the broadcasters' official discourse, as in the article collection about the American network Nickelodeon (Bryant, 2006).

In addition, sources can be problematic when producers or cultural industries themselves create the official discourse on the genesis of their products. For example, they can produce "making-of" or "behind-the-scenes" documentaries, books or DVD bonuses, which are more self-promotion or "industrial reflexivity" (Caldwell, 2008), and always require a kind of deconstruction from researchers. In this regard, directly interviewing professionals (and not using secondary interviews) and ethnographically documenting their work seems a more relevant methodology to reduce some of these biases. Unfortunately, such approaches remain scarce within the academic field of animation and are relatively recent: Valérie-Inés de la Ville and Laurent Durup's work (2008) about the creation of the French-Canadian cartoon *Totally Spies!* (2008), Dafna Lemish's on international cartoon producers and their perception of gender (2010), Ian Condry's on work in Japanese animation studios (2013), or Jeanette Steemers' on the production of preschool TV in the United Kingdom (2010), remain exceptions to some extent. Guided by such examples, however, we have therefore tried to embrace the entire production process (i.e. the preproduction, the actual production and finally the broadcasting) of one animated series to study the position of children within this process, as well as the constitution of cultural value in this industry of cultural value in this industry.

1.2. An "atypical" cartoon

Thanks to a contact at the CNC (the French National Centre for Cinema and the Moving Image), in May 2015 we got the opportunity to contact Delphine Maury, the original creator of the *Long Long Holidays*, a ten-episode animated series (26 minutes each) which was about to be broadcast at that time. It became clear that Maury was the perfect entry point to meet and interview a large range of professionals involved in the creation of the cartoon: the producers, the broadcaster, i.e. some managers from the "Youth Unit" (*Unité Jeunesse*) at France Télévisions (the French national television broadcaster), members of staff of the *LLH* animation studio, Blue Spirit (its CEO, some animators and X-effects professionals), its dubbing studio (Piste Rouge), the three main screenwriters, one of the storyboarders, the film director, the author of the graphic charter, the international distributor, as well as two people in charge of *LLH* tie-ins (i.e. a couple of books and a serious game). Our interviews took place after the cartoon's production, preventing our study from being completely synchronic, but by interviewing the main actors within the first year following the first broadcast – while some were still being asked to lead masterclasses about *LLH* or while the cartoon was receiving various professional rewards – we gained access to vivid and reliable testimonies, as well as first-hand materials retracing the exchanges between professionals and the continuity of the project.

In order to have a first insight into this "saga on WWII" (World War II), one may read the presentation available on the website of Cyber Group Studio, the cartoon's international distributor[4]:

> Adventures, laughter, poetry and emotion in a poignant depiction of WWII.
>
> The *Long Long Holiday* recounts the daily life of 2 kids brother and sister [*sic*], who are left by their parents at their grandparents' house near the Normandy coast for a few weeks at the beginning of World War II. As the war rumbles on, those weeks become five years.
>
> This series sheds new light on a unique historical context – a war epic, patriotic actions, etc.– all viewed through the eyes of two young urban children who know nothing of life in the country. Despite the war, they will experience the most wonderful adventures while coming into contact with nature, making new friends and even with the farm animals.

Even though this synopsis was clearly created for advertising and commercial purposes, it is nonetheless interesting because it sheds light on some of the cartoon's specificities. *LLH* is indeed an original creation

4 https://www.cybergroupstudios.com/productions/kids-6-12/the-long-long-holiday/.

and not an adaptation of a pre-existing cultural content, whereas animated TV series are very often derived from successes in children's literature (Chelebourg, 2013; McCallum, 2019). The historical background of the story also offered the opportunity to air it during spring 2015, for the official celebrations related to the 70th anniversary of the end of World War II, which gave a patrimonial veneer to the cartoon. Finally, its serial construction – the fact that its 10 episodes cannot be watched out of sequence – also made *LLH* special, since broadcasters usually prefer independent episodes for young TV audiences for segmented and multiple airings (Stabile and Harrison, 2003).

These three characteristics may explain why *LLH* has often been described as "atypical" or even "risky," in reference to the professionals' own terms, but in our perspective, it is also because they pursued clear broadcasting and production goals at the same time. Thus, from the very beginning, producing the cartoon was considered as more challenging than common animated content for children's TV. That is simultaneously one of the reasons why the broadcaster and the producer constantly provided moral and financial support to the project, first by encouraging Maury to develop her initial ideas, and then by motivating the various production teams to achieve their respective tasks.

Ultimately, the cartoon received a very favorable reception: it won several prizes in France such as the "*Nouveau Talent Animation*" award from the SACD (Society of Authors and Drama Compositors), and the "*Laurier jeunesse*" award for radio and television. It was also recognized abroad, with prizes for the best international animation series in Stuttgart or at the Kecskemét Animation Film Festival in Hungary. Its audience reception was also exceptionally good: one-and-a-half million viewers for the first airing in France on average[5], to which should be added those from the TV rebroadcasts, DVD sales, and international exports.

From various points of view, *LLH* was evidently not representative of the general production of animated contents on French television. Even though numbers have mostly remained confidential, we have been told that its cost per minute was significantly above average (*cf.* CNC, 2019). Similarly, even though animation projects, in particular animated movies, can take years to be released, the cartoon was even given extra time to

5 For partial comparisons with daily audiences among young viewers, see the report from the French regulator on audiovisual contents (CSA, 2018, p. 35–37).

mature at different steps of the production process, and especially at the beginning when it was essentially Delphine Maury's idea. The cartoon consequently had a very particular status, which also made it relevant to discuss the construction of cultural and artistic values in animation, which we consider here as a constitutive part of the production process.

2. Producing and legitimating a cartoon series

2.1. Authorship and cultural valorization

The production process of *LLH* appears to have greatly contributed to the fast legitimation of the cartoon's quality – on multiple levels – especially through the "quality" of the professionals involved in the project themselves. One of the originalities of the series lies first in the presence of Delphine Maury all along the preproduction and development process: she was said to be the "artistic director" or the "showrunner" in reference to the TV shows in the US or in the UK. If this is also a characteristic of "prime-time animation" (Stabile and Harrison, 2003) in those countries, this remains very unusual in France, where the role of an original author is usually limited to the design of the graphic charter. In animation (but also more generally in fiction TV – cf. Boutet, 2017, p. 103), as projects require years and large teams of workers, authorship is usually very diluted: in France, only a couple of producers have managed to occupy such a position, even though they were not always the original creators of the cartoons, for example Jean Chalopin (for *The Mysterious Cities of Gold* or *Ulysses 31*) or Albert Barillé (for the Once upon a time… series) in the 1970–1980s or more recently Vincent Chalvon-Demersay (for *Totally Spies!* or *Martin Mystery*). As a result, Delphine Maury embodied the project on multiple occasions and left her mark on the final product even though it was a collective production. For instance, before contacting any producer – which is the usual procedure in this industry – she was the recipient of a support fund for audiovisual creation from the CNC[6], which plays a major role in the so-called "French model" of cultural industries (Noesser, 2016), by strongly supporting "original creation." Delphine Maury also directly dialogued with almost all the major actors

6 All along the production process, *LLH* was helped by this public institution, in addition to other public and private sources of funding, such as France Television, Canal+, Les Armateurs, the PROCIREP, the Poitou-Charentes region, etc.

in the process (writers, graphic designer, broadcaster, CNC, casting/dubbing, producers, director, etc.) and her involvement lasted up to the presentation of *LLH* in festivals, competitions, etc. Following her emphasis, during the interviews, on the importance of the author as the warrant of what cultural goods for children should be, be it a book, a journal or a cartoon, Maury has clearly had a form of authority and authorship over the cartoon. As is the case with TV show with identifiable showrunners (Newman and Levine, 2012, p. 38–58), this was an important argument to differentiate *LLH* from other TV animated contents.

It is also essential to notice that the legitimacy of *LLH* also comes from its strong ties with the field of children's literature, which is visible through the trajectories of some actors, such as Delphine Maury, who worked for Bayard (a famous French children's press company), before entering the "small world" of animation. Similarly, an important member of the Youth Unit at France Télévisions was recruited after a first career in the children's literature publishing sector. Among others, one of the writers who helped to construct the scenario of *LLH*, Timothée de Fombelle, is a prominent author of novels for young people. Finally, the graphic designer, Emile Bravo, is also a renowned author of comic strips for children. In this regard, *LLH* series cannot be compared to the cartoons whose link to children's literature solely rests upon the adaptation of existing works. It is a creation that directly benefited from some of the most legitimate actors in children's literature field, even if this field is a subordinate position within the literary field (Ferrier, 2009; Prince, 2015, p. 23–25). In addition, if *LLH* does not derive from an existing novel, the cartoon's content remains nourished by some classic works from children's literature, with explicit references, such as the book *Robinson* (*Crusoe*) which gives the name to the children's secret group, or more implicit ones such as *Tom Sawyer* in which children were already propelled, without their parents, in the countryside and more precisely into nature, to experience intense and formative adventures. This kind of intertextuality, which is not only literary, but also audiovisual (see below), was recalled by several of our interviewees and constituted further added value for the cartoon.

All professionals recognized Delphine Maury's central role and place all along the "chain of cooperation" (Becker, 1982) that led to the final version of *LLH*, even if this implied discussions or sometimes conflicts: for instance, Maury's choice to hire Syd Matters, a pop music band she was fond of and not aimed at children, was highly debated. However, the richness of the final product comes both from her strong lead and the cooperative process which nourished the cartoon – and the characters themselves (Garnier and François, 2018) – through the professionals' own "personalities". From a dispositional perspective (Bourdieu, 1979), one could actually say that the numerous professionals involved in the project shared a social and a cultural habitus, so to speak the habitus of the intellectual fringes that one can find within contemporary creative industries (Hesmonlagh and Baker, 2010). However, a large proportion of the professionals whom we interviewed also shared "generational resources" (Glevarec, 2019), i.e. resources related to animation and children's cultures that function as shared references in the field of cultural production and as common ground to express their personal "sensitivities" in their choices. For instance, a lot of professionals independently admitted that Miyazaki's cartoons were a clear inspiration, especially for *LLH*'s depiction of nature. Thus, such references, with a strong authorship and artistic claims too, directly participated to the "arty" dimension of the cartoon and to the collaborative process.

2.2. A collective and sociotechnical legitimation

From the first idea and presentation to the CNC to its first airing in May 2015 on France 3, a national public television channel and a member of France Télévisions, the completion of the project took more than six years. The involvement of France Télévisions from the very beginning of the project is also specific to *LLH*: generally, producers first contact France Télévisions with projects which have already partly advanced. In *LLH*'s case, however, the broadcaster was a direct partner for the development almost from the beginning. This early supervision explains why the project was given a long time of "maturation," which made it possible to question the first version of *LLH*'s scenario and to change the potential director several times. For example, one of the possible directors was described as not sufficiently "audacious," whereas the final one admits that he had to move from a "cartoony" to a more "realistic" style of animation to be recruited. The "small world" of French animation indeed seems to be composed of different "families", a word used at least by one of the professionals: Each "family" apparently shares more or less the same vision of animation, with specific styles and techniques, and relies on people who are used to working together, while newcomers are "tested" before they can be accepted into a family. Incidentally, a rigorous inquiry on the existence and boundaries of such families still needs to be done within French animation studies.

Nevertheless, the association with the production studio Les Armateurs, the company behind the famous *Kirikou*, the *Triplets of Belleville*, *Ernest and Celestine*, effectively contributed to the artistic and cultural legitimation of *LLH*. Les Armateurs' producer-in-chief at that time, Didier Brunner, who now leads the studio Folivari, is indeed famous for his professional skills and experiences regarding "arty" cartoons. He has also played a major role in the international notoriety of French cartoons and the elaboration of the "French touch" idea (Comin et al., 2017). More unexpectedly, *LLH* was distributed by Cyber Group Studios, a French company founded in 2005, which has become one of the leading animation studios worldwide, but essentially through licensed and more commercial cartoons, internally or externally produced. *LLH* was very different from the company's other cartoons, like *Zou* or *Zorro, the Chronicles* which was distributed by 41 broadcasters all over the world. Its involvement in *LLH* should be understood as a rather individual decision by its CEO, Pierre Sissman, who put his personal interests for an "edutainment" series about WWII over commercial considerations: during his interview, he underlines how much it was important to have such a "good" cartoon in his catalog, even if he does not expect a financial profit. The cartoon's cultural and artistic value is the issue here: generating more symbolic profit than economic outcomes, *LLH* was an exception that Cyber Group could amortize with the sales of more standardized, licensed series, which can be multiplied into several seasons. Ultimately, *LLH* highly benefitted from this partnership since it helped to export the cartoon in various countries (e.g. in Germany on ZDF, in Switzerland on RTS, in Denmark on DR) and beyond via Netflix.

Celebrated abroad as the "French flag" in the specialized press, *LLH* was also valued as being made in/by France, which is almost true: only a limited part of the layout was made in China, and only few professionals of the animation studio Blue Spirit worked in Montreal, under French supervision in Angoulême. The series' reputation was also helped by the international renown of the French schools of animation (Nagorny, 2014; Mérijeau and Roffat, 2015), for example through the participation of some students from La Poudrière, one of the most selective and famous schools in this field, since each episode is followed by a one-minute sequence, in different animation styles, directed by selected students.

Even the specific cel shading software[7] developed by the French studio Blue Spirit, which was often mentioned by our interviewees, participated in the artistic recognition of *LLH*, by combining efficiency and tradition: numerous scenes from the cartoon are clearly indebted to the use of the most recent graphic technologies, while the audience noticed the familiar "ligne claire" aesthetics in French-language comics (McKinney, 2008, p. xiv).

Finally, what is noteworthy is that all the professionals we met profoundly enjoyed the project and said that they were "lucky" or "proud" to have been involved (one of the writers says for instance it has been really difficult for him to come back to more "ordinary" animation). From their point of view, the first quality of *LLH* rests upon its story, rooted in the historical depiction of WWII, as experienced by children. Nevertheless, the creation of the cultural value cannot be reduced to the subject matter of production, and it is important to reveal its interplay with reception issues, in particular regarding how its assumed audience was embedded in the cartoon's very content.

3. What does "appropriate for children" mean? Production of cultural value through audience design

3.1. What cartoons "for children" should be like...

Historically, French TV cartoons have been closely associated with childhood, even if some clearly address adults, as early as the end of the 1960s, for instance with the famous TV show *Les Shadoks* (Denis, 2016). Similarly, the reception of Japanese animation in France at the end of the 1970s and in the 1980s was biased because it was initially broadcast within children's TV shows, and ignoring the fact that a great deal of it was created for older audiences in Japan (Allamand and Morand, 2016). For Cécile Noesser (2013, p. 423), "the resistible ascent" of animation in France is also closely associated with the development of "films designed for adults, that help[ed] their qualification as authors' films". This is why Michel Ocelot for example, the "father of *Kirikou*", has several times

---

7 Cel shading is 3-D technique that creates the impression that animated objects are in 2-D, mimicking the appearance of comic books or traditional cartoons.

criticized the "drag" of animation which is automatically associated to childhood, and claimed that he was addressing everyone, and not only children. From the professionals' point of view, this probably explains why the "small world" of animation is confronted with contradictory imperatives. On the one hand, what can be shown to children, especially on TV, is conceived and prepared very carefully, in relation to moral issues, and in relation to the presumed sensitivity of young audiences. On the other hand, professionals point out the fact that they feel free to do what they want, because cartoons "for children" are still under-considered or seen as being of little value among cultural goods, especially when compared to contents aimed at adults. In their perspective, improving the quality of children's cartoons entails working against moral panics and the devaluation of cartoons "for children."

The expression "for children" actually carries two meanings. Firstly, it contains the idea of a target and the necessary adaptation to childhood: cartoons should be specifically designed for this audience category characterized by its (young) age. Obviously, what can be seen by children can also be watched by older audiences, and in some cases, like *LLH*, cartoons can be assigned to a "family" category too, which explicitly focuses on an intergenerational audience (Garnier, 2018). But the second meaning of "for children" leads to the idea of value: what is "for" someone is supposed to be "appropriate" or, in a pejorative sense, "good enough" for this person. Not only should cartoons be "appropriate for" to children (defined as a specific age group of beings and becomings, cf. Garnier, 1995; James et al., 1998), but, reciprocally, they perform and institute what children can appreciate and how they can appropriate them.

Accordingly, it seems that the question of children's age, in combination with the representations of children and childhood that are integrated in the cartoon, worked on a double level in the creation of *LLH*, both at a moral and at the cultural and artistic level. From a moral perspective, the professionals tested all the constraints related to children's cartoons: "This project was particularly atypical, because it breaks almost all the rules of seemliness for youth (contents)", explains a professional from France Télévisions. And at a cultural level, the professionals wanted to produce a "high-quality" program instead of those they described as "poor", "very normative", with a "very repetitive dramatic structure", aimed at keeping children quiet in front of the television before "the departure to school".

3.2. Between risks and moral constraints: Taking children seriously

The French public authority for audiovisual broadcasting, the CSA (Conseil Supérieur de l'Audiovisuel) has implemented numerous regulations and age categories for children's TV programs (Jullier, 2008). However, for the professionals we met, it is first of all the broadcaster who is responsible for what children watch on television and who should control *a priori* future contents. That involves discussions, and sometimes disagreements, such as the ones Delphine Maury recounts about her choice of showing the main female character, the young Colette, sleeping in her brother's bed at the very beginning of the story, when she is afraid of sleeping alone in another room. Maury contests the possible suspicion of pedophilia mentioned by the broadcaster, arguing that children are able to contextualize the characters' actions. She also insists on the importance of that sequence for the story and the relationship between siblings. She also stresses the importance of children's emotions and capacities, in particular the fact that they are perfectly able to distinguish fiction from reality. She was perfectly confident in her choices as an author and the scene finally remained in the cartoon.

Even more so, the context of the story and the violence implied by World War II (especially bombings, military fights, deaths, injuries, etc.) led to numerous moral issues regarding what should be shown to young spectators. When a realistic point of view was chosen, professionals at the same time developed strategies to let spectators understand this violence, but without directly showing it. For instance, in the third episode, *LLH* children found a (dead) soldier in the countryside during the Exodus[8]. However, its position, sitting under a tree, and the perspective on screen, avoid showing the dead body; similarly, in the dialogue on screen, Colette, the little girl, thinks that the soldier is sleeping, while the older children explicitly choose not to tell her the truth.

In addition to war, the remoteness of many adults (above all, Ernest and Colette's parents) and the rural context of the 1940s also gave the opportunity to show children with greater freedom than those in today's cartoons: some children in *LLH* use knives, three of them go on a bicycle

8 In the historiography of WWII, the *Exodus* refers to the episode in which millions of French (and other European populations) people left their houses to flee the German army's progresses at the beginning of the conflict in 1940.

without any helmet, etc. Unlike contemporary cartoons too, the professionals explain that they took the risk to show people drinking wine or smoking – but only adults – because it was completely coherent with the historical context and the story, and because it could not be withdrawn without losing the quality of the narrative. Sometimes, they even suggested ideas they knew to be "unacceptable" during the production process in order to divert the broadcaster's watchfulness and introduce other polemical subject matter regarding children. Nevertheless, it must also be said that the Youth Unit of France Télévisions was supportive of the realistic point of view and wanted to get some distance from the "over-protected children" approach that dominates animated productions, according to their perception of the children's TV market: "I am myself bad at self-censorship", one of its members says in contrast. Like other professionals, he emphasizes the "subjective" dimension of his moral judgment, and consequently the importance of the normative discussions between professionals to overcome a kind of "self-righteousness" or orthodox vision related to children's vulnerability. As we will see below, this position values both the agency of the young spectators and the agency of the characters within cartoons.

3.3. From characters to "real" children

Regarding children's TV, the "prohibition logic", as one professional called it, has a long history (Cohen, 2004): children should be prevented from watching risk-taking situations they could replicate in real life. But what is at stake today for the international animation industry is the cultural dimension of these prohibitions. Some of the professionals involved in the production of *LLH* have underlined how hard it can be to work with countries such as Canada and more broadly in North America, where prohibition tendencies are stronger, even though some professionals from these countries at the same time proved able to overcome their "fears" and "prudery". In any case, what is also different is the importance assigned to the tests with "real" children organized during the creation of cartoons, which seem very rare in France compared to English-speaking countries. This may be linked to the importance assigned to psychologist advisors in North America or to the incorporation of "developmentally appropriate practices" (i.e. "appropriate" practices which are supposed to follow the stages of children's moral and cognitive development) during the production process (Steemers, 2010).

Thus, such tests were not implemented at all for *LLH*: the professionals rather projected in the series their own childhood and/or their family life, sometimes with the influence of their own children (cf. Zafirau, 2009), in particular to fuel the characters' behaviors on screen (Garnier and François, 2018). In the meantime, they addressed rude critics regarding the age categorizations ordinarily used for TV programs. In doing so, they wanted to leave open the different levels of interpretation of the series according to the variety of ages in the potential audience. This was epitomized by the off-screen voice introducing each of the ten episodes and in charge of the continuity between them: one can hear an old woman speaking, who is supposed to be an old Colette today, but from the professionals' point of view, it is something children can perfectly miss without any misunderstanding of the storytelling. It is precisely this conception of the young audience's skills that contributed towards enhancing the cultural content of the cartoon.

3.4. Historical realism and children's games

If the realism of *LLH* seems to be a threat from a moral point of view, it was also a resource for the professionals since it gave a "true" historical content to the series. *LLH* was not designed just as an entertaining program, but also as an educational tool contributing to the culture of its audience, i.e. working for the memory of younger generations. In this sense, the historical realism greatly contributed towards enhancing the cultural value of the series as an enrichment of the past by its present meaning.

The professionals involved therefore paid great attention to the historical accuracy of what was shown, especially to small details such as the design and even the noises of war engines, and, of course, to the WWII events integrated in the ten episodes of the series. A historian specialized in the history of women during this period was employed to check the historical content, whereas one of the writers was also a former history teacher. Emile Bravo, the author of the graphic charter, is also a specialist of this period since he had already worked on this historical context for some of his comics. Above all, Delphine Maury had gathered a large documentation on the period and realized ethnographic interviews with people who were children themselves during the war. This material obviously nourished the content of the series: for instance, "Gadou" the pig, which becomes Colette's friend before being eaten, or the story of the

Jewish yellow star that all children wear at school in solidarity with one of them, are clearly borrowed from the interviewees' lives. Their testimonials also became the subjects of the short animated sequences at the end of each episode recounting their memories.

But *LLH* is not only a "history lesson" about WWII. It is also an entertaining show aimed at attracting kids, and more broadly their family. In line with the three historical missions of the French national broadcasting public service – "to inform, to entertain, to educate", as the head of the TV Youth Unit explains – the broadcaster emphasizes both the "playful" and the "didactic" logic of the series. The young characters also enjoy the discovery of nature and the countryside. They have a lot of fun together, while Colette and Ernest develop a network of friends, a group of children from 6 to 11 called the *Robinsons*, in a little town of Normandy where they are forced to stay. There, they share games, jokes and secrets, enjoying their friendship while the adults' world is turned upside down. As a result, the project also gained supporters through this balance between didactic and entertaining dimensions, which reminds us that "quality TV" for children is not assessed solely through this first criterion.

Likewise, the attention to children's diversity on screen should be highlighted: socio-economical, religious, and geographical differences between children are clearly drawn, far from the model of an "universal child" (Garnier, 2014)[9]. The show is also noticeable for its two leading girl characters, Colette and the older Muguette, who echo the will of Delphine Maury and other professionals to promote gender equality (cf. Lemish, 2010) and to remember women's role during WWII. Finally, throughout the five years of WWII, the young characters grow up. The choice of the professionals was, however, to show less the physical aspects of the characters' development than the growing moral value of their behavior during the war (in fact, they are graphically almost the same from the first to the last episode). In this perspective, becoming older means becoming more conscious of outside events, and finally getting involved in the fight against the Nazi occupation. The children gradually become members of the Resistance and happen to be able to help, even to save, adults.

---

9 The question of the diversity of the children's characters and the intergenerational dimensions of *LLH* was also elaborated in two other articles (Garnier & François, 2017; Garnier, 2017).

The context of WWII therefore offered multiple opportunities to show the reality of children's agency, from a moral and didactic perspective. Again, this refers to some historical truth, in reference to the children's participation into the war, which had long been underestimated (see for example the work of Mayall and Morrow, 2011 about English children during WWII). Young characters put at risk their innocence, by mixing or confusing their children's games with acts of sabotage or spying. Thus, the five-years narrative arch has been constructed as an increasing empowerment of children, who take risks and become aware of their responsibilities, far from the images of vulnerability and weakness generally associated with childhood (cf. Annett, 2018). The quest of a balance between the "entertaining" and the "informative" modes is therefore a constraint that many professionals integrate well in their daily work The potential of *LLH* to fulfill objectives on the both sides of the spectrum was said to be very quickly identified, but some actors also seized the project to further develop their conception of the curious and active child. This demonstrates that the "cultural" valorization of a cartoon is not limited to the deepening of its educational aspects.

For that reason, another crucial element of this balance between playfulness and didacticism is the professionals' decision regarding how to tell and show the story (both in its historical and fictional meanings) through the eyes of children. This approach has had many consequences all along the creation of the series. For instance, even in the script, adults' characters did not give many explanations to children and, in *LLH* episodes, informative news about the war remain rare and are always mediated (through adults, through direct experiences for the children, etc.). This also works with the complexity of the vocabulary that children (both on screen and among the audience) can listen to: for example, the word "*Boches*" (used in French as a negative term for the German occupants), is used on purpose, with no explanations, and was not presented by professionals as an obstacle but as a "resource" to raise curiosity among children because today most of them are not able to understand the word immediately. Moreover, even the frame and the visual perspective in *LLH*, from the storyboard to the final product, were adapted to the size of the young characters' body, which reinforced the project's initial goal from a formal and narrative perspective.

To sum up, the animated series shows some strong children as characters, designed for a capable young audience. From that point of view, one can understand why the professionals so much criticize the "childification" or "infantilization" of children, or what has also been called the "islandisation" of childhood (Christensen et al., 2000), i.e. the fact that children should be protected and isolated from all the problems of adult's world. By playing on the relations between fiction (story and entertainment) and realism (history and education), the cartoon therefore invites "real" children to participate in the heroic adventure of the characters, who are becoming "big ones" at a young age. This process of children's empowerment regularly appeared in the interviews and it suggests that this shared conception of childhood probably helped to bind the actors towards the final product. The valorization of children, both as characters and as an audience, also led to the growth of the series' value.

If this analysis of the *Long Long Holidays* does not claim to extensively explain its critical and popular success, it shows how the creation of the series contributed to its own legitimation, long before it was broadcast. The collective organization required by the project, supported by the cartoon's topic, was itself a means to (at least symbolically) distance *LLH* from the ordinary production of animated shows.

The series acquired a specific identity both because it criticized the vulnerability of childhood and the traditional "moral panics" about children and media, and because it had found an interesting compromise between entertainment and education. The fact that *LLH* rests upon a strong narrative rather than iconic characters, unlike the majority of TV cartoons adapted from existing works (Brougère, 2017), is also a sign of its distinctive approach and can also explain the nature of its circulation strategy, with only scarce and very particular merchandising: one novelization, one activity book and one serious game. This limited conversion into other media has not been an obstacle neither to its audience records in France, nor to its successful international exportation.

This case study also opens new paths within media production studies, as well as animation studies. Among other things, it questions previous works on quality TV for children (Oswell, 2002; Steemers, 2010 and 2016), in particular their focus on pedagogical goals over others. Similarly, it strengthens the understanding of cultural industries and the tensions between the standardization of children's mass culture (and its diffusion through licenses), and the "arty" position of some creations, which constitutes an exceptional good for selected consumers. Here we have described a process of cultural valorization through the use of a historical theme and the singularization of *LLH*'s storytelling. They both constitute characteristics of the new capitalist economics in developed countries like France, where public cultural policies can provide funding for the creation of such "exceptional goods" (Boltanski and Esquerre, 2017). While worldwide diffusion and complex transmedia strategies require a high degree of standardization through protected licenses, French animation partly develops other tactics, with animated films or series entering into an economic system of scarcity and singularization. Art and culture represent an investment into economic growth and foster the development of some geographical territories, such as those of the companies involved in the production process, in the French animation industry (Benneworth and Dauncey, 2016). At the same time, however, the increasing production of animation contents for and by subscription video-on-demand websites (e.g. Netflix) creates new challenges for the animation industry as well as national policies and regulations (Potter, 2018): studying and assessing its impact on the French industry would be another way to refine our comprehension of the valorization process in cultural industries.

References

Allamand, C. & Morand, E. (2016). Distribution et promotion des films du studio Ghibli en France: stratégie marketing et logique sérielle, éléments d'analyse. In M. Pruvost-Delaspre (Ed.), *L'animation japonaise en France. Réception, diffusion, réappropriation* (p. 115–140). L'Harmattan.

Annett, S. (2018). From Vulnerable Minds to Cosmopolitan Affect: Child Fans of Anime in the 1960s–1980s. *Mechademia: Second Arc, 11*(1), 25–43.

Baton-Hervé, E. (2000). *Les enfants téléspectateurs. Programmes, discours, représentations.* L'Harmattan.

Benneworth, P. & Dauncey, H. (2016). Cultural Policy, Creative Clusters and the Complexity of Higher Education: Notes from the Case of Enjmin in Angoulême, France. *International Journal of Cultural Policy, 22* (1), 80–99.

Bermejo Berros, J. (2007). *Génération Télévision: la relation controversée de l'enfant avec la télévision.* De Boeck.

Boltanski, L. & Thévenot, L. (2006). *On Justification. Economies of Worth.* Princeton University Press.

Boltanski, L. & Esquerre, A. (2017). *Enrichissement. Une critique de la marchandise*. Gallimard.

Bourdieu, P. (1984). *Distinction. A Social Critique of the Judgement of Taste*. Harvard University Press.

Bourdieu, P. (1996). *The Rules of Art: Genesis and Structure of the Literary Field*. Polity Press.

Boutet, M. (2017). Un Village français. A French auteur(s) series on a public network. *Series – International Journal of TV Serial Narratives, 3*(2), 101–114.

Brougère, G. (2017). Personnage et captation de l'enfant dans la production "transproductive". In G. Brougère & A. Dauphragne (Eds.), *Les biens de l'enfant. Du monde marchand à l'espace familial* (p. 73–104). Nouveau Monde Éditions.

Bryant, A. J. (Ed.) (2006). *The Children's Television Community*. Routledge.

Buckingham, D. (1993). *Reading Audiences: Young People and the Media*. Manchester University Press.

Buckingham, D. (2009). Children and Television. In J. Qvortrup, W. Corsaro, & M. Honig (Eds.), *The Palgrave Handbook of Childhood Studies* (p. 347–359). Palgrave Macmillan.

Buckingham, D. (2011). *The Material Child*. Polity Press.

Caldwell, J. T. (2008). *Production Culture. Industrial Reflexivity and Critical Practice in Film and Television*. Duke University Press.

Caronia, L. & Caron A. H. (2008). Television Culture and Media Socialization across Countries: Theoretical Issues and Methodological Approaches. In K. Drotner & S. Livingstone (Eds.), *The International Handbook of Children, Media and Culture* (p. 371–389). Sage.

Chambat-Houillon, M. & Jost, F. (2003). Parents-enfants: regards croisés sur les dessins animés. *Informations sociales, 111*, 62–71.

Chelebourg, C. (2013). *Les fictions de jeunesse*. Presses universitaires de France.

Christensen, P., James, A. & Jenks, C. (2000). Home and Movement. Children Constructing 'Family Time'. In S. L. Holloway & G. Valentine (Eds.), *Children's Geography. Playing, Living, Learning* (p. 139–155). Roultedge.

CNC. (2019). *Le marché de l'animation en 2018*. Centre national du cinéma et de l'image animée.

Cohen, K. F. (2004). *Forbidden Animation: Censored Cartoons and Blacklisted Animators in America*. McFarland & Co Inc.

Commin, J. P., Ganne, V. & Brunner, D. (2017). *Kirikou et après… 20 ans de cinéma d'animation en France*. Actes Sud – Institut Lumière.

Condry, I. (2013). *The Soul of Anime. Collaborative Creativity and Japan's Media Success Story*. Duke University Press.

Critcher, C. (2008). Making Waves: Historical Aspects of Public Debates about Children and Mass Media. In K. Drotner & S. Livingstone (Eds.), *The International Handbook of Children, Media and Culture* (p. 91–104). Sage Publications Ltd.

CSA (2018). *Programmes jeunesse: offre et consommation*. Conseil supérieur de l'audiovisuel.

De la Ville, V.-I. & Durup, L. (2008). Managing the Stakes of Inter-Textuality in Digital Cultures. In R. Willett, M. Robinson & J. Marsh (Eds.), *Play Creativity and Digital Cultures* (p. 36–53). Routledge.

Denis, D. (2016). *Les Shadoks: histoire, esthétique et pataphysique*. INA Éditions.

Denis, J. (2008). Projeter le marché dans l'activité. Les saisies du public dans un service de production télévisuelle. *Revue française de socio-économie, 2*, 161–180.

Drotner, K. & Livingstone, s. (2011). Children's Media Cultures in Comparative Perspective. In V. Nightingale (Ed.), *The Handbook of Media Audiences* (p. 405–424). Wiley-Blackwell.

Duccini, H. (2013). Histoire d'une illusion: la télévision scolaire de 1945 à 1985. *Le Temps des médias, 21*(2), 122–133.

Ferrier, B. (2009). *Tout n'est pas littérature! La littérarité à l'épreuve des romans pour la jeunesse*. Presses universitaires de Rennes.

Fisch, S. M. & Truglio, R. T. (Eds.). (2000). *G Is for Growing: Thirty Years of Research on Children and Sesame Street*. Routledge.

Furniss, M. (2017). *Animation: The Global History*. Thames-Hudson Ltd.

Garnier, P. (1995). *Ce dont les enfants sont capables: marcher, travailler, nager, XVIIIe, XIXe, XXe siècles*. Métailié.

Garnier, P. (2014). Childhood as a Question of Critiques and Justifications: Insight into Boltanski's Sociology. *Childhood, 21*(4), 447–460.

Garnier, P. (2015). L'agency des enfants. Projet politique et scientifique des 'childhood studies'. *Éducation et sociétés, 36*, 159–173.

Garnier, P. (2018). Comment adresser une série animée aux enfants? Analyse de la conception des *Grandes grandes vacances*. In M. Loïc, A. Seurat & I. Feroc-Dumez (Eds.), *Les cultures médiatiques de la petite enfance et de l'enfance* (p. 28–42). http://jeunesetmedia.wixsite.com/jeunesetmedias.

Garnier, P. & François, S. (2017). Des modes d'existence du dessin animé. Création et coordination dans le domaine de l'animation. Journée d'étude *La fabrique de l'animation. Une industrie culturelle saisie par les sciences sociales*, LabEx ICCA/ NEF Animation, Paris, 6 juin 2017.

Garnier, P. & François, S. (2018). Les enfants du dessin animé: genèse d'une série télévisuelle et incarnations du jeune public. In G. Brougère & S. François (Eds.), *L'enfance en conception(s). Comment les industries culturelles s'adressent-elles aux enfants?* (p. 125–151). Peter Lang.

Glevarec, H. (2019). *La différenciation. Goûts, savoirs et expériences culturelles*. Le Bord de l'eau.

Hendershot, H. (Ed.) (2004). *Nickelodeon Nation. The History, Politics, and Economics of America's Only TV Channel for Kids*. New York University Press.

Hesmondhalgh, D. & Baker, S. (2010). 'A Very Complicated Version of Freedom': Conditions and Experiences of Creative Labour in Three Cultural Industries. *Poetics, 38*(1), 4–20.

James, A., Jenks, C. & Prout, A. (1998). *Theorizing Childhood*. Polity Press.

Jouët, J. & Pasquier, D. (1999). Les jeunes et la culture de l'écran. Enquête nationale auprès des 6–17 ans. *Réseaux, 17* (92), 25–102.

Jullier, L. (2008). *Interdit aux moins de 18 ans: Morale, sexe et violence au cinéma*. Armand Colin.

Lemish, D. (2010). *Screening Gender on Children's Television: The Views of Producers around the World*. Routledge.

Mayall, B. & Morrow, V. (2011). *You Can Help Your Country: English Children's Work during the Second World War*. Institute of Education Press.

McCallum, R. (2019). Adaptations for Young Audiences: Critical Challenges, Future Directions. In C. Hermansson & J. Zepernick (Eds.), *The Palgrave Handbook of Children's Film and Television* (p. 37–54). Springer International Publishing.

McKinney M. (Ed.). (2008). *History and Politics in French-Language Comics and Graphic Novels*. University Press of Mississippi.

Mérijeau, L. & Roffat, S. (2015). L'animation à l'université française, un enseignement en quête d'identification, *Mise au point. Cahiers de l'association française des enseignants et chercheurs en cinéma et audiovisuel*, 7. https://journals.openedition.org/map/1972#bodyftn24.

Morrow, R. (2008). *Sesame Street and the Reform of Children's Television*. Johns Hopkins University Press.

Nagorny, F. (2014). Histoire des formations en cinéma d'animation. In S. Denis, C. Duchet, L. Mérijeau, M. Pruvost-Delaspre & S. Roffat (Eds.), *Archives et acteurs des cinémas d'animation en France* (p. 199–208). L'Harmattan.

Newman, M. Z. & Levine, E. (2012). *Legitimating Television: Media Convergence and Cultural Status*. Routledge.

Noesser, C. (2016). *La résistible ascension du cinéma d'animation. Sociogenèse d'un cinéma-bis en France (1950–2010)*. Thèse de doctorat, Université Paris 4.

Oswell, D. (2002). *Television, Childhood and the Home. A History of the Making of the Child Television Audience in Britain*. Oxford University Press.

Pecora, N., Murray, J. P. & Wartella, E.A. (Eds.). (2006). *Children and Television: Fifty Years of Research*. Routledge.

Perlmutter, D. (2014). *America Toons: A History of Television Animation*. McFarland.

Pilling, J. (Ed.). (1998). *A Reader in Animation Studies*. John Libbey Publishing.

Poels, G. (2013). De Televisius à Gulli: l'invention des enfants de la télé (1949–2005). *Le temps des médias, 21*, 104–120.

Potter, A. (2018). Creating Children's Television for SVODs: The Alignment of Global Production Practices with National Screen Policies in the Netflix Original 'Bottersnikes and Gumbles'. *Media Industries, 5*(2), 111–127.

Prince, N. (2015). *La littérature de jeunesse. Pour une théorie littéraire* (2nd ed.). Armand Colin.

Souriau, E. (2009). *Les différents modes d'existence*. Presses universitaires de France.

Stabile, C. A. & Harrison M. (Eds.) (2003). *Prime Time Animation: Television Animation and American Culture*. Routledge.

Steemers, J. (2010). *Creating Preschool Television. A Story of Commerce, Creativity and Curriculum*. Palgrave Macmillan.

Steemers, J. (2016). International Sales of UK Television Content: Change and Continuity in the Space 'In between' Production and Consumption. *Television and New Media, 17*(8), 734–753.

Steinberg, M. (2012). *Anime's Media Mix: Franchising Toys and Characters in Japan*. University of Minnesota Press.

Strenae, (2011). Special issue "Les formes de la fiction dans la culture pour la jeunesse", 2. https://journals.openedition.org/strenae/264.

Wells, P. (2002). *Animation: Genre and Authorship*. Wallflower Press.

Wells, P. (2010). *Les fondamentaux de l'animation*. Pyramyd.

Zafirau, S. (2009). Audience Knowledge and the Everyday Lives of Cultural Producers in Hollywood. In V. Mayer, M. J. Banks & J. Caldwell (Eds.), *Production Studies: Cultural Studies of Media Industries* (p. 190–202). Routledge.

11

Gord Downie and Jeff Lemire's graphic narrative *Secret Path*: Analysis of a transmedia adaptation

Dr. Alison J. Halsall

In 2016, Canadian troubadour Gord Downie published *Secret Path*, the story of Chanie Wenjack, a twelve year-old Ojibwe (Anishinaabe) boy who died on October 22, 1966, after running away from the Cecilia Jeffrey Indian Residential School located near Kenora, Ontario, to walk home to the family he was taken from over six hundred kilometers away[1]. Downie was moved by the story of Chanie Wenjack (misnamed "Charlie" by his teachers) after reading a story written by Ian Adams that was published in *Maclean's* magazine in February 1967. Wenjack's heartbreaking ordeal inspired Downie to turn to poetry to memorialize this young person's unacknowledged history. Downie's ten poems eventually transformed into the ten-song album *Secret Path*, which accompanies the graphic narrative adaptation of the same name (illustrated by Canadian comics artist Jeff Lemire). In turn, Downie's music and Lemire's illustrations inspired *The Secret Path*, an animated film broadcast publicly by the Canadian Broadcasting Corporation (C.B.C.) in October 2016, in an hour-long commercial-free television special[2]. All of these texts – musical, graphic, filmic – are packaged together under the title

1 Joseph Boyden's poetic novella *Wenjack* (2016) tells Chanie Wenjack's story too, though largely from the perspective of the Manitous, spirits of the forest, who comment on his journey, taunt him, and ultimately offer him a type of comfort on his journey home. Illustrated by Cree artist Kent Monkman, the novella beautifully and sorrowfully describes Chanie's death.

2 *The Secret Path* was created, written, and directed by Gord Downie; it was composed by Downie with Kevin Drew and Dave Hamelin, and illustrated by Jeff

Secret Path and are as such available to readers and viewers. All proceeds are donated to Canada's National Centre for Truth and Reconciliation, the archival repository for all of the material collected by the Truth and Reconciliation Commission, whose purpose is to document the history and lasting impacts of the Canadian Indian Residential system on Indigenous students and their families[3]. Wenjack's story exposes the treatment and abuse of these children in the residential schools that were established to assimilate them into Euro-Canadian culture. "Chanie haunts me. His story is Canada's story," writes Gord Downie.

> This is about Canada. We are not the country we thought we were. History will be re-written. *We are all accountable*, but this begins in the late 1800s and goes to 1996. 'White' Canada knew – on somebody's purpose – nothing about this. We weren't taught it; it was hardly ever mentioned. […] I am trying in this small way to help spread what Murray Sinclair said, 'This is not an aboriginal problem. This is a Canadian problem. Because at the same time that aboriginal people were being demeaned in the schools and their culture and language were being taken away from them and they were being told that they were inferior, they were pagans, that they were heathens and savages and that they were unworthy of being respected – that very same message was being given to the non-aboriginal children in the public schools as well… They need to know that history includes them.' ("Secret Path," 2017)

So reads Gord Downie's statement on Secretpath.ca, made at Ogoki Post in September 2016, a statement whose basic principle reminds readers, listeners, and viewers of the importance of "relating," of Canadian settler culture working to achieve better outcomes for Indigenous children and youth. The particular transmedial format of *Secret Path* works to encourage transcultural reconciliation, its dynamic visuals and hauntingly beautiful music attempting to convey this story to as many audiences as possible to inspire the Canadian government and its people to start on the road to truth even before they can think about reconciliation.

Lemire. The film was executive produced by Mike Downie, Patrick Downie, Gord Downie, and Sarah Polley.

3 I use the term "Indigenous" and "Indigenous peoples" to refer to the First Nations, Métis, and Inuit sovereign nations living in what is now called Canada, to honor the hundreds of culturally and linguistically distinct nations, and those of mixed ancestry, that inhabit North America and especially Canada.

1. Visual storytelling as living resistance: Indigenous representation in graphic narratives and picture books

Comics and graphic narratives that visualize the intergenerational traumas experienced by Indigenous peoples in Canada because of European and Canadian governmental colonialism is a bourgeoning trend in the comics industry. These comics are responding to the call made by Canada's Truth and Reconciliation Commission (T.R.C.) in its 2015 Executive Summary to educate. "Using the power of the graphic medium to both show and tell" (Wolf, 2016, p. 221), they tackle hard-hitting issues that affect Indigenous populations across Canada, such as chronic poverty, social exclusion, suicide, homelessness, violent death, substance and solvent addiction, disease, incarceration, colonialism and cultural dislocation.

Although the practices of child removal and forced assimilation were classified as cultural genocide by the United Nations in 1948, residential schools for Indigenous children were not fully abandoned as a practice in Canada until 1996. Ongoing is recognition by Canadians of the profoundly negative impact of the schools on Indigenous peoples, and of the effect that these stolen generations continue to have on Indigenous cultures. As the bourgeoning Indigenous comics industry testifies, Indigenous experiences and resistance have become "narratable" as a valid and valuable testimonial discourse. As more and more narratives about child removal have emerged (*The Outside Circle*; *Lost Innocence*; *Betty: The Helen Betty Osborne Story*; etc.), these visual stories are especially powerful resources with which to educate readers in Canada (and throughout the world) about the crises that Indigenous peoples continue to experience in Canada. This chapter explores the affordances of word and image, myth and worldview in making use of the healing power of transmedial storytelling to address the long-lasting legacies that systemic racism has burdened Indigenous peoples with.

Relocations of Indigenous peoples and even whole communities in Canada have been frequent since contact. In 1991, the Royal Commission on Aboriginal Peoples (R.C.A.P.) report enumerated the many tragic consequences that these relocations have had for Canada's first peoples: they severed Indigenous people's relationship to the land and environment, and weakened their cultural and communal bonds; these dispossessions led to a loss of economic self-sufficiency, including, in some cases, increased dependence on government transfer payments; they also led to a decline in standards of health, and changes in social and political relations in the relocated population (Vowel, 2016, p. 191). From Confederation in 1867, the new Canadian government practiced internal colonialism in the biopolitical and geopolitical management of its people: it used modes of control (like prisons, reserves, schools, policing, minoritizing) to ensure the ascendency of a nation and its white elite (Tuck and Yang, 2012, p. 5). It drafted policies that looked to displace Indigenous peoples who were seen as obstacles to settlement; to control the proliferation of Indigenous languages and stories; and to help them adapt to contemporary civilization by encouraging them to sign treaties, move onto reserves, and take up farming, in the process disrupting kinship and governance systems further, and removing Indigenous peoples from their traditional economies and sources of food. The conclusion of the report filed by the R.C.A.P. in 1991 after engaging in 178 days of public hearings, visiting 96 communities, doing research, and consulting with experts, reads as follows: "Our central conclusion can be summarized simply: *The main policy direction, pursued by more than 150 years, first by colonial then by Canadian governments, has been wrong*" ("Highlights from the Report," 1991). Since 1991, Indigenous populations continue to be at risk of removal from what remains of their homelands to enable growing immigration, urbanization, and the exploitation of natural resources like oil and gas pipelines run by corporations. They continue to suffer the highest rates of poverty, suicide, homelessness, violent death, drug and alcohol addiction, disease, imprisonment, and cultural dislocation (Fast and Collin-Vezina, 2010, p. 127). Life's basics – clean drinking water, adequate housing, education, and child welfare – are still substandard, such that Canada has been admonished by the United Nations Economic and Social Council for the significant disparities that still exist between Canada's Indigenous and non-Indigenous peoples.

Doris Wolf writes about the systemic injustices committed against Indigenous peoples and argues that non-Indigenous Canadians must be involved in the truth and reconciliation process in ways that are genuinely intercultural. The "restorying" of the past, as she calls it – the destruction of the foundational myth of Canada as a benevolent peacemaker by focusing on the violence it has directed against entire communities and peoples – must be accomplished by *non*-Indigenous Canadians to understand and acknowledge that forced removals and relocations of Indigenous peoples and whole communities in Canada to make room for white settlement and education were principal components of Canada's racist policies. Paulette Regan (2010) also insists that non-Indigenous Canadians must recognize and acknowledge that the Indian Residential School legacy is a settler problem rather than an Indigenous problem before the real reconciliation process can begin (p. 63).

In Canada, residential schools operated for 150 years, beginning in the 1840s. By 1932, there were more than 80 schools in operation. 150,000 Indigenous children attended these schools; approximately 6000 died in the system. 67 % of the schools were run by the Catholic Church, 20 % by the Anglican Church, the rest were run by other Protestant denominations (Vowel, 2016, p. 171). In 1850, attendance at the residential schools became compulsory for all Indigenous children between the ages of 6 and 15; parental non-compliance was punishable by prison terms. Often at these schools the children were not getting much of an education at all, since they spent most of the day doing hard labor around the property. The residential school legacy is a story about racist and paternalistic educators, church officials, and government who wanted to assimilate Indigenous children into mainstream Canadian society for "their own good." Children were forcibly removed from their families by Indian agents or police officers and forbidden to speak their own languages or practice their cultural and spiritual traditions. The other part of the story is about the cultural, psychological, and emotional harms and traumatic abuses that were inflicted upon small children, "an intergenerational history of dispossession, violence, abuse, and racism that is a fundamental denial of the human dignity and rights of Indigenous peoples" (Regan, 2010, p. 5).

A rash of apologies for the many types of abuse practiced in the Indian Residential Schools appeared from 1986 onwards, as testimonies from survivors began to circulate: in 1986, from the United Church of Canada; in 1991, from the Missionary Oblates of Mary Immaculate; in 1993, from the Anglican Church; and in 1994, from the Presbyterian Church. In 1988, then Minister of Indian Affairs, Jane Stewart, offered the first official apology from the Canadian government. On June 11, 2008, Canadian Prime Minister Stephen Harper offered an apology on behalf of Canada, an apology that Cherokee writer Thomas King (2013) characterizes as "a stingy thing," limited only to the abuse that Indigenous peoples had endured in the residential school system (p. 122–123), one that ignored the treaty violations, the thefts of land and resources, and the institutional racism that Indigenous people have endured since contact. Harper's apology was made doubly insufficient on September 25, 2009 when, during the G20 Summit, he affirmed that "We (Canada)... have no history of colonialism." In stark contrast to Harper's convenient blindness, current Prime Minister Justin Trudeau has committed his Liberal government to full federal action on the Truth and Reconciliation Commission's final report and, while there is still much important work to be done to balance Indigenous rights and the creation of oil and gas pipelines on their traditional lands, the focus Trudeau has given to truth telling and acknowledging is undeniable.

History of the Indian Residential Schools is still very present. Although the last school closed in 1996, approximately 80,000 former students are still alive. Public knowledge about the Indian Residential School legacy has certainly increased because of the work done by the Truth and Reconciliation Commission of Canada (T.R.C.) that was established in 2008, the same year as Stephen Harper's apology. Even before that, 2006 saw the Indian Residential Schools Settlement Agreement (I.R.S.S.A.), the largest class-action settlement in Canadian history that responded to the over 12,000 individual abuse claims filed against the federal government and church entities. The I.R.S.S.A. consisted of a number of components that were intended to address the needs of survivors. These included: monetary reparations; an independent assessment process that adjudicated physical and sexual abuse claims and awards for financial compensation; a health support program for survivors administered by Health Canada; a commemoration program for memorial projects; and the creation of the Truth and Reconciliation Commission of Canada. The T.R.C. was charged with gathering testimony from former students, collecting documents relating to the schools, producing a report on the residential school system and its aftermath, and making recommendations to the government based on its findings[4]. The first paragraph alone of the T.R.C.'s Executive Summary is searing in its condemnation of Canada's long history of racist policies towards the Indigenous peoples whom it has dispossessed:

---

4 The T.R.C. issued an executive summary in the summer of 2015, eventually releasing six volumes of its final report on December 15, 2015. Its work has been transferred to the National Centre for Truth and Reconciliation housed at the University of Manitoba, which is now the permanent home for all statements, documents, and materials gathered by the T.R.C.

> For over a century, the central goals of Canada's Aboriginal policy were to eliminate Aboriginal governments; ignore Aboriginal rights; terminate the Treaties; and, through a process of assimilation, cause Aboriginal peoples to cease to exist as distinct legal, social, cultural, religious, and racial entities in Canada. The establishment and operation of residential schools were a central element of this policy, which can best be described as 'cultural genocide'. ("Truth and Reconciliation," 2016)

Although the Executive Summary specifically identifies "education institutions and what they have taught, or failed to teach" (Vowel, 2016, p. 175) as the source of the troubled relations between Indigenous peoples and non-Indigenous Canadians, the Commission maintains that education is key to reconciliation. In a national benchmark survey conducted in May 2008, results confirmed that although Canadians were somewhat familiar with the physical and sexual abuse that occurred in the Indian Residential Schools, very few had any substantive knowledge about the policy goal of assimilation that motivated this system (Regan, 2010, p. 41–42). Truth and Reconciliation Commissioners warned in their *Interim Report* that "The Commission continues to face huge challenges in raising awareness, among non-Aboriginal Canadians, of the residential school history and legacy. This presents an enormous limitation to the possibility of long-term understanding and meaningful reconciliation" ("Interim Report", 2012, p. 9).

In response to this lack of awareness, education becomes a primary concern and focus in these Indigenous comics in Canada that are directed at young readers, education about Canada's past and present, and education between and among communities, Indigenous and non-Indigenous alike. As the comics industry testifies, Indigenous experiences and resistance have become "narratable" as a valid and valuable testimonial discourse. Indeed, they are "necessary interventions" (2016, p. 24), Sarah Henzi claims, whose Indigenous epistemologies provide an antidote to the conventional history of the Americas and call for an urgent change in worldview, from creators and readers. Métis writer Jo-Ann Episkenew (2009) argues that contemporary Indigenous literature serves two transformative functions: "healing Indigenous people and advancing social justice in settler society" (p. 15). For Indigenous creators and readers, creating and reading these stories can bring healing by giving voice and validation to their collective experiences (Episkenew, 2009, p. 16). They can also affect healing by advancing social justice, by educating settler readers about Indigenous perspectives and knowledges in Canada and by challenging settler myths (Episkenew, 2009, p. 17). Even more importantly, the transformation of trauma into narrative can enable Indigenous creators and readers to begin to distance themselves from the trauma. "By re-experiencing these emotions in a safe environment and by expressing them in language, we are often able to come to terms with emotional injuries and then move our emotional lives forward to a place of health and contentment" (2009, p. 70), Episkenew claims optimistically. In this way, Indigenous stories validate experiences and offer opportunities for critical reflection and catharsis. As more and more comics about child removal emerge, such as Gord Downie and Jeff Lemire's *Secret Path* (2016) and Brandon Mitchell's *Lost Innocence* (2013), these visual stories are powerful resources with which to educate readers in Canada (and throughout the world) about the land struggles, historical erasure, pain, and dislocation that Indigenous peoples experience in Canada.

2. Acknowledging: Learning from the residential school system

That two white men are telling the story of a dead Anishinaabe boy in *Secret Path* is an obvious epistemological and ideological problem, however. Ojibwe (Anishinaabe) writer Lenore Keeshig-Tobias (1991) writes about cultural theft, "the theft of voice" that occurs when a white writer writes in the voice of an Indigenous character (p. 64). Okanagan writer Jeanette Armstrong (1992) echoes these ideas: "What's at issue here is the ability of… non-native writers – without malice in most cases – to draw a picture of Native contemporary lifestyle and thinking and so on which creates a false image in the mind of the reading public, and which creates problems for contemporary Native people" (p. 11). Gord Downie attempts to counteract the paternalism of white culture towards Indigenous peoples by not speaking *for* Wenjack, but *about* him. He accomplishes this by redeploying the most canonized form of literature (the epic) to "restory" Chanie's journey. The transmedial format – exploring Chanie's "odyssey" across poetic, musical, visual, and filmic media – harnesses the wide-reaching potential of oral storytelling to confront readers, listeners, and viewers with a testimonial about Canada's colonial past and present. As Canada's revered bard, Downie positions Wenjack as an extraordinary hero typical of the epic, but an ignored hero of Canada, one who endured systematic injustices committed by the Canadian government and white, settler culture, and whose epic journey home to Ogoki Post in Northern Ontario was motivated by powerful forces of love and fear. In his appropriation of one of the oldest literary forms to "restory" Chanie's trauma, Downie blows apart the peacemaker myth of the Canadian nationalist narrative and replaces it with a searing indictment of the abuse institutionalized by the Canadian system. Downie accomplishes all of this with the full support of the Wenjack family.

Doris Wolf writes at length about the systemic injustices committed against Indigenous peoples, and argues that non-Indigenous Canadians must be involved in the truth and reconciliation process in ways that are genuinely intercultural. Downie is one such storyteller, and *Secret Path* as a transmedial project has the potential to unsettle foundational myths about Canada in the hopes that young Canadians will learn about that past to gain empowerment in their present. However, Wolf, along with critic Sidonie Smith, raise the prospect that the creation of comics like *Secret Path* about Indigenous issues can actually be more limiting than helpful. That such visual narratives provoke empathy rather than a targeting of structural inequalities and forms of exploitation within and across nations is not productive, they argue, because they are fundamentally apathetic (Wolf, 2016, p. 214; Smith, 2011, p. 65). Critic Paulette Regan, however, claims that it is important for non-Indigenous Canadians to move beyond passive empathy to something she calls testimonial reading, which emphasizes collective responsibility for the history of colonialism (2010, p. 49). This is exactly what Downie and Lemire perform in their transmedial project. In reading, listening to, and watching *Secret Path*, viewers bear witness to this story and in the process reflect on the racism that the government has directed at its Indigenous peoples for centuries. This transmedial project becomes an important component in the truth-telling process. Not the end-all be-all, of course. But a meaningful step, nonetheless.

Critic Sarah Henzi (2016) argues that popular culture has an ability to "speak beyond linguistic, cultural, and intergenerational gaps" in an effort to bring up issues for "diffusion and discussion" (p. 24). *Secret Path* exemplifies such synergies. All of the media that it employs produce effects that are greater together than each of its parts. Poetry, music, visuals, and animation work together to "restory" the tragedies of abused young people in the residential school system, in a very approachable and dynamic format. Through image and song, Wenjack's story gains immediacy and vividness, and it becomes less seemingly fictitious as an abstract narrative. The interdependence of image, song, and animated film thus offers a new space for resistance, a space to "rectify the falsity of colonial imagery" (Henzi, 2016, p. 36–37). Comics artist Jeff Lemire speaks about the transcultural reach of *Secret Path*:

> Music is universal. It crosses languages and cultures and speaks to everyone, and I've always felt the medium of comics could do the same. It's our hope that one day *Secret Path* will be taught in schools and that it will help to shed light on this all too often ignored part of Canada's past. I think, above all else, that's what Gord and I wanted to create: something that can't be ignored. Every Canadian should know Chanie Wenjack's name and I hope *Secret Path* helps to make that a reality. ("Secret Path," 2017)

Even in its physical shape, *Secret Path* (the comic) makes a statement: it refuses to sit on a shelf easily and fit in with the other books and graphic novels that line a bookshelf. In its large size and scale, the book sets itself apart and calls attention to its presence as a book, but more importantly, as a story. An untold story. A story that *demands* to be told. In its long, rectangular panels and oversized pages, Downie and Lemire paint a larger-than-life picture of Chanie's terrible odyssey across harsh terrain and unforgiving weather, setting out to walk the 600 kilometers that separated him from his family in northern Ontario. In many – if not most – of the panels, Chanie plods along the railway track that he thinks is taking him home. A powerful recurring image in the comic and animated film (a variation on the fixed epithet of the literary epic) is this train track that Chanie follows, the track that represents his supposed "secret path" of escape, the path that in fact leads to his death, but also the "path to truth and reconciliation" that the restorying of Chanie's epic journey could help Canadians and Indigenous peoples make progress on. Most importantly, these tracks evoke the "trains of tears" that transported so many Indigenous children away from their families and communities. Through the large individual panels of the comic, its long, establishing shots and close-ups of searching and anguished eyes and faces, Downie and Lemire slow down a reader's consumption of this narrative, encouraging readers – forcing them, even – to "see" and to face the abuses that Chanie experienced.

Sadly, this story is not simply one boy's odyssey, but an odyssey shared by 150,000 Indigenous children across Canada, as Downie and Lemire's comic reminds readers. Similar to David Alexander Robertson's *7 Generations* (2012), the panels that depict Chanie's time at the residential school are moody and fragmented, suggesting that the boys are together yet separate, isolated and alienated. Chanie lacks any power and control in the school. He is a victim of emotional, physical, and sexual abuse at the hands of the adult teachers. Priests and nuns are largely faceless figures, terrifying in their anonymity. Lemire captures the indescribable horror of the sexual abuse by not depicting it. A diptych juxtaposes two comics panels, one of Chanie's grimacing, terrified face as the priest approaches his bed at night in the dormitory, and the other of the priest's outstretched hand, threatening in its reach, so different from the comforting hand that Chanie's father extends to him in his dreams. In stark contrast to the busy panels before and after this diptych, the whiteness of the page suggests the threatening whiteness of the priest, and creator Lemire's unwillingness to represent this act of physical and sexual violation.

The strict regulation of the panels that depict life at the residential school stands in contrast to the more fluid and colorful panels and pages that depict Chanie's happy life back home. Clipped, shorn, and "cleaned" in an effort to wash the Indigenousness out of them, the boys become interchangeable upon their arrival at the residential school. Because of Wenjack's minority group status (as an Indigenous person *and* as a child) he is exploited and discriminated against, deprived of the basic human rights that other Canadians took for granted. The sheer size of the pages and the size of individual panels paint a big picture of some of the horrors that these children endured. In reading this graphic narrative and accompanying Wenjack on his tragic journey, there is no way to escape the meaning. It is written large, so that readers cannot miss the point.

A 10-song album download accompanies *Secret Path*, the comic. The poems appear on the album in the order that they appear in the comic, and in turn become the soundtrack that accompanies the images. The music is generally moody, in the vein of Tragically Hip albums. With the strong presence of a guitar and a piano, Downie's soulful crooning describes Wenjack's imagined thoughts, feelings, experiences, just as Homer and his group of bards once told the story of Odysseus's homeward journey and imagined his thoughts. Album and comic open with the powerful claims, "I am the Stranger/You can't see me/I am the stranger/Do you know what I mean?"[5]. The quiet insistence of Chanie's

[5] This first stanza of Downie's lyric "I am the Stranger" evokes a short poem by Mi'kmaq poet and songwriter Rita Joe: "I am the Indian/And the burden/Lies yet with me." Both poems reference the "burden" and the "strangeness" associated with

subject position as a stranger, as a blank space, announces from the outset the importance of the transmedial platform in "restorying" the unsung odyssey of this Anishinaabe boy. The song "Swing Set," accompanied by an electronic, techno beat, demonstrates the powerful synergy between comic and music. In this sequence three boys play at a swing set and watch from afar while another Indigenous child is physically abused by a priest. On the album, the diegetic sound of the twining of the swing's chains draws attention to the importance of this sound as a metaphor for the governmentally-sanctioned chains that bind the youngsters. The techno beat mimics Chanie's pounding heart as he readies himself for escape. "Now?/Not yet./Now?/Not yet" form the refrain of poem and song. That this refrain is repeated three times with mounting intensity in both song and animated film underscores the desperation of Wenjack and his friends to escape their awful situation. The climax of the song mirrors the exhilaration Chanie feels upon his escape: the repetition of an angry and affirmative "yes" over and over captures the exhilaration of the boys as they finally escape these literal and metaphorical chains.

The transfer of the narrative to animated film triples the effectiveness of the comic because it brings the story to life, following the visual narrative almost panel by panel as a storyboard. Jeff Lemire and his team of animators employ different color palettes to contrast Wenjack's happy life before with his experiences of deprivation, sadness, and abuse at the school. In one particular sequence, thanks to the power of the moving image, Chanie walks closer and closer to the camera, forcing viewers not only to confront the abuse of these children but also to "see," to accept their complicity in this intergenerational trauma, as part of the nation of Canada. The sequence entitled "The Only Place to Be" captures Chanie's epic journey to death. A two-page spread shows Chanie walking diagonally from upper left to lower right, with extreme close-ups interspersed of his trudging feet. The forgotten hero Chanie is defined by this act of putting one foot in front of the other, through sheer strength of will. The harsh rain and sleet break across the panel frames and the gutters, as though the natural elements are the one constant across time and space. The accompanying song communicates Downie's imagining of Chanie's acceptance of death through the song's tempo that is much

---

Indigenous peoples in North America, as well as the ideological and racial chasm that separates settler from Indigenous peoples. Canadian poet and songwriter Gord Downie in turn looks to bridge that gulf in this transmedial project.

slower, more reflective and comforting: "I'll just close my eyes/I'll just catch my breath/This is the only place to be/I've got lots of time/My whole life ahead/This is the only place to be." Repeated seven times, the line "This is the only place to be" alludes to Chanie's quiet resignation to his inevitable end. Beginning and ending with that line, this sequence is meditative, and the song's short length reflects Chanie's fragmented grasp of reality as he nears death. The diegetic sound of humming, and the soft piano and guitar provide a humbling tribute to Chanie's tragic death. "Here, Here and Here" is a song, poem, and moving sequence that emphasizes the verbs that define Chanie's life: "I feel", "I hurt", "I lived", "I died" are all curt statements about the basics of human life, a life cut short by the Canadian government's biopolitical and geopolitical management of Indigenous peoples. The panels of the comic and the animated sequence capture the "here" that Chanie inhabits as he moves from life into death and the "here" of his father's embrace. Implicit in this is a double-entendre: poems, comic, and animated film in turn call listeners to "hear" the story so that Chanie's life, and the lives of 150,000 other Indigenous children, will not be forgotten.

Secret Path is a silent graphic narrative, in that there are no dialogue boxes, no thought balloons. *The Secret Path* is an animated film with a powerful soundtrack, but no dialogue of any sort, conscious as this transmedial project is of the power of language. Poem, song, and animated sequence entitled "Don't Let This Touch You" liken words metaphorically to things that are impermanent and, worse, ineffective. "Words are birds/Words are snow/Words whisper/Words don't make the rain go/[...]/Words are blanks/Words are ghosts/Words are god/Words don't make the rain go." All three media platforms emphasize that English words have justified this abuse for too long. The animated film clarifies this association of words with oppression, as Chanie throws the Canadian National Railway Route Map on the last fire he lights. Significantly, Kenora and Ogoki Post do not even feature as stops on any of the rail lines, not worthy it seems of an official stop on a Canadian train route. The map's English lettering changes into Indigenous letters, in Chanie's last act of resistance. Chanie rewrites the map according to his own language before burning it in the last fire he lights; the letters rise up in smoke before disappearing into the dark sky. Cross-cutting in turn juxtaposes this colonial map with a frame in which a priest at the residential school is teaching the boys English, the language of the oppressor. A phrase written on the blackboard – "See the Boy Run" – provides an ironic commentary about just what Chanie does, propelled by the abuse he experienced at the hands of his so-called teachers. In an act of resistance, Chanie rewrites the map according to his own language before burning it. Because there is no dialogue or narrative exposition on the page or the screen in *Secret Path*, readers and viewers become a part of the storytelling process, making meaning between and among the media platforms. This participatory reading and viewing practice in turn invites the white settler voice to begin to reflect on and acknowledge the horrors of its colonial past.

The animated film concludes with the illustration of Chanie dissolving into the photograph that currently hangs in his sister Pearl Wenjack's contemporary living room back in Ogoki Post. In *Secret Path*, the transmedial platform "restories" Chanie's epic odyssey across poetic, musical, visual, and filmic media to confront readers, listeners, and viewers with a testimonial about Canada's colonial past and present, the systemic racism that has led to the state of crisis that many Indigenous peoples still experience today. Gord Downie and Jeff Lemire certainly fall into the category of white advocates who speak for and about Indigenous people and communities, but Downie's powerful influence as a rockstar, and Lemire's as a celebrated comics artist, have an undeniable potential to communicate this important story to many who remain ignorant of the intergenerational traumas that Indigenous populations in Canada continue to suffer.

The right to self-determination on the part of Indigenous peoples was affirmed at the international level by the ratification of the United Nations Declaration on the Rights of Indigenous Peoples in 2007. Although Canada ratified the United Nations Convention on the Rights of the Child in December of 1991, thereby committing itself to upholding the rights of *all* children in Canada, as of January 2010, Canada, the United States, and New Zealand had not signed this particular declaration about the rights of Indigenous peoples (and children, more specifically). As recently as May 2016, Carolyn Bennett, Minister of Crown-Indigenous Relations and Northern Affairs, affirmed that Canada had finally become a full supporter, without qualification, of the U.N. declaration. As this recent development attests, there is still an urgent need to challenge the Euro-Canadian colonial status quo, and Indigenous comics are effective tools with which to do so. These texts provide opportunities to think about how to represent and how to interpret, in the process exploiting the visual and narrative possibilities of unsettling commonplace frames of difference, and thematizing the practices of truth telling, acknowledging, restoring, and relating.

Michael Cromer and Penney Clark (2007) argue that "To look at graphic literature as a product of its time and place is to catch a glimpse of the political and cultural zeitgeist of a nation" (p. 578). That this new trend in Indigenous comics is so recent speaks to the very urgent need on the part of Indigenous and non-Indigenous peoples to question the Canadian peacemaker myth. As Kate Cregan and Denise Cuthbert (2014) remind us, the status of a nation's children is an index for the development and advancement of the nation itself (p. 113). That so many Indigenous young people still do not have access to clean drinking water, adequate housing, education, and child welfare is a terrible example of Canada's prioritization of settler issues and concerns over those of its Indigenous young people. Canada has failed the Indigenous children who inhabit its land, as these comics consistently attest. As the Commission for Truth and Reconciliation makes clear, education is "an effective peacemaking tool," and perhaps even more importantly, a "weapon" (Regan, 2010, p. 99). This rich tradition of Indigenous comics for young readers speaks to the power and possibility of sequential and transmedial narratives in helping to align the needs of Canada with the worth of *all* of the nation's children.

References

Armstrong, J. (1992). The Body of Our People. *Paragraph, 14*(3), 9–12.

Boyden, J. (2016). *Wenjack*. Hamish Hamilton.

Cregan, K. & Cuthbert, D. (2014). *Global Childhoods: Issues and Debates*. Sage Publications.

Cromer, M. & Clark, P. (2007). Getting Graphic with the Past: Graphic Novels and the Teaching of History. *Theory and Research in Social Education, 35*(4), 474–491.

Downie, G. & Lemire, J. (2016). *Secret Path*. Simon and Schuster.

Episkenew, J. A. (2009). *Taking Back Our Spirits: Indigenous Literature, Public Policy, and Healing*. University of Manitoba Press.

Fast, E. & Collin-Vezina, D. (2010). Historical Trauma, Race-Based Trauma and Resilience of Indigenous Peoples: A Literature Review. *First Peoples Child & Family Review, 5*(1), 126–136.

Henzi, S. (2016). 'A Necessary Antidote': Graphic Novels, Comics, and Indigenous Writing. *Canadian Review of Comparative Literature, 43*(1), 23–38.

Highlights from the Report of the Royal Commission on Aboriginal Peoples. (1991). Retrieved from http://www.aadnc-aandc.gc.ca/eng/1100100014597/1100100014637.

Keeshig-Tobias, L. (1991). Not Just Entertainment. *Whole Earth Review*, 64–66.

King, T. (2013). *The Inconvenient Indian: A Curious Account of Native People in North America*. Anchor Canada.

LaBoucane-Benson, P. (2015). *The Outside Circle: A Graphic Novel*. Art by K. Mellings. House of Anansi Press.

Mitchell, B. (2013). *Lost Innocence*. Illustrated by T. Audibert. The Healthy Aboriginal Network.

Regan, P. (2010). *Unsettling the Settler Within: Indian Residential Schools, Truth Telling and Reconciliation in Canada*. UBC Press.

Robertson, D. A. (2008). *The Life of Helen Betty Osborne: A Graphic Novel*. Illustrated by M. Blackstone. Portage & Main.

Robertson, D. A. (2012). *7 Generations*. Illustrated by S. B. Henderson. Highwater.

Robertson, D. A. (2015). *Betty: The Helen Betty Osborne Story*. Illustrated by S. B. Henderson. Highwater.

Secret Path. (2017). Retrieved from http://secretpath.ca/#Book.

Sium, A. & Ritskes, E. (2013). Speaking Truth to Power: Indigenous Storytelling as an Act of Living Resistance. *Decolonization: Indigeneity, Education & Society, 2*(1), i–x.

Smith, S. (2011). Human Rights and Comics: Autobiographical Avatars, Crisis Witnessing, and Transnational Rescue Networks. In M. Chaney (Ed.), *Graphic Subjects: Critical Essays on Autobiography and Graphic Novels* (p. 61–72). University of Wisconsin Press.

Truth and Reconciliation Commission of Canada: Interim Report. (2012). Retrieved from http://www.trc.ca/websites/trcinstitution/index.php?p=580.

Truth and Reconciliation Commission Report Executive Summary. (2016). Retrieved from http://www.standcanada.org/truth-reconciliation-commission-report-summary/.

Tuck, E. & Yang, K. W. (2012). Decolonization Is Not a Metaphor. *Decolonization: Indigeneity, Education & Society*, *1*(1), 1–40.

Vowel, C. (2016). *Indigenous Writes: A Guide to First Nations, Métis & Inuit Issues in Canada*. Highwater.

Wolf, D. (2014). Confronting the Legacy of Canada's Indian Residential Schools: Cree Cultural Memory and the Warrior Spirit in David Alexander Robertson and Scott B. Henderson's *7 Generations* Series. In C. Sugars & E. Ty (Eds.), *Canadian Literature and Cultural Memory* (p. 337–353). Oxford University Press.

Wolf, D. (2016). Unsettling and Restorying Canadian Indigenous-Settler Histories in David Alexander Robertson's *The Life of Helen Betty Osborne* and *Sugar Falls*. In C. Rifkind & L. Warley (Eds.), *Canadian Graphic: Picturing Life Narratives* (p. 207–234). Wilfrid Laurier Press.

About the authors

Gilles Brougère is a Professor in sciences of education at University Sorbonne Paris Nord. He is specialised in research about Early childhood education, play and games, toys, childhood culture, childhood sociology, comparison and intercultural aspect of education, informal education and learning. He is member of a research centre about education and culture, EXPERICE. He is responsible for a master's degree on play and toys.

Email: brougere@univ-paris13.fr

Florence Cherigny is Associate Professor at the Law and Social Sciences Faculty of Poitiers University. She is specialized in research about law of information and communication technologies, internet law, competition law, intellectual property. Her publications deal with social media, connected objects, digital uses of young people, learning analytics. She is member of a research center for interdisciplinary legal studies and cooperation (CECOJI). She participates in an interdisciplinary project about "The future of the creative cultural industries: towards an economy of access or digital goods?".

Email: florence.cherigny@univ-poitiers.fr

Natalie Coulter is Associate Professor in Communication Studies and Director of the Institute for Digital Literacies (IRDL) at York University, Canada. Her research explores the promotional ecologies of children's media and entertainment, girls studies, and digital media. She is co-editor of *Youth Mediations and Affective Relations*, with Susan Driver (2019, Palgrave Macmillan) and author of *Tweening the Girl* (2014, Peter Lang). She is a founding member of the Association for Research on the Cultures of Young People (ARCYP).

Email: ncoulter@yorku.ca

Valérie-Inès De La Ville is a Professor in management and marketing and member of the research centers CEREGE and MSHS de Poitiers. Her publications deal with the economic socialization of young consumers, the innovation processes in industries targeting families and children and the corporate social responsibility of companies operating in children's markets. She launched the 1st international conference "Child and Teen Consumption" in 2004, and is currently supervising an interdisciplinary research project: "The future of the creative cultural industries: towards an economy of access vs digital goods?"

Email: valerie.ines.de.la.ville@univ-poitiers.fr

Sébastien François is Assistant Professor in Media Studies at UCO (Université Catholique de l'Ouest, Nantes campus) and a member of a research team dedicated to digital uses, mediatization and mutations, MUTANUM. His research interests include young people's creative practices (especially online) in relation to media and popular cultures, cultural industries addressing children and teenagers, such as TV animation or app editors, as well as fan studies and fans' practices.

Email: sebastien.francois@uco.fr

Professor **Pascale Garnier** is a specialist of a reflexive and pragmatic sociological approach of age classifications. Her main fields of study are early childhood, body and cultural resources, professional practices with children and more recently the production of cultural goods for children. She belongs to two research networks for the sociology of childhood and children, with the European Sociological Association and the International Association of French Speaking Sociologists.

Email: pascale.garnier@univ-paris13.fr

Quentin Gervasoni is a PhD candidate in sciences of education at Université Sorbonne Paris Nord and member of the research center EXPERICE, and of the LabEx ICCA (Cultural Industries and Artistic Creation). His research deals with the online reception of the Pokémon franchise. His work is situated at the crossroads of fan studies, sociology of culture and sociology of emotions.

Email: gervasoni.quentin@gmail.com

Alison J. Halsall is an associate professor in the Department of Humanities at York University, Toronto, Canada. She holds a Ph.D. in English literature, with specialties in Victorian and Modernisms. Her current research examines world "crisis comics" for young readers. She is also co-editing the first-ever collection of LGBTQ Comics Criticism, under contract with the University Press of Mississippi. She has published articles about H.D., the Pre-Raphaelites, Penny Dreadful, South Park, Harry Potter, and neo-Victorianism in contemporary graphic novels.

Email: ahalsall@yorku.ca

Yelyzaveta Hrechaniuk is a PhD student at the Department of Thematic Studies – Child Studies, Linköping University, Sweden. Her doctoral thesis uses a case of children's charity to explore how concerns about and values of children are produced in social practice. The thesis combines the interdisciplinary field of Child Studies and Science and Technology Studies-inspired field of Valuation Studies. Her research interests also include child consumption, media, popular culture, and material culture.

Email: yelyzaveta.hrechaniuk@liu.se

Stephen Kline is Professor Emeritus at Simon Fraser University, Canada where he spent the last 30 years engaged in critical historical research into mediated social communication focused on commercialization of the cultural industries and its relationship to changing family lifestyles.

Email: kline@sfu.ca

Ève Lamendour is an associate professor in management sciences and member of the research centers CEREGE and MSHS de Poitiers. Her research focuses on the articulation between fiction and management. She devoted her first book, Le manager à l'écran, to the representation of executives and managers through French cinema, between 1895 and 2005. Since then, her work has retained an historical perspective and focuses on a field of investigation extended to television series and novels. Today, she works on the part of fiction that penetrates the organizations. For example, she coordinated, with Yannick Lemarchand, an issue of the journal *Entreprises et Histoire* entitled "The magic of numbers." The fictional aspect, which is inherent to the production of figures, is an enlightening element in understanding contemporary managerial aberrations. Her current research focuses on how works of fiction can be a source of inspiration for research in management sciences.

Email: eve.lamendour@univ-lr.fr

Mary Grace Lao is a PhD Candidate in the joint Communication and Culture Program at York and Ryerson Universities. Her PhD research is a genealogy of rape culture, tracing sexual violence discourse from the second wave feminist movement to #MeToo. She is a researcher on a SSHRC funded project on girlhood culture, feminist fashion, and tween digital practices with Dr. Natalie Coulter.

Email: mglao@yorku.ca

Stine Liv Johansen is Associate Professor, Ph.D. at Center for Children's Literature and Media, Department of Communication and Culture, Aarhus University. Stine's research field is related to children's media use, especially in relation to playful practices and children's co-production of media content. Her research applies a practice-oriented perspective to the role of media and technologies in children's everyday life, focusing particularly on the ways digital and mobile technologies are used as communicative tools, transgressing social and spatial spheres in children's lives. Stine Liv Johansen is chair of the Danish Media Council for Children and Youth.

Email: stineliv@cc.au.dk

Esther Martinez Pastor, PhD in Advertising and Public Relations, Universidad Complutense de Madrid (UCM), and Bachelor's Degree in Advertising and Public Relations (UCM) and in Law (UNED, the Spanish National Distance Education University. I am an Associate Professor (Profesor Titular) at the Faculty of Communication Sciences of Universidad Rey Juan Carlos de Madrid. My lines of research focus on the regulation of advertising, advertising relating to children and transparency.

Email: esther.martinez.pastor@urjc.es

Patricia Núñez-Gómez, PhD, is Professor in the Media & Communication Faculty at Complutense University (Madrid, Spain). Within the European Communication Research and Education Association, my research interests are focused on digital competences for future, Digital Natives, and Media Literacy. I participate in the European project Safe Internet for Kids with NGO's and Spanish Government and hold the chair *Teens and Communication TMKF*: www.catedratmkf.es. The Chair works in collaboration with more than 5000 students from primary to secondary schools developing educational projects related to media literacy, social networks and privacy, youtubers and different audiovisual contents.

Email: pnunezgo@ccinf.ucm.es

Index

ICCA

Industries culturelles, création, numérique

Titres parus dans la collection

Vol. 11 – Valérie-Inés de la Ville, Gilles Brougère and Pascale Garnier (Eds.), *Cultural and Creative Industries of Childhood and Youth. An interdisciplinary exploration of new frontiers*, 2021.

Vol. 10 – Hélène Fleckinger, Kira Kitsopanidou et Sébastien Layerle (dir.), *Métiers et techniques du cinéma et de l'audiovisuel : sources, terrains, méthodes*, 2020.

Vol. 9 – Mélanie Boissonneau et Laurent Jullier (dir.), *Cinéphilies et sériephilies 2.0. Les nouvelles formes d'attachement aux images*, 2019.

Vol. 8 – Christiaan De Beukelaer, *Développer les industries culturelles. Leçons de Palimpseste de la Pratique*, 2018.

Vol. 7 – Maya Bacache, Marc Bourreau et François Moreau (dir.), *Les musiciens et la transformation numérique. Un nouvel équilibre*, 2018.

Vol. 6 – Philippe Bouquillion et François Moreau (eds), *Digital Platforms and Cultural Industries*, 2018.

Vol. 5 – Philippe Bouquillion, Julie Peghini et Catherine Servan-Schreiber (dir.), *Artisanat et design. Un dessein indien ?*, 2018.

Vol. 4 – Gilles Brougère et Sébastien François (dir.), *L'enfance en conception(s). Comment les industries culturelles s'adressent-elles aux enfants ?*, 2018.

Vol. 3 – Emmanuelle Savignac, Yanita Andonova, Pierre Lénel, Anne Monjaret et Aude Seurrat (dir.), *Le travail de la gamification. Enjeux, modalités et rhétoriques de la translation du jeu au travail*, 2017.

Vol. 2 – Sophie Noël, Aurélie Pinto et Olivier Alexandre (dir.), *Culture et (in) dépendance. Les enjeux de l'indépendance dans les industries culturelles*, 2017.

Vol. 1 – Laurent Creton et Kira Kitsopanidou (dir.), *Crowdfunding, industries culturelles et démarche participative. De nouveaux financements pour la création*, 2016.

www.ingramcontent.com/pod-product-compliance
Ingram Content Group UK Ltd.
Pitfield, Milton Keynes, MK11 3LW, UK
UKHW021921120926
8556IPUK00042BA/1094

9 782807 616011